Psychoanalytic and Cultural Aspects of Trauma and the Holocaust

Psychoanalytic and Cultural Aspects of Trauma and the Holocaust presents interdisciplinary postmemorial endeavors of second-, third-, and fourth-generation Holocaust survivors living in Israel and in the Jewish diaspora.

Drawing on a wide range of fields, including psychoanalysis, Holocaust studies, journal and memoir writing, hermeneutics, and the arts, this book considers how individuals dealing with the memory, or postmemory, of the Holocaust possess a personal connection to this trauma. Exploring their role as testimony bearers, each contributor performs their postmemorial work in a unique and creative way, blending the subjective and the objective. The book considers themes including postcolonialism, home, displacement, and identity.

Psychoanalytic and Cultural Aspects of Trauma and the Holocaust will be key reading for academics and students of psychoanalytic studies, Holocaust studies, and trauma and cultural studies. It will also be of interest to psychoanalysts working with transgenerational trauma.

Rony Alfandary, Ph.D., is a clinical social worker, psychoanalytic psychotherapist, and photographer. He is a lecturer at the School of Social Work at the University of Haifa and the former director of the Post-Graduate Program of Psychoanalytic Psychotherapy at Bar-Ilan University, Israel. His recent publications include *Exile and Return: A Psychoanalytic Study of Lawrence Durrell's The Alexandria Quartet* and *Postmemory, Psychoanalysis and Holocaust Ghosts: The Salonica Cohen Family and Trauma across Generations*, both published by Routledge.

Professor Judith Tydor Baumel-Schwartz is the director of the Arnold and Leona Finkler Institute of Holocaust Research, the Abraham and Edita Spiegel family professor in Holocaust Research, the Rabbi Pynchas Brener professor in Research on the Holocaust of European Jewry, and professor of Modern Jewish History in the Israel and Golda Koschitzky Department of Jewish History and Contemporary Jewry at Bar-Ilan University, Israel.

Psychoanalytic and Cultural Aspects of Trauma and the Holocaust

Between Postmemory and Postmemorial Work

Edited by Rony Alfandary and Judith Tydor Baumel-Schwartz

LONDON AND NEW YORK

Designed cover image: © R. Alfandary, 'A Suitcase Full of Postmemories'

First published 2023
by Routledge
4 Park Square, Milton Park, Abingdon, Oxon OX14 4RN

and by Routledge
605 Third Avenue, New York, NY 10158

Routledge is an imprint of the Taylor & Francis Group, an informa business

© 2023 selection and editorial matter, Rony Alfandary and Judith Tydor Baumel-Schwartz; individual chapters, the contributors

The right of Rony Alfandary and Judith Tydor Baumel-Schwartz to be identified as the authors of the editorial material, and of the authors for their individual chapters, has been asserted in accordance with sections 77 and 78 of the Copyright, Designs and Patents Act 1988.

All rights reserved. No part of this book may be reprinted or reproduced or utilised in any form or by any electronic, mechanical, or other means, now known or hereafter invented, including photocopying and recording, or in any information storage or retrieval system, without permission in writing from the publishers.

Trademark notice: Product or corporate names may be trademarks or registered trademarks, and are used only for identification and explanation without intent to infringe.

British Library Cataloguing-in-Publication Data
A catalogue record for this book is available from the British Library

Library of Congress Cataloging-in-Publication Data
Names: Alfandary, Rony, editor. | Baumel-Schwartz, Judith Tydor, 1959– editor.
Title: Psychoanalytic and cultural aspects of trauma and the Holocaust : between postmemory and postmemorial work / edited by Rony Alfandary and Judith Tydor Baumel-Schwartz.
Description: First edition. | Abingdon, Oxon ; New York, NY : Routledge, 2023. | Includes bibliographical references and index. |
Identifiers: LCCN 2022034037 (print) | LCCN 2022034038 (ebook) | ISBN 9781032228884 (hbk) | ISBN 9781032228891 (pbk) | ISBN 9781003274650 (ebk)
Subjects: LCSH: Holocaust, Jewish (1939-1945)—Psychological aspects. | Generational trauma. | Holocaust survivors—Family relationships. | Children of Holocaust survivors—Mental health. | Holocaust survivors—Mental health. | Holocaust survivors—Biography.
Classification: LCC RC451.4.H62 P79 2023 (print) | LCC RC451.4.H62 (ebook) | DDC 940.53/18019—dc23/eng/20220923
LC record available at https://lccn.loc.gov/2022034037
LC ebook record available at https://lccn.loc.gov/2022034038

ISBN: 978-1-032-22888-4 (hbk)
ISBN: 978-1-032-22889-1 (pbk)
ISBN: 978-1-003-27465-0 (ebk)

DOI: 10.4324/9781003274650

Typeset in Times New Roman
by codeMantra

To all our family members whom we lost in the Holocaust but whose memory lives with us forever.

Contents

List of figures ix
List of contributors xi

1 Aftermath: Memory, Postmemory, and Postmemorial Work After the Holocaust 1
RONY ALFANDARY AND JUDITH TYDOR BAUMEL-SCHWARTZ

PART I
Cultural and Psychological Aspects of Postmemorial Work 7

2 Searching, Searching, Searching… Are There Any Relatives in the Room? 9
RONY ALFANDARY

3 Then Came Hitler: A Lifetime of Choices on My Path of Postmemorial Work 31
JUDITH TYDOR BAUMEL-SCHWARTZ

4 Reflections on Postmemory – With Some Notes from Ireland and Greece 44
RICHARD PINE

5 Traumatic Childhood and Growing Up in the Shadow of Trauma: When Post-Trauma Meets Postmemory: The Story of David, a Holocaust Survivor 60
MAIA JESSICA SHOHAM

6 From Stone Tomb to Flourishing Vineyard: Moving from
Silent Testimony to Living Creativity in "Creating Memory", a
Bibliotherapy Initiative for Third Generation Holocaust Survivors 72
BELLA SAGI

7 Never Forget – The Net Will Remember: Connective Memory
as a Form of Postmemory in the Age of Digital Platforms 87
OSHRI BAR-GIL

PART II
Postmemorial work in Literature and Art 109

8 Letting the Monster In? Illustrating the Holocaust in
Contemporary Israeli Children's Picture Books 111
ERGA HELLER

9 "Where's the Little Girl? What Little Girl? Was There
Ever a Little Girl?": From Narrative Memory to Emotional
Postmemory in Nava Semel's Book *And the Rat Laughed* 124
NAAMA RESHEF

10 The Presence of Absence; Postmemory in My Life 137
NAOMI SHMUEL

11 *I Was a Child of Holocaust Survivors*: Second Generation
Postmemory in Animated Documentary 146
LIAT STEIR-LIVNY

12 "If It's ME Reading the Signs": Carl Jung's Synchronicity and
the A-Causal in Holocaust Postmemory at the Movies 157
MICHELLE LISSES-TOPAZ

13 Writing the Erasure 175
ILANA EILATI SHALIT

Index 187

Figures

1	Bondy and Benjamin Cohen	18
2	Bondy and Edmond	18
3	Edmond and Benjamin	19
4	Bondy, Benjamin, and Bondy's mother, Mazeltov	19
5	Bondy, Benjamin, and Rosette	20
6	Parc Zoologique de Paris (Lion)	21
7	Librairie Hachette (Le Paradisier)	21
8	La Grande Marque Française Cambodge	22
9	Labortorie Bouty Le Sirop de Gaïarsol	22
10	Blecao Hippocampe	23
11	Bon Points S' Germian	24
12	1939 – Benjamin's billet de satisfaction	24
13	Postcard to Benjamin	25
14	Benjamin's diary	26
15	Benjamin's témoignages de satisfaction	26
16	Benjamin's Bookmark, July 1942	27
17	The list that started our journey	88
18	Map location of our virtual journey based on the stations mentioned in her notes	89
19	The first page of testimony	97
20	The second page of testimony	97
21	List of people from Drujsk who were murdered. Automatically linked by the Yad Vashem algorithms	98
22	Consolidation suggestion at the Yad Vashem archive. The human needs to connect the dots for the machine	98
23	Screenshot of connected archives search from Jewishgen.org website. Each line is a search in records found in different databases	99
24	Savta Hanna and I	101

25	Moshe and Salvator Segura	166
26	Salvator Segura in 1987, at the age of 73. Moshe Segura in 2018, at the age of 93	166
27	Advertisement for the film "Gunga Din"	169
28	Advertisement for children's Chanukah program at the movie theater	170
29	Partial Segura Family Tree	172

Contributors

Rony Alfandary, Ph.D, is a clinical social worker, psychoanalytic psychotherapist, and photographer. He is a lecturer at the School of Social Work at the University of Haifa and the former director of the Post-Graduate Program of Psychoanalytic Psychotherapy at Bar-Ilan University, Israel. His recent publications include *Exile and Return: A Psychoanalytic Study of Lawrence Durrell's The Alexandria Quartet* and *Postmemory, Psychoanalysis and Holocaust Ghosts: The Salonica Cohen Family and Trauma across Generations*, both published by Routledge.

Oshri Bar-Gil, Ph.D. is the grandson of the deceased Hanna Kugler. He has graduated from the psychoanalysis, culture, and hermeneutics post-graduate program at Bar-Ilan University, Israel. His dissertation, titled "The Google Self", explored the ways in which usage of digital platforms changes our self-perception.

Prof. Judith Tydor Baumel-Schwartz is the director of the Arnold and Leona Finkler Institute of Holocaust Research, the Abraham and Edita Spiegel family professor in Holocaust Research, the Rabbi Pynchas Brener professor in Research on the Holocaust of European Jewry, and professor of Modern Jewish History in the Israel and Golda Koschitzky Department of Jewish History and Contemporary Jewry. Born in New York in 1959, she immigrated to Israel with her parents in 1974 and completed her undergraduate and graduate degrees at Bar-Ilan University (Ph.D. History 1986). In 1980, she joined the staff of the Institute for the Study of Diaspora Jewry, and after its inception in 1981, she worked in the Arnold and Leona Finkler Institute of Holocaust Research until 2002. She directed the Institute for the Study of Religious Zionism (2009–2011), the Fanya Gottesfeld Heller Center for the Study of Women in Judaism (2011–2017), and the Helena and Paul Schulmann School for Basic Jewish Studies (2013–2018), all at Bar-Ilan University. She has written and edited numerous books and articles about religious life during and after the Holocaust, gender and the Holocaust, descendants of Holocaust survivors and Holocaust commemoration, and public memory in the State of Israel. She is married to Prof. Joshua Schwartz and together they have a large blended family.

Erga Heller, Ph.D., is a senior lecturer at Kaye Academic College of Education, Be'er Sheva, Israel. She teaches in the departments of art history and Hebrew and children's literature. Dr. Heller is also the editor-in-chief of Lexi-Kaye, a lexical peer-reviewed Hebrew journal on education and teaching. She is a member in an international research team, CoHLit-21 (Antwerp University), that studies contemporary Holocaust literatures. She has published widely in both Hebrew and English.

Michelle Lisses-Topaz is a developmental and educational psychologist who was born and raised in the Los Angeles area. In the 1990s, she immigrated to Israel, where she studied at the Hebrew University in Jerusalem. Today, she has an active career in both the public and private sectors, where she works with children, parents, and educators. She also teaches at the Open University of Israel and is the proud mother of two. As often as possible, she still loves to take in a movie, as does her sister, their seven cousins, and the combined 11 great grandchildren of Salvator and Sarah Segura.

Richard Pine is director of the Durrell Library of Corfu (Greece) where he lives (www.durrelllibrarycorfu.com). He is the author of 20 books, including *The Diviner: the art of Brian Friel* (1990/1999), *Lawrence Durrell: the Mindscape* (1994/2005/2023), *The Disappointed Bridge: Ireland and the Post-Colonial World* (2014), *A Writer in Corfu: an essay on Borderlands, Exile and Metaphor* (2020), and *The Quality of Life: essays on Cultural Politics 1978–2018* (2021).

Naama Reshef is the head of the literature department, a teacher, and a researcher at the Kaye Academic College of Education in Beer Sheva, Israel. Reshef is researching various aspects of the concept "identity" and focuses on literary texts as a space for shaping and formulating identity consciousness. Her current research project focuses on identity, trauma, and memory in literary texts.

Bella Sagi, Ph.D., is a bibliotherapist (Private Practice) and lecturer at David Yellin Academic College of Education and at the psychotherapy program at the psychological service of the Hebrew University of Jerusalem. Her work focuses specifically on the junction point between literature, gender, and psychology, especially trauma. She studies writing after trauma, especially sexual trauma and childhood abuse. She recently published a short stories book, called *Greenstick Fracture* (2021), that deals with trauma and recovery, and wrote an epilogue for Holocaust survivor's diary that was published in Berlin (Voigt, 2014) and now translated into Hebrew.

Ilana Eilati Shalit is a clinical psychologist and a member at the Tel Aviv Institute of Contemporary Psychoanalysis. Ilana has been involved in psychotherapy and psychoanalysis for over 20 years at a private clinic and serves as an individual and group counselor in several facilities teaching psychotherapy. In addition, Ilana is a writer and has published short stories. Among her publications are "Living on a tree", in Hamusach 62 - Articles and Essays (www:blog.nli.org.il); "The face is the bars", in Hamusach 81- Articles and Essays (www.blog.nli.org. il). Ilana focuses on the relationship between psychoanalysis and writing, literature, poetry, art, and creativity.

Naomi Shmuel, Ph.D., is an author, illustrator, and anthropologist living in Israel. She is the daughter of the author and poet Karen Gershon, who came to England on the Kindertransport from Germany in 1938. Naomi's original prize-winning children's books are widely used in Israeli schools to foster inter-cultural understanding and tolerance. Naomi was awarded the Israeli Prime Minister's prize for literature in 2011, teaches in various academic institutions, and runs workshops training professionals to work with human diversity.

Maia Jessica Shoham is a clinical psychologist, psychotherapist, and supervisor. She is also the founder and director of B-Tnua Psychotherapy Clinic. She teaches at the University of Haifa in the seminary for advanced studies in educational psychology the course: emotional aspects in psychodiagnostics. Maia is a Ph.D. candidate at Bar-Ilan University, Psychoanalysis and Hermeneutics Track. For many years, she worked as a clinical psychologist at AMCHA, the Israeli center for psychological and social support for Holocaust survivors and their descendants. Maia was also the senior psychologist at the Talpiot Children's Village – Day Center department.

Liat Steir-Livny is an associate professor in the Department of Culture at Sapir Academic College. She also teaches in the Cultural Studies MA program and in the Department of Literature, Language, and the Arts at the Open University of Israel. Her research focuses on Holocaust commemoration in Israel from the 1940s until the present. It combines Holocaust studies, memory studies, cultural studies, trauma studies, and film studies. She is the author of many articles and five books: *Two Faces in the Mirror* (Eshkolot-Magness, 2009, Hebrew) analyzes the representation of Holocaust survivors in Israeli cinema; *Let the Memorial Hill Remember* (Resling, 2014, Hebrew) discusses the changing memory of the Holocaust in contemporary Israeli culture; *Is it O.K to Laugh About It?* (Vallentine Mitchell, 2017) analyzes Holocaust humor, satire, and parody in Israeli culture; *Three Years, Two Perspectives, One Trauma* (The Herzl Institute for the Study of Zionism, University of Haifa, 2019, Hebrew) analyzes the media of prominent Jewish organizations in the United States and Eretz-Israel in the aftermath of WWII; *Remaking Holocaust Memory* (Syracuse University Press, 2019) analyzes documentary Cinema by Third-Generation Survivors in Israel. She is the recipient of the 2019 Young Scholar Award given jointly by the Association for Israel Studies (AIS) and the Israel Institute.

Chapter 1

Aftermath

Memory, Postmemory, and Postmemorial Work After the Holocaust

Rony Alfandary and Judith Tydor Baumel-Schwartz

Introduction

Warsaw 1988. Judith Tydor Baumel-Schwartz makes her first trip to Poland, where her father was born 85 years earlier. The country to which he was deported from Nazi Germany as a Polish citizen in 1938. Poland is in the grip of a communist regime that will only fall a year later. Buildings are gray, streets are clean, and stores are stocked with a strange array of goods, many shoddily made. She reaches the Krasinski Gardens, where Warsaw Jews once strolled on Sabbath afternoons, now full of local children at play. From all directions, Polish washes over her, a language that she rarely heard as a child, but has surprisingly begun to understand.

Salonica 1993. Rony Alfandary visits Greece, on his way back to Israel after ten years spent in England. He went there to follow up addresses of his family, found on the back on envelopes that were part of a huge collection of letters exchanged between family members who died in the Holocaust.

Strangely, both Judith and Rony felt at home on these visits, as if they are remembering places never visited and experiences never had. Among those experiences is not only Judith's father's deportation to Poland, but the five-and-a-half years that he spent in Nazi camps, Auschwitz and Buchenwald. Her father is a Holocaust Survivor.

Rony did not find any of the original houses, as they were all bombed during the war. What he did find was a sense of the uncanny, that elusive Freudian term which denotes both familiarity and strangeness. That impossible but residual feeling has not left him since as the journey began.

Both Judith and Rony, editors of this collection of essays, were born after the end of the Second World War. And yet, they both feel that the events of that period have left an indelible stamp upon their psyche. It is not a unique experience among members of their generation and those who follow.

The most important event in their lives, one that shaped much of their lives, occurred long before they were born. Judith is a member of the "Second Generation", daughter of a Holocaust survivor. Rony comes from a family devastated by the Holocaust. Both have their own memories, but they are interspersed with, and at times even overwhelmed by, "Postmemory", memories of traumatic events that the previous generation experienced, transmitted to them through stories, images, rituals, and other behaviors.

How can one address a complex Holocaust legacy that often defies comprehension? In what way can we keep these memories of others alive, while ensuring that they do not overwhelm our own memories and life? One way is through postmemorial activity, a positive enterprise that keeps transgenerational postmemory from becoming toxic. Such activity can be expressed on the personal level such as in journal and memoir writing, or on the public level in spheres such as Holocaust studies, psychoanalysis, hermeneutics, and the arts. It can be carried out by the second, third, or fourth generation – those who have a direct family connection to the Holocaust – or by those whose ancestors were untouched by the cataclysm. Whether linked to the Holocaust by blood or by choice, postmemorial work transforms all those involved into memorial candles for the dead. Yet, at the same time, it also helps them retain their own identity by channeling postmemory into contemporary action.

Such writing is even more challenging than usual. The choice of words is delicate and involves careful monitoring of the transformation of unconscious processes into tangible linguistic forms.

For instance, what word should one use when describing the fate of the Jews and other victims of the Nazi regime in Europe and the trauma that is still resonating?

Were they slaughtered like animals?

Did they perish in the sense of the disintegration of their civil rights and then of their bodies?

Were they murdered like helpless victims in a well-planned criminal act?

Were they annihilated in a way that would leave no sign whatsoever of their existence?

Were they exterminated like vermin and parasites which lived off the bodies of superior beings?

Or did they simply die, as is the natural and inevitable fate of every living organism?

The trauma suffered is not "just" the terrible loss of all those millions of individuals and communities, the places where they lived, and the traditions they upheld. Trauma, by its nature, refers to what is not being spoken, what is not being able to be expressed through ordinary language and action.

The essays included in this volume strive to describe the effects and repercussions of those traumatic events. It is a book about postmemorial work carried out both by descendants of Holocaust survivors, and by those whose connection to the cataclysm was more tangential. Its genesis was an International (Zoom) Conference on Postmemorial Work, held in January 2021 under the auspices of The Finkler Institute of Holocaust Research, the Louis and Gabi Weisfeld School of Social Work at Bar-Ilan University, the School of Social Work at the University of Haifa, and the Steinmetz-Hershcovitz Foundation. Each of the dozen scholars whose chapters appear in this volume focuses on a different aspect of postmemorial activity, but all have a common denominator: an attempt to come to terms with the past and its legacy through positive, present-day endeavors.

To assist the reader in following the narrative we have grouped the chapters into two sections. The first deals with postmemorial work in the cultural and psychological spheres and contains seven chapters.

Rony Alfandary writes about his search for pre-Holocaust and Holocaust-related family history on three continents, through the use of family letters and documents. He explores the aspects of postmemorial work which have extended beyond the translation, compilation, and interpretation of family letters that belonged to victims of the Holocaust. He demonstrates how the search for more information to fill up the gaps in the matrix of memory becomes, and remains, a Sisyphean endeavor governed by *repetition compulsion*. Working through a small collection of postcards and personal notes discovered recently, he illustrates *the uncanny* aspects of the preoccupation with the past and some of its creative and hopeful outcomes.

Judith Tydor Baumel-Schwartz focuses on her personal life and professional choices as a member of the Second Generation. She explores the concept of *goral*, a Hebrew word translated as "fate" or "predestination", and its role in shaping her personal choices of Holocaust-related postmemorial work on both the personal and professional levels. She analyzes her choice to specialize in Holocaust Studies and discusses the difference between destiny and predestination, the need for individuality while making decisions, the role of being a "Second Generation" memorial candle, and various outside influences on postmemorial work.

Richard Pine reflects about Postmemory while bringing examples from Ireland and Greece. Referring to traumatic periods in the history of Ireland and Greece, he suggests that local folk memories of the trauma, that in the first instance are transmitted orally, can become transformed into literary narratives in novels, plays, and memoirs that continue to embody and represent the memories of trauma as part of a national or ethnic narrative.

Maia Jessica Shoham writes about the story of David, a Holocaust survivor. She presents the case of a post-traumatic Holocaust survivor who was separated from his family between the ages of 6 and 11. This long separation was traumatic for him. At age 11, he reunited with his mother and they lived together until she died. However, they failed to go through a processing process. She describes the patient's therapeutic journey and processing of multiple layers of trauma: his own traumatic experiences, and his mother's, which he absorbed through intergenerational transfer.

Bella Sagi reviews the findings of a study about a new Israeli program, called "Creating Memory", that includes creative work in bibliotherapeutic methodology. The project brings together texts written by survivors and creative writing by young members of the third and fourth generations. The study concludes that young participants engage in the program through observation, intrinsic connection, and creativity that enable them to revive the past and make it part of their story.

Oshri Bar-Gil explores the way new digital technologies (search engines, genealogy websites, and social networks) are allowing connections between memory fragments that once belonged to living people. With the help of Big Data, it has become possible for the third generation to discover names, faces, places, and records that skipped generations and uncover new dimensions of the Holocaust memory. His chapter, a very contemporary one that ends this section, describes the changing patterns in memory that follow technological changes. Using his own personal story, he illustrates the transition from personal to collective, mediated by the connected society – the connective postmemory.

The second section of this volume contains six essays and focuses on post-memorial activity in Literature and the Arts.

Erga Heller writes about illustrating the Holocaust in contemporary Israeli children's picture books. She focuses on illustrations in Israeli picture books about the Shoah published between 2000 and 2020 as representations of the Shoah's postmemory. Although illustrations are known to be significant mediators, there is lack of discussion about illustration in Israeli Holocaust picture books. This chapter tries to fill this gap by studying the construction of postmemory through book illustrations.

Naama Reshef writes about the transition from narrative memory to emotional memory in Israeli author Nava Semel's book *And the Rat Laughed*. Semel, one of the first Israeli authors to write about the influence of Holocaust trauma on the second generation, asserted that the narrative, integrative, and coherent memory does not have the power to carry the burden of the memory of trauma, which is often a silent memory. Semel points to an alternative – Emotional Memory – "which is beyond the facts and the events themselves". In her book *And the Rat Laughed* (2001), she indicates the main realm through which the silent memory permeates the second and third generations and is transformed into emotional postmemory: the work of art.

Naomi Shmuel focuses on the presence of absent postmemory in her life. Being the daughter of Kindertransport child from Germany Kaethe Loewenthal, later to become the poet and writer Karen Gershon (1923–1993), she presents her unique experiences of postmemory and their effects on her life. Her analysis includes an attempt to understand her mother's writing both as a form of self-therapy and as the voice of the Kindertransport generation, a voice which has accompanied Naomi on her own journey from England to Israel in search of a viable home. This chapter follows the delicate thread connecting the generations, woven into families and books, creating meaning and continuity despite – or perhaps because of – the tragedies of history.

Liat Steir-Livny describes and analyzes second-generation postmemory in animated documentary. Since the 1980s, numerous representations in the Western world have introduced second-generation Holocaust survivors as protagonists, and described growing up in the shadow of the parents' trauma. She explores the first animated documentary dealing entirely with postmemory of a second-generation Holocaust survivor "I was a Child of Holocaust Survivors". The film is based on the graphic novel of the same name by Bernice Eisenstein (2006) in which she gives a first-person description of growing up in the 1950s in Toronto's Kensington Market neighborhood. The chapter analyzes how through the particularities of the animation's textures, the film opens up new ways of visualizing themes that previously eluded live action films: Holocaust-related fantasies, dreams, and hallucinations.

Michelle Lisses-Topaz presents the unusual manner in which she was spurred on by her maternal grandfather's legacy from a very young age, and how this quest developed and reached an apex in the last few years. Her grandfather's family's livelihood in the movie theater business in Salonica, Greece, during the decades prior to the Holocaust, serves as the stage upon which her personal journey to discover more about his past took hold, beginning more than 40 years ago, and culminating in the present.

In a very personal chapter that ends this section, Ilana Eilati Shalit discusses the possibility of the possible representation of personal trauma by writing a text of a postmemory. Working against the danger of nullification and obliteration associated with experiences of the Holocaust, writing a postmemory is an attempt to perform a contrary (mental) act: an act of creating attendance and of continued development and growth. This act helps build a representation of the experience and engage in communication with respect to it. She presents an imaginary letter written to her grandmother, whom she had never met, and discusses the psychological processes related to creating (concrete and symbolic) attendance in the events, creating an illusion of a responsive and beneficial internal presence, and through this further processing the mirroring and containment processes cut short due to the Holocaust.

Together, these essays comprise a personal, and yet scholarly corpus, that sheds light on the processes by which traumatic fragments of events from the past are contained through postmemorial work, neutralizing their toxic elements that continued into the present.

Event, memory, and postmemory are a never-ending dialectic. Even before an event comes to an end, it has often sown the seeds of memory. Those, in turn, open the door to postmemory, and thus to postmemorial work, long before the event is relegated to the distant past. As we see in this volume, the varied forms of postmemorial activity in the aftermath of a cataclysmic event such as the Holocaust, help us in re-placing the legacy of that event within our lives as a positive force, enabling us to join past and present, while allowing us to move forward into the future.

Part I

Cultural and Psychological Aspects of Postmemorial Work

Chapter 2

Searching, Searching, Searching... Are There Any Relatives in the Room?

Rony Alfandary

Introduction

Once the sensitivity for the dimension of the postmemory had been evoked, there can be no stopping. In the following pages, I will explore a postmemory tale of remembering events taking place more than 20 years before I was born, yet having a continuing impact upon the way I view the world, history and myself. It is a case study of a larger issue to which this volume is devoted: how postmemory affects us, the questions it raises, and our attempts to find answers.

Simultaneously, it is the story of my search to understand how the events of the Holocaust have left an indelible mark upon my psyche. It is not just my own story but that of my generation, 2nd and 3rd generation of Holocaust survivors, trying to make sense of the most profound period in modern times that still shapes today's world.

Throughout 2021, I put the final touches to my book about the collection of hundreds of letters, photographs, postcards, and other artifacts belonging to the Salonica Cohen family.[1] The collection is based upon the triangular exchange of letters between Rita Cohen Parenti (1903–1986) in Palestine, Leon (1901–1942) and Isaac Cohen (1898–1942) in Paris, and the rest of the Cohen family in Salonica. All members of the Cohen family in Europe, more than 30 adults and children, perished in Auschwitz. The only survivor was my grandmother, Rita Cohen Parenti, who immigrated to Palestine in 1934 where she and her husband raised five children, begetting in turn 14 grandchildren and 28 great grandchildren to date.

The book's publication recalled the Hebrew proverb: "finished but not completed" (*Tam ve-lo-nishlam*). Beyond the fact that the book's scope precluded an exhaustive and comprehensive study of a correspondence that survived its authors, and despite my honoring my grandmother's command to remember her murdered family, my own deep wish to put my preoccupation with the Holocaust aside remained unsatisfied. I hoped that once the book was published, I could return to other interests in my life. But despite doing just that, I remained haunted by the memory of my own family in

DOI: 10.4324/9781003274650-3

particular, and that dark period in the history of humankind in general. I was still drawn to reading more material, organizing a conference on the subject and of course, editing this volume of essays with my colleague, Prof. Judith Tydor Baumel-Schwartz.

Hence my chapter's title. I believe that once you realize that a *postmemory* lives within and in a sense, dominates you, you will be always guided toward postmemorial work. In other words, once you have begun searching for your lost relatives, knowing well that they are not to be found, the search itself will become a driving force in your life.

When does a postmemory come into existence? Here, a psychoanalytic approach is useful. I suggest that there must be some external stimulus in the shape of an artifact, whether a photograph, letter, film, or even a remembrance of a story once told. This becomes an encounter with a significant other, a testimony to a life lived before one's time. That testimony is elaborated and begins to become one's own memory, i.e. a postmemory, sending its psychic roots into the individual's own history. The link formed between that external stimulus, an echo of someone else's experience, and the internal representation, which is intrinsic to one's being, creates a web of relations and association, a matrix of meanings and possibilities, engaging one in the search.

This is not an ordinary search that one can easily abandon if it does not immediately yield satisfactory results. Rather, it is an obsessive search that becomes a goal in itself, leaving its subject matter somewhat in the shadow. A search that outsiders view with a slight worry, lest you dedicate unreasonable amounts of time, emotional and mental energy, and sometimes even considerable resources to it; a search that ultimately consumes you.

The Cohen Collection

The letters inspiring this study are documents found on four separate occasions in varied locations. They were written in four different languages: most in French, some in Ladino, a few in Solitreo, and a few legal documents in Greek.[2] The choice of languages, including the dominance of some, is indicative of the Cohen family's national and cultural complexity in Salonica, not unlike other Jewish families at that time.

Ladino was the language of Jews in Salonica, and other Central and Southern parts of Europe, used for more informal and daily usage.[3] It was a language acquired in transit during the expulsion of Jewish communities from 15th-century Spain. Thus, it is a language of exile, travel, and longing.[4]

This memoir is written in yet another language, English. Undoubtedly, some aspects of the original idioms are lost through translations, which the circumscribed scope of this study does not allow us to properly explore.[5] Much can be learned by analyzing the Cohen's choice to use one language or another. French was the formal language that placed them in the social and cultural position to which they aspired, while Ladino was the home language, their mother tongue, a language of idioms and playfulness, allowing them to convey messages, sometimes clandestinely, which French could not. This will have to wait for another study.

It is a Tower of Babel where confusion and misunderstanding are prevalent, where multiple voices are heard simultaneously. It is also indicative of the times we live in. How apt that such a memoir, a tale of loss and survival, will be told out of such linguistic confusion and multiplicity. As Jacques Derrida (1930–2004) wrote in his essay about Babel, the Tower of Babel not only represents the multiplicity of language, which cannot be reduced, but it points to a defect, an inability to complete a story.[6] There will always remain a sense of incompleteness, of something missing. The familiar language contains an unfamiliar sound, thus evoking the Freudian sense of The Uncanny, *Das unheimlich*.[7] The translation process does not aim to purely transfer meaning from one language to another in this memoir but to show the links created by discovering and reading the letters.

The first box was left behind by Rita and Samuel in their apartment in Israel. The letters in that box were received from Rita's mother, brothers, and sister from Salonica, and brothers in Paris between 1930 and 1941. That box contained about 80 letters, handwritten in French and Ladino, as well as their envelopes and some postcards and photographs.

The letters' physical state is often quite poor as the box went through serious physical mishaps. It was subjected to at least two floods, while the family lived in a small neighborhood called Sova, located in the Ayalon Wadi in South Tel-Aviv, during the 1930s, soon after they arrived in Palestine from Salonica.[8] Numerous letters cannot be read due to their poor condition. Some of them are badly smudged.

When the box was opened in 1993, the addresses in Paris from which Leon sent his letters captured the readers' attention. Especially the last address: 5 Rue le Goff. Rita's children began investigating. Through hard work, perseverance, and good luck, they found a lead. Benjamin's wife, Elly, and Esther's friend, Ines Cohen (no relation), came across a photograph of Leon and Bondy in a publication by Serge Klarsfeld (b. 1935). They contacted Serge and his wife, Beate (b. 1939), who provided them with the name of the person who gave them that photograph, Mireille Florent Saül from Paris. After intensive overseas telephone conversations with the French telephone company, Mireille was indeed found. In a very emotional telephone conversation, she confirmed that she was the daughter of Leon Cohen's wife's sister, Rosette Saül, who lived in Provence.

Thanks to Mireille's insistence, the **second box** of letters was "found" among Rosette's possessions in 1999. The box had apparently been kept in the 5 Rue le Goff apartment from soon after the war, and was there for two decades, while Rosette's and Bondy's brother, Edmond, was in residence.

Only after Edmond left the apartment during the late 1950s was the box given to Rosette and kept at her home in Provence.[9]

The third box of letters and documents was discovered, again "accidentally", in the same house in Provence in 2014 by Rosette. It contains about 80 letters, 70 postcards, and about 50 photographs received by Leon Cohen from his mother and siblings in Salonica, Paris, and Palestine, between 1927 and 1940, along with letters and documents that Leon took with him to Paris after leaving Salonica.

The discovery of **the fourth box**, early in 2017, was an even bigger surprise. It contained more about 100 letters, 100 photographs, and 150 postcards along with many other items such as Leon's business stamps, diary, check book, various legal documents, visiting cards, two small paintings done by an unknown artist, and other objects, covering the period between 1924 and 1931. It was apparently found in the same house in Provence, but for some reason it was only spoken of recently.

All attempts to understand how that was possible were met with nondescript answers, ranging from *"there was a big mess when we moved"* to a simple *"I just don't know. I just found it"*. It is most tempting to speculate about the real and deeper layers of such a denial, but being a sensitive issue, perhaps covering a family secret that risked causing unnecessary pain, we dropped it for the time being, leaving much to wonder about. What is the story behind the boxes' gradual revelation? What secret narratives lie beyond? As we shall see, the sense of secrecy and surprise lingers on.

Who Is the Story About?

Of all the narratives, which is the more significant in this postmemorial tale? To whom should we draw attention? Is it necessary to point to figures at the expense of others, to make it a better story? Using these literary ploys seems almost inappropriate when dealing with such subject matter, and yet, these considerations are inevitable. Decisions need to be made, and better out in the open. There's a story to be told, and it needs to be told in the best possible way.

Four key figures feature in the letters: Leon Cohen in Paris, who received the majority of the letters, his older brother Isaac, their sister Ines in Salonica, and their sister Rita in Tel Aviv. The paterfamilias, Shabtai Cohen, a wealthy Salonica merchant, died at a relatively young age sometime after 1917 (no exact date available). This would also explain Isaac and Leon's move to Paris in search of financial security and stability. Rachelle, the widow, relied upon her children's support.

The first personal letter Leon received after moving to Paris is from his younger brother Eli in Salonica, dated January 22, 1925. The letter is written on the back of a photograph of Ines' oldest son, Solomon.

I'm sending you a postcard of cute Solomon. He seemed to be annoyed. I have received two letters from you, including the content in the envelopes [Money?].[10] *I'll reply in more length tomorrow. We are very happy that you are progressing in your work and becoming more independent.*

At home everyone is fine. As in Marseilles, the weather is very good, and it hardly feels like winter. We received a postcard from Isaac, and are also still waiting for a letter from him.

Yours,
Eli

Leon first letter is addressed to Samuel Parenti in Salonica, who is about to marry Leon's sister, Rita, and dated October 14, 1930.

Dear Sam,

Allow me to address you in such an intimate way even before I can call you my dear brother-in-law? Is it necessary to greet you? Is it necessary to compliment you on your choice of a bride? I will only say that I wish you much happiness and a long life. I am beginning to grasp that that is true happiness: home, a loving, beautiful, clever, loyal, and good-natured wife, one of us.

After one is married to such a woman, one can face life with more courage. I will be brief today and hope that you respond quickly so that we can get better acquainted. My brother Isaac also sends his greeting. He and his wife Martha are always busy. Even I only see him once or twice a week here in Paris, and even that only briefly.

Yours,
Leon

The wedding took place in Salonica on March 11, 1931. The young couple soon left Greece and settled in Palestine. Young Samuel Parenti was a Zionist activist. He was elected by the Zionist Federation of Greece to be a member of the organizing committee appointed to arrange the 8th Greek Zionist Congress.[11] This was based upon his local activity in the Zion Flag (*Degel Sion*), a Salonica Zionist Association, that included being the Treasurer of the local Jewish Zionist football team. In 1930 the Zionist Federation elected Parenti to be a member of the Hirsch Quarter committee, a Jewish group responsible for local Jewish affairs in that predominantly Jewish district. It was the very same district where years later, the Jews of Salonica were rounded up before being sent to their deaths in Auschwitz.[12]

The last letter in the collection was sent to Bondy's sister, Rosette. It is dated November 16, 1942 and needs no explanation.

M[elle] *Denise Ertzlichoff to Paul and Rosette Paris, Wednesday, November 16, 1942*

… The concierge from 5 rue Le Goff has asked me to say she would very much like to have news as she liked your sister dearly… As you have heard, I was at the Broussais hospital where I had been since October and from which I

came out last week. I was being treated for arthritis of the upper foot and bone decalcification. You probably heard these details from your sister Bondy as she came to see me on November 2 with the two little ones on her way to put flowers on her uncle's grave...So when Melle Froment (The concierge) came to tell me the dreadful news, how they were all arrested, your poor sister, your brother-in-law, the two little ones, your dear parents, your sister Suzanne, I could not believe in such a terrible misfortune.

Is it possible that such things can be done, taking young men away is one thing, we are at war, but women, poor little children, and elderly people, it is too horrible, especially in the way the concierge from 5 rue Le Goff described it, it is unthinkable and so appalling, your poor sister crashing down on the floorboards with eyes of dread, I am so worried about her health and above all little Benjamin and little Elaine, if they had at least been left with you, or with me, I would have taken care of them, and I am sure she would have felt easier knowing them to be safe.

I was told that the friend across from them got a letter in November telling him they were at Drancy but were going away that very evening, to where they did not know.

Maybe you have some news as I heard you were left free though I cannot believe this arrest is about religion, I suppose it is to do with them being Turkish citizens, as I read in the papers about Turkey siding with England and Russia. They should have gone away early in November for I know many who are safe and well in Lyon and Marseille.

I should very much have liked to come to see you and talk in person about all these sad things, but I cannot walk and am still in the same state regarding my foot which gives me a lot of pain, and then I worry so much about your sister and the two poor children, they were so sweet.

If you have any news, I beg of you dear Mme Rosette let me know, or if you can come to see me it would make me so happy; hoping you will come – please pass on my regards to your husband...
Denise

Leon Cohen

The first letters that Leon received and kept during the 1920s describe a young man working as an accountant, first in Paris, then in Marseilles, and later back in Paris. After considerable initial difficulties, including a failed business venture with his brother, he did well, and remained in business as a freelance accountant during those economically turbulent years. He maintained close ties with friends from Salonica, who also served as both a social and professional network. Like many at that time, he was an *émigré*, finding a home away from home within the Greek immigrant community in Paris, which was a very cosmopolitan, cultured, and lively city during the *roaring twenties* and thirties.[13] Some of these letters are very jovial, showing strong friendly connections between young men who enjoy their years as popular single men, seeking fun in their personal lives, and promotion in their professional ones.

Later, in the mid-1930s, Leon married Bondy Saül, from a family of Salonica Jews, who had immigrated to France,[14] an occasion for much celebration and greetings. The letters from that period describe domestic happiness as well as longing for the families back home. Leon hopes that his brothers, sister, and mother will join him in Paris. He even hopes for his sister in Palestine to come and join him with her family, even though he acknowledges that the life they have made in the growing Jewish community there, binds them to that remote land. In reality, after he left Salonica in 1925, Leon Cohen never again saw his Salonica family, nor his sister in Palestine.

Once married, Leon and Bondy seemed to lead a relatively comfortable family life in Paris. Dozens of postcards from their trips in France attest to that. In many photographs, one sees them enjoying the countryside, the sea, and friendly encounters. Soon, they have two young children, Benjamin (1935), and Rachelle (1939).

Isaac Cohen

Many of the letters Leon received were from his older brother, Isaac, and his Christian wife, Martha. Isaac is much of a mystery. No one really knows what he did for a living. He was involved in various commercial activities, including attempts at starting a restaurant. Some activities involved export and import. However, he did not fare well in business, was often in debt, and, more than once, escaped debtors. On more than one occasion, he had to leave Paris, or at least to pretend that he was leaving, to avoid them. The couple had no children, at least while the correspondence was taking place. Isaac seldom wrote letters that did not contain requests for financial assistance. His brothers, sisters, and mother often reproached him for not keeping in touch. He seemed to vacillate between excesses: either deep in somber moods, prepared to sell his wife's dowry to rescue himself, or enjoying apparent success, taking lavish holidays in France, and sending postcards from his tours. His whereabouts during the war, or the question of what actually happened to him, remained unresolved to this day. Numerous archival and online searches, including Beate and Serge Klarsfeld's book documenting lists of Jews taken from France to concentration camps, revealed no evidence of his fate. An attempt to gather information was also made through the French Commission for the Compensation of Victims of Spoliation Resulting from the Anti-Semitic Legislation in Force during the Occupation, a governmental agency established by the French President Jacques Chirac in 2000, which so far has not yielded results.

Ines Cohen Matarasso

Ines is portrayed as the loving, benevolent, and caring elder sister. Married to Moise Matarasso, she was the mother of three children, and Rachelle Cohen's main source of comfort in the difficult years. She remained near her mother, taking her into her household. She led a stable family life and was the backbone of the Cohen family in Salonica. Leon turned to her when in need. Isaac the maverick shied away, fearing her disapproval. It was with her that Rita conducted the most moving exchanges through letters. Like her mother and sister, she dealt with increasingly difficult health issues, just as the economic situation in Salonica worsened. In her letters, she appears as an honest and direct woman, stern but empathic when she realized that it was expected of her. In the letters she wrote to her brother in Paris and her sister in Tel-Aviv, she always tried to keep them updated with family developments. Apart from informing them of her children's achievements, such as academic success, or reaching Bar-Mitzva age, she was always concerned with her younger brothers' futures. The main goal, common to many Jewish families, was to see them marry into good families, as well as having lucrative jobs that would allow them to provide for their future wives and children. Ines, her husband, and his parents and siblings, as well as their three children, were sent to the concentration camps like the vast majority of Salonica Jewry in 1943. No trace was found of their burial place.

Rita Cohen Parenti

The fourth figure, Rita, my grandmother, was the fifth child. She was an independent woman who worked as a teacher in the *Alliance Israélite Universelle* in Salonica.[15] She did not marry in haste, but only at age 30, quite unusual for a woman in those times, and usually attributed to having disqualifying characteristics. That was apparently not the case with her. She refused to compromise and had been in a relationship with a colleague at school, which her family did not approve of.[16] She was eventually married off to Samuel Parenti, introduced to her by her beloved brother Benjamin who knew him through their mutual work at the Theodor Herzl Association in Salonica.[17] The two were married in 1930. Rita became pregnant soon after and gave birth to their first of five children, Esther, in 1932. From the outset, Samuel stated that he wished to immigrate to Palestine, and despite Rita's reluctance, the young couple and their child (Rita was also pregnant with their second child) made their way by boat to Jaffa in 1933. As the letters sent to Salonica from Tel-Aviv in the following years showed, those were very hard times. Rita gave birth to four more children, including twins, and had to live at a much lower standard of living to her accustomed one. Like many immigrants, Samuel took on menial work and could not continue in his original occupation as a journalist. Eventually, he managed to open a stall at the Carmel Market in Tel-Aviv and was able to provide for his children, all of whom acquired a respectable profession, married, and had children through his support. The two maintained a humble way of life, but provided a safe and loving home for their five children during the difficult pre-state years in Israel, going through many riots that preceded the State's establishment. Not a Zionist, Rita often regretted the move, but was torn by the knowledge that otherwise, her fate would have been that of her siblings' – death in the concentration camps. After she parted from her mother, sister, and brothers in 1933, she never saw them again. That was her constant sorrow, projected onto future generations, a sorrow that had developed into my sense of being a living monument for all she had lost. A memory of her loss had developed into my postmemory.

Postscript: Benjamin's Secrets

After long deliberation among Rita's descendants, the collection was handed over to Yad Vashem in early 2020. It was almost like putting it to rest, a kind of a collective burial rite. The lingering hope that something else might be found was also put to rest.

But then, during May 2021, some more material was found. In Benjamin Parenti's apartment, Rita's youngest, who had compiled a beautiful booklet of some of the letters before he died in 2012, found a blue envelope containing some very special items. They were clearly taken from the Second box, originally discovered in 1999, but were secretly kept by him for all those years without his family's knowledge.[18]

Why did he keep these precious items in his own private collection, tucked away on a top shelf? Once that envelope was opened, even a cursory glance through the items provided a possible, painful, and moving explanation.

There were 27 items in that blue envelopes which can be divided into three categories: five family photographs, 13 painted cards, and a few personal notes and school evaluation sheets.

In the first photographs, Bondy holds her young son Benjamin as a baby which meant they were taken sometime during 1935 (Figure 1).

Another photograph shows Bondy with Edmond, her older brother, in a composition very similar to a photograph showing her with Leon, on a beach holiday (Figure 2).

Edmond survived. He appears in yet another photograph where he is holding Benjamin (Figure 3).

Suzanne, Bondy's youngest sister who also survived, was a young girl at the time, and is shown in a photograph, as is their mother, Mazaltov, who did not survive (Figures 4 and 5).

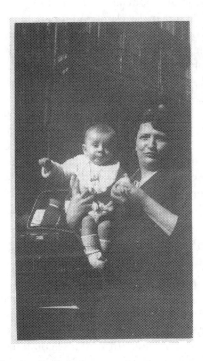

Figure 1 Bondy and Benjamin Cohen.

Figure 2 Bondy and Edmond.

Searching, Searching, Searching... Are There Any Relatives in the Room? 19

Figure 3 Edmond and Benjamin.

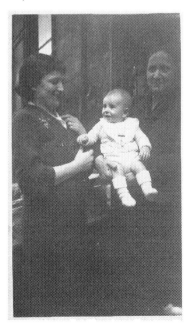

Figure 4 Bondy, Benjamin, and Bondy's mother, Mazaltov.

Figure 5 Bondy, Benjamin, and Rosette.

The collection of cards can be divided into several sub-groups. One contains colored painted cards showing animals (a lion and an American rhea) which was published by the Parisian Zoo, *Parc Zoologique de Paris*, in the second arrondissement, 6 kilometers away from where the Cohens lived at that time, on 5 Rue le Goff (Figure 6).

The second contains three colored painted cards of animals (a Bird of Paradise, a polar bear, and a Cobra snake), published by *Librairie Hachette* in Paris, a publishing and bookstore enterprise still in operation today (Figure 7).

The third is a color card published by *La Grande Marque Française*, which on one side carries a small map of Cambodia with various illustrations surrounding it, while on the other side is a printed text describing the country, which then was still a French colony (Figure 8).

The fourth contains color painted postcard-sized advertisements given with purchase. In this group, we find an advisement for a cough syrup made by the French *Labortorie Bouty* company, still in existence (Figure 9).

One can easily find similar cards from that period for sale on the internet, from five euro per card and upward. They have become collectors' items.

Figure 6 Parc Zoologique de Paris (Lion).

Figure 7 Librairie Hachette (Le Paradisier).

22 Rony Alfandary

Figure 8 La Grande Marque Française Cambodge.

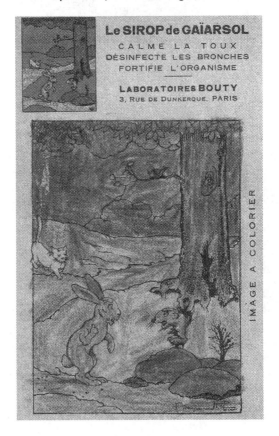

Figure 9 Labortorie Bouty Le Sirop de Gaïarsol.

Other advertisement cards in this group belong to *Blecao,* a coffee beverage firm, with one side showing an image of a Sea Horse while the other side describes the qualities of the drink (Figure 10).

Similar cards and posters from that period can also be found on internet auction sales. The fifth subgroup has three *Bon Points* issued by *Reseau De La Mer Vivante*, with one side showing a train, a car, and a drawing of the St. Germaine train station, while the other side beckons people to take a holiday at the beach. These *bons points* are the kind of rewards that used to be handed out to good pupils in French schools and were still in existence in the late 1960s (Figure 11).

The third category contains items easily identified as belonging to Benjamin. The first is a report card from Benjamin's kindergarten, at Place de la République in Brive, issued on 1939. On the back of the card, Leon writes to his four-year-old son: My darling *Jamin, Papa is very happy you are going to school and sends his love because you are a very good boy. Soon he will go to Brive to hug you along with the little sister and darling mummy* (Figure 12).

See you soon, Papa

Figure 10 Blecao Hippocampe.

Figure 11 Bon Points S' Germian.

Figure 12 1939 – Benjamin's billet de satisfaction.

The second item, dated December 22, 1939, is picture postcard Leon sent to Benjamin where Leon wrote:
A thousand tender kisses to my little darling, sending wishes for your good health and have a good holiday over merry Christmas.
See you very soon,
Papa (Figure 13)

The third item is a booklet in which Benjamin seems to have written. It is very delicate, tiny, ostensibly handmade, and delicately sewn. Most of the pages are blank but there are two notes that Benjamin wrote. It is certain that they are Benjamins, as they have the kind of spelling mistakes a child of his age would make (ché instead of chez, vé instead of vais). The first note is: *On Thursday I'm going to Auntie Rosette* (Bondy's sister) and the second: *On Thursday Dad is going to go to the shop* (Possibly Bondy's parents' shop) (Figure 14).

The fourth item is from July 1942, a few months before they were sent to Auschwitz, and is Benjamin's *témoignages de satisfaction*, an evaluation report from his primary school in Paris (Figure 15).

The last item is a piece of narrow paper that seems to have served Benjamin as a bookmark. It has his name on it, and the date, July 1942 (Figure 16).

That the Cohens spent considerable amount of time in Brive, some 460 km south of Paris, during 1939, raises some questions, particularly as the family knew nothing about it throughout their research. There was no indication of such a move in the other letters sent to Salonica or Tel Aviv. Why did they go

Figure 13 Postcard to Benjamin.

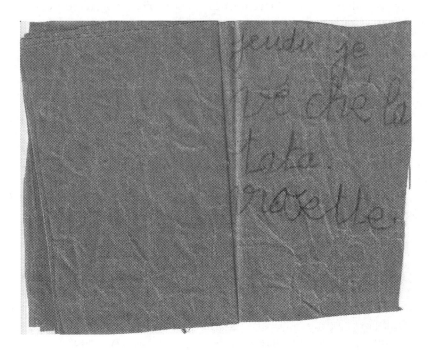

Figure 14 Benjamin's diary.

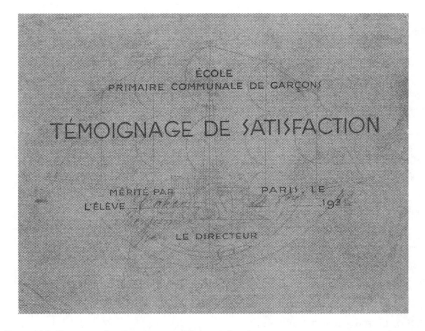

Figure 15 Benjamin's témoignages de satisfaction.

Figure 16 Benjamin's Bookmark, July 1942.

there? Clearly, it was not just for a holiday as Benjamin went to kindergarten there. It is possible that only Benjamin and his mother were there, and that Leon had stayed in Paris and commuted for weekends and holidays. Possibly, Leon had sent his infant daughter Rachelle (born February 1939) and wife to relative safety in the South of France after the beginning of what is thought of as the "Phoney War". "The Phoney War" was a period of eight months, beginning in September 1939 when France and England declared war on Germany, with very little military action. It ended abruptly in April 1940 when Germany invaded France. Many French families moved to the South during that time, and the Cohens may well have been a part of that trend. While unclear when they returned to their Rue le Goff apartment, it was probably after December 1939, the date of Leon's card to Benjamin. We know from previous correspondence that they spent 1940–1942 in their flat in Paris. A memorial plaque hangs at Benjamin's primary school in Paris, 14 rue Victor Cousin, commemorating his death and that of other Jewish pupils.

The bigger mystery is why did Benjamin Parran (Rita's son) keep those precious items secret even from his closest family for all those years? As he has passed away in 2012, we can only speculate.

The first clue is the significance and the circumstances of his name, in view of the Sephardic Jewish tradition of naming babies in honor of their deceased and living ancestors. Let us connect the dots. In 1935, Benjamin Cohen, Rita's brother, died of illness in Salonica. A few months later, Leon Cohen's son, born in Paris, was named Benjamin after his late uncle. In 1939, Benjamin Parenti (later Parran) was born in Tel-Aviv, named after his mother's beloved brother. Thus, the name Benjamin is loaded with significance. Is it possible that upon discovering these documents in 1999, Benjamin Parenti (Parran) in Israel, himself married with two children, decided to keep the items (which celebrate Benjamin as well as his connection with his father) as his own personal memorial?

Whatever the real reason, he, too, was caught up in the never-ending search for a connection to the memory of his lost family. Keeping those items in a private place in his house was akin to storing them in a private section of his consciousness, perhaps attempting to secure the memory of his lost family away from the passage of time and the erosion of forgetfulness.

Final (?) Thoughts

A postmemorial story is never over. The memories passed down to us, the 2nd, 3rd, and 4th generations, whether directly through stories of those who survived, the letters of those who didn't, or through unconscious inter-generational transmission of indigestible psychic content, continue to grow.

We are doomed, or blessed, to live under the shadow, or illumination, of those past experiences of the Holocaust which remain beyond expression and comprehension. And yet, they will also continue to guide, motivate, and command us onwards in our journey to make better sense of what had happened in the past, so that we can attempt to better shape our present lives.

Notes

1 Alfandary, 2021.
2 A cursive form of the Hebrew alphabet, traditionally, a Sephardi script, Solitreo is nonetheless the predecessor of the modern Ashkenazi Cursive Hebrew currently used for handwriting in modern Israel and for Yiddish. In Judaeo-Spanish ("Ladino") of the Balkans and Turkey, it served as the standard handwritten form that complemented the Rashi script character set used for printing.
3 Ginio, 2002.
4 Rafael, 2001.
5 Various people took part in the translations of the letters: the letters in the first two boxes were translated by Moshe Bacher, Rachel Wolf, Avner Peretz, Helen Lotan and Eliezer Papo. The Solitreo letters were translated by Dr. Dov

Hacohen. The letters from the third box were translated by Lizette Leichner, and the letters from the fourth box were translated by Dr. Emanuel Cohen and Marianne Leloir.
6 Derrida, 1960.
7 Freud, 1919.
8 A small barracks neighborhood where around 80 people lived during the mid-1930s, on the banks of the Ayalon (Wadi Musrara). The neighborhood was adjacent to Sova Bakery (nowadays, the route of the tunnel that descends from La Guardia Junction to South Ayalon Highway).
9 Edmond Saül, was Bondy's older brother. When the war broke, he was conscripted into the French army but was placed in prison during his entire military service. Rosette and Suzanne, Bondy's younger sisters, survived as they were in a part of Paris where the Nazis were less vigilant in their search for Jews.
10 Comments written in the letters by Rony Alfandary will appear in brackets.
11 One of the signatories on that appointment letter was Shlomo Nehama, a relative of Joseph Nehama who wrote the definitive, seven-volume *Histoire des Israélites de Salonique* published in 1935.
12 For a thorough survey of the various political groups in the Jewish community of Salonica in the inter-war years can be found in Naar's 2016 book. For further details about the life in the Hirsch Quarter and the deportation of the Jews from it, read Matarasso's 2020 book.
13 For further reading, refer to Aymard's 2014 article.
14 One of the outcomes of the dominance of the *Alliance Israélite Universelle* in the educational scene of Salonican Jews was a cultural affinity to life in France. Apart from the obvious advantage of being fluent in French, it was a country many middle-class, educated Salonica Jews aspired to live in, not unlike the draw Zionist Jews had toward emigrating to Palestine.
15 Founded in Paris in 1860 by a group of emancipated French Jews, the *Alliance Israélite Universelle*'s goal was to "offer effective support to those who suffer for being Jewish". In order to achieve its aim of "working everywhere towards the emancipation and progress of Jews", the Alliance concentrated on the creation of a vast educational network in the Balkans, the Near and Middle East and in North Africa. The Salonica branch opened in 1874. The *Alliance* was not a pro-Zionist organization and saw its aim to integrate the Jewish communities in their European countries. Rita's association with the *Alliance*, therefore, throws further light upon her reluctance to emigrate to Palestine with her Zionist husband. For further reading, refer to Molho's 1993 article "Education in the Jewish Community of Thessaloniki in the Beginning of the 20th Century".
16 In his 1997 novel, *Gioconda*, the Greek author Níkos Kokántzis wrote about an illicit love affair between a Jewish Salonica woman and a Greek man in the years before World War II. In the novel, their love affair is brought to a tragic stop when he was not able to save her from being sent by the Nazis and the local police to her death in Auschwitz. Would that have been Rita's fate if she had been allowed to continue her relationship with her Christian lover?
17 Theodore Herzl Association and Degel Sion (mentioned later) were Salonica-based Zionist organizations. More information about them can be found in The Central Archives for the History of the Jewish People in Jerusalem (CAHJP).
18 My deepest thanks to my great cousin, Marianne Leloir, Bondy's great niece, who helped me in the deciphering and translation of these items. In addition, it was with her that I was able to share the sense of excitement and amazement with the discovery and the puzzlement with the questions raised.

Bibliography

Alfandary, Rony, 2021, *Postmemory, Psychoanalysis and the Holocaust Ghosts: The Salonica Cohen Family and Trauma across the Generations.* London: Routledge.

Aymard, Maurice, 2014. "Salonica's Jews in the Mediterranean: Two Historiographical Perspectives (1945–2010)", in *Jewish History*, Vol. 28, No. 3/4, Special issue on Salonica's Jews, pp. 411–429.

Derrida, Jacque, 1960. *Des Tours de Babel.* Paris: Galilee.

Freud, Sigmund, 1919. "The Uncanny", in *The Standard Edition of the Complete Psychological Works of Sigmund Freud*, Ed. & trans. J. Strachey, Vol. 17. London: Hogarth Press, pp. 217–252.

Ginio, Eyal, 2002. "Learning the Beautiful Language of Homer:' Judeo-Spanish Speaking Jews and the Greek Language and Culture between the Wars'", in *Jewish History*, Vol. 16, No. 3, pp. 235–262.

Kokántzis, Níkos, 2003. *Gioconda.* Palermo: L'epos Societa Edtrice.

Matarasso, Isaac, 2020. *Talking until Nightfall – Remembering Jewish Salonica 1941–1944.* London: Bloomsbury Continuum.

Molho, Rena, 1993. "Education in the Jewish Community of Thessaloniki in the Beginning of the 20th Century", in *Balkan Studies*, Vol. 34, No. 2, pp. 259–269.

Naar, Devin E., 2016. *Jewish Salonica: Between the Ottoman Empire and Modern Greece.* Stanford: Stanford University Press.

Rafael, Shmuel, 2001. "Current Methods and Methodology in Ladino Teaching", in *Shofar*, Vol. 19, No. 4, Special Issue: Sephardic Studies as an Interdisciplinary Field, pp. 85–95.

Chapter 3

Then Came Hitler
A Lifetime of Choices on My Path of Postmemorial Work

Judith Tydor Baumel-Schwartz

Introduction

There is a Jewish concept that a person's *goral*, a Hebrew word translated as "fate" or "predestination", is determined at their conception. But that, as my father once explained, isn't the term's only meaning. *Goral* can be either "fate" or "destiny". Fate is unchangeable, while destiny lies in a person's own hands. *Goral* is a combination of the two, half fate and half destiny. If a person's *goral* is determined at conception, only part is predestined. The rest is the result of their choices, decisions, actions, and responses.

Was my *goral* to be the daughter of a Holocaust survivor? That was predetermined by being my father's daughter, born after the war's end. But what about the other Holocaust-related parts of my life? It may have been my destiny to become a Holocaust scholar, but that was my choice, as was the rest of my professional identity. "You had no choice", a friend of mine, also 2g (Second Generation) often said to me. "Coming from a home like yours, always liking history, being so connected to family, and family being so connected to Holocaust – what else were you about to do with your life?!"

How correct was she? At first glance, I certainly felt that I had a choice. Or did I? Initially, I began a different professional direction. Only because of a life-altering dream, mirroring a memory that was not mine but nevertheless shaped the rest of my life, did I decide to change my original trajectory and ended up where I am today. Emphasis on the words "decide". My choice. But let's look at it differently. Could it be that my subconscious, predestined by my being born when, where, and to whom I was born, conjured up that dream as part of a pre-ordained direction with a pre-determined end? Albeit, I may have zigzagged toward it throughout my early years, but eventually I caught up with my destiny. Or was it my fate? Is that what our sages mean in Ethics of the Fathers (3:19) when they write "Everything is foreseen [by G-d], yet freewill is granted [to human beings]"? Is that total freewill, or only the decision as to how one eventually will reach their predestined goal?

In any case, I'm getting ahead of myself. To begin answering those questions we first need to understand a bit about memory and postmemory, and of course, pre-determination or predestination.

Memory, Postmemory, Choices, and Predestination

Thought is the process of using one's mind to manipulate information, form concepts, engage in problem-solving, reason, and make decisions. Psychologists now claim that we think anywhere between 6,000 and 6,200 thoughts a day, many of them negative, and most about things that never occur.[1] Memory is the process through which we acquire, preserve, and later retrieve information about things we experienced or learned, the complex structure that organizes all our knowledge.[2] Thought and memory are based on personal experiences and acquired information, often combining the two.

Postmemory is one's relationship to the memory of others which one has taken upon oneself. Originally a term coined by Marianne Hirsch in 1992 to describe the relationship between children of survivors and their parents' memories,[3] it was quickly expanded to mean the relationship that later generations bear to the traumas which they did not experience, but were transmitted to them by those who experienced them. When dealing with a traumatic event such as the Holocaust, postmemory can become a toxic and negative element in one's life. To alleviate the negative aspects of those memories, one solution is to turn to "postmemorial work", the metamorphosis of negative trauma to positive action.

How common is "postmemory" among the Second Generation? As Shmuel Refael and I wrote in the dedication to the book we edited about Second Generation Researchers: "For our parents and grandparents who survived the inferno in order to bequeath us memories of lives we did not live, that will live inside us forever".[4] No surprise there; after all, he and I are researchers who have devoted large portions of our lives to studying elements pertaining to the Holocaust. But many of the researchers who participated in the book worked in medicine, gerontology, physics, engineering, etc., with no professional connection to the cataclysm. Yet they, too, often realized that they were making personal and professional decisions, based on their Holocaust heritage.

How does one make decisions? What mechanism steers people to choose X and not Y or decide to do A and not B? Influencing factors include past experiences, cognitive biases, age and individual differences, escalation of commitment, and belief in personal relevance.[5] Regret, satisfaction, and an evaluation of the positive and negative aspects of choices are three of the post-decision factors influencing future decisions.[6] Choices begin with identifying the problem, examining alternatives, examining criteria for a beneficial decision, choosing among alternatives, and taking action. Choices are often the result of value and efficiency. What one values most at a particular time often guides one's decisions, and one usually chooses the most efficient way of reaching one's goal.[7]

How do the concepts of predetermination or predestination fit the dynamic of making choices? Much has been written about theological predestination and predetermination, the concept of something being unable to be prevented or changed because of a higher power such as G-d or fate.[8] In Judaism, divisions over the question of free will versus fate, determinism, or Divine foreknowledge have existed since ancient times, and have continued among modern Jewish thinkers. Although most speak of human beings having free will, the question is the degree to which human freedom is restricted by G-d's knowledge and providence.[9]

All these issues come into play when trying to understand what guided me to the decision to specialize in the Holocaust as an academic choice. How is that decision connected with my co-founding the first national organization of children of Holocaust survivors in Israel in 1980, an organization that lasted less than a year? To what degree did my personal and professional identities mesh or clash as part of those choices? How did the continuous interplay between my personal and professional identity and choices reflect various issues in my life such as attachment and separation, individuality and appeasement, my relationship with my parents, siblings, spouses and children, or my feeling of being a "memorial candle", the candle Jews traditionally light on the anniversary of a close relative's death, but symbolically, a constant reminder of their memory? To answer these and other questions, I will discuss the personal\professional crossroads in my life that led to my becoming who I am today, analyzing the background to my choices in view of the double meaning of *goral*.

How I Got There in the First Place

Having set the theoretical grounding of this adventure, we can now explore who I am and how I got there in the first place. So, let's go back to the beginning before Hitler and his henchmen came on the scene, and see where I might have ended up had it not been for his untimely appearance in my family's history.

I was born in New York City in 1959 and moved to Israel at 15 with my parents, ten months after the Yom Kippur War of October 1973. My formative years were spent in the tiny Orthodox Jewish community in Woodside, Queens, but we were anything but your typical American-Jewish Orthodox family. Not even your typical American Jewish Orthodox Holocaust survivor family, if such a thing even existed.

My father, Chaskel Tydor, was born at the beginning of the 20th century in Bochnia, a small Polish town in Western Galicia. During the First World War his family became refugees in Germany, eventually settling there permanently. In 1930, he married a woman from his Polish hometown, and the couple had two children. They could have had a wonderful life together as a family, but they didn't, because a year later Hitler came to power. By the time they applied for visas to England, they arrived too late to save him from five-and-a-half years of Nazi camps, and his wife from being murdered in Poland. Founding a survivors' kibbutz in postwar Germany and bringing it to pre-State Israel where he lived until 1951, he ended up managing a travel agency in New York to be near his children, rescued to America in late 1941.

Then there was my mother, Shirley Kraus, born in New York in the late 1920s, raised by a traditional mother and atheist father. She ultimately ascribing to her father's communist ideology, that is, until she met my father: an Orthodox Holocaust survivor twice her age, a widower with grown children, and her boss at the travel agency. Differing in background, belief, age, and temperament, they fell in love, marrying five years later. For two years, they lived out west, in Deer Lodge, Montana, and Rapid City, South Dakota, where my father managed uranium mines. Eventually, they returned to New York for my birth, also returning to the travel business where they first met.

Throughout my childhood the Holocaust was always present, hovering in the background as a story of devastation, but also one of survival and victory. From a young age, I heard how my half-sister and half-brother had fled wartime Europe as refugee children and knew, like so many of my classmates in my Orthodox Jewish Day School, that we were "memorial candles" for those who perished, compensating our parents for what they had lost.

Then, the idea of having anything to do with the Holocaust professionally was the last thing in my mind. When asked what I plan to be when I grow up, I would answer "a travel agent like my parents", then a nurse, and finally, a secretary, to ensure constant employment. I knew that one must always learn a trade, no matter what academic subjects one decides to study. No wonder I requested a typing course as a high school graduation present, working my way to a proficient speed in two languages to be able to support my family if everything fell apart. Judy the typist would save the world, or at least, the family's finances.

In the middle of this my parents, maternal grandmother, and I found ourselves in Ramat Gan, Israel. Despite the difficulties, the move was a blessing for me in terms of friends, school, and discovering how much I really loved history. I even took college history courses at the nearby Bar-Ilan University while in my last year of high school and throughout my voluntary national service.

At the same time, I was slowly being immersed in Holocaust-related matters without even being aware of it. Watching my father view the 1978 mini-series "Holocaust"[10] (while the rest of us tried to pretend it wasn't being shown), accompanying him to Holocaust commemorative evenings, and of course, participating in family Holocaust-related gatherings such as the one we traditionally held on the eve of my father's liberation from

Buchenwald. But to me, these were personal events and not guidelines toward my professional future. I was studying history because I enjoyed it, and not for any other reason. "What are you going to do with a degree in history and no teaching certificate?" asked my always-practical father, to which I replied that I was going to be a secretary, like my mother. The answer must have satisfied him as he didn't ask me again.

One Step Forward: The Dream that Started It All Off

Having finished my BA (and marrying a fellow student along the way, agreeing to support us while he continued for a graduate degree), I found work immediately as a personal assistant to a well-known architect. For two months, I earned an unimaginable salary for a 20-year-old college graduate, but soon realized that this job was not for me. By the middle of August, my husband was away on army reserve duty, and my level of despair rose daily.

One night I dreamed that I was standing on the ramp in Auschwitz bathed in fog. A train approached and a group of my relatives who had been killed in the war disembarked. Helplessly I watched them being led to their death and shouted: "wait for me!", but they continued marching into the darkness. Suddenly my grandmother Esther, my father's mother for whom I was named, turned around and said: "My child, remain here. You have a task. To make sure they won't forget us". And then they all disappeared into the fog.

I awoke in a cold sweat, alone in our sweltering apartment. What now? What should I do so to make sure that "they won't forget us"? Like most of my important decisions, my mind went "click" "click" "click" as the puzzle pieces fell into place. I would quit my job, return to school, specialize in the Holocaust, and then write about it and teach it. But what about my being the family breadwinner? That morning I told my boss about the dream and my decision. He listened attentively, leaned back in his chair and said: "Return to school, study Holocaust, and one day you will be a famous historian". Smiling, he continued: "And I will proudly tell everyone that you were once my assistant!"

My spirits lifted and I registered for graduate studies in Jewish history at Bar-Ilan University, finding an advisor under whom I would write my thesis on the Holocaust. Not just anything about the Holocaust, but my family history. What could be better than beginning with my brother and sister's story, that of Jewish refugee children who escaped Nazi-occupied Europe! Family, history, and Holocaust all bound together. Little did I know that these would be the opening chords of a lifetime symphony of writing about family in one form or another.

Until then, the idea of continuing for a graduate degree was nowhere on my radar. I wasn't thrilled with my administrative job, but there were other jobs available. In my circles, people were doctors, lawyers, teachers, rabbis, and business people. Why did I turn my life upside down because of a dream? What thought and decision process was at work here? One didn't have to be a psychoanalyst to understand how my subconscious conjured up Auschwitz, but why did I dream about this grandmother of whom I had never dreamed before?

Was the only way to make sure "they won't forget us" to become a Holocaust historian? Other 2g children addressed this credo by having large families or naming their children after Holocaust victims. Some spent time with elderly survivors. Others volunteered in Holocaust-related organizations. Around then, 2gs in the United States were responding to their heritage after having read the first book to be written by a child of Survivors about children of Survivors, but not by dropping everything else and making the Holocaust the center of their lives. Why, then, did I give up an exorbitant salary to take a secretarial position at the university that paid a tenth of it while I went back to school?

There are no simple answers. That I was unhappy on my well-paying job was a given, but my response to the dream was not. The need to make a change was a given, but not necessarily the direction it took. Certainly not one that would change my family equation without consulting with other family members, including my husband at that time, who returned from reserve duty several days later to find almost everything in his life turned upside down: finances, social life, short-term plans, and long-range expectations.

One makes decisions bearing in mind values and efficiency. The Holocaust, which had always been a not-so-silent accompaniment to my life, now began playing its symphony full force. It would eventually become "a major part of my religion", as my closest relatives have often somewhat facetiously said in a subtly ironic way. So, this was certainly a decision guided by values. As for efficiency, in those days, taking a graduate degree in Jewish history was certainly the fastest way to become a Holocaust scholar. But it was not the only way to carry out my dream-grandmother's last request. Could one say that it was a decision that was "stronger than me", and that I felt guided by something outside of me, to move in that direction? Maybe. Particularly as I was always known in my family for craving stability and trying to plan out my life years in advance, while here I was, turning everything stable in my life upside down, and embarking on a roller coaster, without any idea of the direction it would ultimately take. I just went and did it. Here we go. Postmemorial activity. Karma. Kismet. *Goral.*

One False Step: Timing is Everything, Including While Probing the 2g Legacy

My husband agreed to the change in plans while expecting me to continue as primary breadwinner, but my parents were the ones who were truly thrilled with my choice of topic; after all, this wasn't just any graduate degree in history, it was HOLOCAUST STUDIES: family history, personal mission, and a sacred cow all in one. My graduate studies indeed felt like a mission. From October 1979 onward, I worked in a university office every day, taking classes every evening, and then went home to write my thesis. Work breaks were spent at the library of the Institute for the Research of Diaspora Jewry (the *Machon*, Hebrew for "Institute") where veteran researchers, some of whom were friends of my father, and almost all of whom were thrice my age, helped perfect my German while teaching me more about the Holocaust than I had learned from any book. Exhausted from never-ending schedule, I would collapse into bed long after midnight, rising early to begin the cycle once again. On *Shabbat* I slept, ate, prayed, and caught up on research literature.

Despite the grueling schedule, six months after beginning my studies I found myself involved in a new Holocaust-related venture, as co-founder of Israel's first 2g organization, a short-lived long-named enterprise with the unimaginative title: "Organization of Children of Holocaust Survivors in Israel".

Didn't I have enough Holocaust in my life? I worked all day, studied all evening, wrote my thesis about refugee children all night, and spent time in-between at the library of the *Machon* that would soon merge with the university's newly established Holocaust Institute. Holocaust-related commemorative events were my family's dinner table conversations. Why did I need to establish a 2g organization? Was I beginning to realize, like my American counterparts who were talking about founding similar groups, that we were a bit different, or to use a kinder term, "unique"? I had actually wanted to start a volunteer group where healthy young 2gs would assist indigent aging survivors and dissolved the initiative when it morphed into group therapy without a therapist. Sick of complaining 2gs, I vowed never again to have anything to do with such organizations.

So why did I do it in the first place? Was this, too, *goral?* Probably not. It was something that I had been strongly encouraged (a.k.a. pressured) to do by my mother, who sent me clippings about American 2g initiatives established following the publication of Helen Epstein's, *Children of the Holocaust*, while stating that I should (must!) start something similar in Israel.[11] At the time, it was definitely *not* a decision about carrying out postmemorial work, but rather the result of my sense of obligation as a "memorial candle". As opposed to my previous decision to turn my life upside-down and go back to school, the values behind this decision were those pertaining to honoring one's parents, and not those connected with a sense of mission, self-definition or identity. There was no mystical component to my decision, nor was it in sync with what 2g organizations were all about. The efficiency was artificial: two newspaper articles, a few letters to the editor seeking members in those pre-Facebook days, and very little emotional involvement on my part.

This also explains the organization's brief existence. At the time, I was barely taking 2g emotional baby steps, being too busy focusing on the survivors, to grant their children independent emotional space in my life. Moral of the story: true postmemorial work has to be an independent choice and not the result of pressure and prodding, as well-meaning as it may be. It also has to come at the right time. This one did not, hence it didn't last. It may have been my fate to establish such an organization but not at that time, and thus, even if I felt it was my destiny, to be successful, it would have had to happen later, as indeed it did.

Two Steps Forward: Right Person, Right Place, Right Time

Six months later, in late 1980, I reached the next watershed event in my postmemorial odyssey. Due to administrative changes, I left my university secretarial job and began working in the law library for graduate student wages. The loss of income was problematic, but it meant that could spend more time at the *Machon's* library where, despite the age differences, I fit in seamlessly with the researchers. The feeling was mutual, and in late 1980, when they began a new project, its secretary suggested to the Director that they hire me as a part-time student-employee.

One project that led to another and I eventually became a full-fledged half-time staff member. Around that time, the *Machon* began working hand-in-hand with the newly established Finkler Institute of Holocaust Research as one academic body, I felt that I had found my academic home. I was a Holocaust researcher! I loved my work and the people I worked with, soaking up the Central European atmosphere and learning as much from my colleagues about the Holocaust as from my graduate classes. Another step toward fulfilling my grandmother's legacy.

Just as I handed in my MA thesis in May 1981, I took the second step. As a researcher, I had gotten to know the administrative coordinator of the university's Program for Basic Jewish Studies. Aware of my academic background and linguistic proficiency, he asked me to teach an English-language Jewish Studies survey course for foreign summer students. Already in high school, I had taught English to groups of children and young adults, and I knew that I could hold my own in a classroom. This, however, was real university teaching, and THE HOLOCAUST. I took a deep breath, answered in the affirmative, and spent the next two months creating a curriculum and reading assignments. Striding into the classroom three weeks after receiving my MA, I felt completely in my element. For five weeks I taught students only three years younger than me, introducing them to the intricate web connecting perpetrators, victims, and bystanders. I loved it, they loved me, and hopefully I made my late grandmother proud.

Here were two professional offers and two calculated choices that I made, both in line with my values, providing efficient ways of bringing me closer to my goal. Were they *goral*? Luck is often being the right person, in the right place, at the right time. By specializing in Holocaust Studies, I took a step toward being the right person to work in the field. In both cases, timing was a given: a project about to begin, a course suddenly became available. But I had made great efforts to be at the right place – becoming friendly with the *Machon*'s staff and being physically present, so that when there was an opening, they might naturally consider me for the position; getting to know people in strategic university positions and letting them know my qualifications, so that any suitable opening might be offered to me. That was the "destiny" part of *goral*, which is in our hands. If a project opened up, and a course became available by fate, it was destiny that I was chosen to research and teach.

One Step Back and Sideways: A Strategic Withdrawal to Save My Professional Life and Personal Sanity

For several years things moved in the right direction. Project led to project and course to course, until I found myself teaching a Hebrew Holocaust course in the Basic Jewish Studies Program. But one can't support a family from a project and a course. While writing my dissertation I began looking for a full-time position in Holocaust studies. By the time I completed my doctorate I was a team member of Israel's Open University's Holocaust course, teaching simultaneously as an adjunct in colleges throughout the country. Eventually, I was offered a part-time Holocaust teaching position at the University of Haifa which I hoped would eventually become a tenured full-time academic position.

I was wrong. In 1996, after teaching there for five years, my newly elected department chair informed me that he had no desire to employ a religious woman with degrees from Bar-Ilan University – "that clerical-fascist institution", in his words – and would not renew my three-year contracts. I had two-and-a-half years to go, and my various research\adjunct positions, but I needed to look for full-time academic employment.

I was also in double jeopardy, as per the title of the book I published two years later about women in the Holocaust. In Haifa, the problem was me: I was targeted for being religious. Elsewhere the problem was my topic: I had little chance of getting an academic teaching position in Holocaust studies. Not only were universities not hiring in that field, but from previous experiences with my former MA thesis advisor, now a well-known Holocaust studies scholar, I feared that as soon as I reached a certain academic rank, or if I tried to progress in Holocaust studies at Bar-Ilan, I would encounter a powerful glass ceiling.

The name of the game was to progress, but in a different specialization without those constraints. I therefore took a step back and sideways, strategically withdrawing from Holocaust studies to specialize in a field with more attractive academic employment options: Israel studies. I had straddled the fence between Holocaust and State of Israel when researching the World War II parachutists from pre-state Israel. Now I began teaching Israel Studies in Haifa alongside my Holocaust courses, publishing articles on the topic and making myself a name in the new field. It was a decision made after examining the alternatives and realizing that if my value was putting food on my family's table by getting a full-time academic position, this was the most efficient way of going about it.

Was this *goral?* I had no say in who became the Haifa department chair – that was "fate" – but I could choose my response to his chessboard move. Having no intention of leaving the game, my destiny was to become a knight, moving back and sideways before moving forward again. In Haifa, as soon as this man became chair, I was the wrong person, in the wrong place, at the wrong time. By changing subjects, even before I changed my geographical location, I moved to a different sphere, hopefully giving me a better chance at getting a permanent position. There also is a good chance that this move had its roots in the "survival instincts" that were a legacy from my father, whose story taught me that there are times one must rapidly make hard decisions to survive. Fate? Destiny? In any case, Postmemorial work would have to wait in view of the acute necessity to make a living.

A Giant Leap Forward

My gamble won. Two years later, when a Professor of Zionism at Bar-Ilan University suddenly passed away, I applied for his position. But my former MA advisor constructed the contest from hell, with me being forced to compete for a year with another candidate, a close friend, in an ugly gladiatorial tournament. Whether by acumen or seniority, I came out victorious while unbelievably remaining friends with my competitor, but I knew that my decision to suspend my postmemorial work had been correct. That decision solidified when I was promoted, and my former advisor informed me that he was not renewing my research contract at the *Machon* he then headed, my first academic home where I would have been happy to remain as a volunteer.

During the next decade-and-a-half, I continued to publish on both Holocaust and Israel studies, but kept a low Holocaust profile so as not to clash with him. Even after retiring, he remained the *Machon's* director for three more years while still retaining influence in the department. Only in 2018, when I was appointed *Machon* director, could I finally return to what I considered my *goral* – my fate and destiny all rolled together. And I did it with a vengeance.

As a tenured Full-Professor and now, the only Holocaust scholar in my department, I could finally mold the Institute as I so desired, choosing a motto that reflected both my dream and the postmemorial work I hoped to carry out for the rest of my professional life: "Remember, Research, Commemorate. Create Communities. Build a Bridge Between Generations". Within two years, the *Machon* had become one of the largest university-based Holocaust institutes in the world, sponsoring ten "communities" (multi-disciplinary national and international frameworks) with close to 600 members. Holding numerous conferences and symposia, it began publishing books, connecting scholars and active participants in Holocaust education and commemoration while promoting Holocaust scholarship throughout the world.

Discussion and Conclusions: Making Choices and Understanding *Goral*

As of the writing of this essay, I am a Holocaust scholar and Director of the Finkler Institute of Holocaust Research at Bar-Ilan University. And since the moment of my birth, I am also a member of the Second Generation, and a half-sister to two members of the First Generation, both child Holocaust survivors. How did these two parts of my personal and professional identity mesh?

From the day I began my postmemorial work, there was continuous interplay between my personal and professional identity and choices. Whether liminal or subliminal, my attachment to and identification with my family background and upbringing affected my postmemorial choice to be a Holocaust researcher. They also came into play through issues of separation and attachment when it became necessary to make a strategic decision and abandon much of that work in order to survive professionally, and when I found it necessary time and again, to nevertheless return to that postmemorial work.

Then there was my need for individuality in making decisions regarding the form and timing of my postmemorial work, which was also influenced by my past experiences, cognitive biases, age, position, and assumptions regarding the immediate and long-term relevance of the decision's potential results. To that one must add a desire to appease my parents by being a "memorial candle", the value that I put on postmemorial work in general, and that of the particular postmemorial enterprise in which I was involved at that time. Throughout the years, all this influenced my relationship with parents, siblings, spouses, offspring, friends, and even colleagues, but most of all, it influenced how I viewed myself, and my regrets and satisfactions in evaluating a particular choice.

And what of *goral*, a concept with which I had been raised, that was also a convenient way of viewing situations over which I felt I had little, if any, influence? To what degree did it influence my postmemorial work? How much does it still influence it today? With the passage of time, I have learned that *goral* can be a valid explanation for events, but it is important to be able to discern the difference between those parts which are "fate" and those which are "destiny". That understanding is the first step in our postmemorial work, which is only possible because of our parents' survival. We, too, are survivors of sorts who have chosen to devote part of our life to remembering theirs. Is that our *goral?* Was it determined at our conception? Those never-ending questions, for which there can never be a definitive answer, will always be at the crux of what we do, and will accompany us, and our postmemorial work, for the rest of our lives.

Notes

1. Tseng and Poppenk, 2020.
2. Anderson, 1976, p. 3.
3. Hirsch, 1992, pp. 3–29.
4. Dedication page in Baumel-Schwartz and Refael, 2021.
5. Deitrich, 2010, pp. 1–3.
6. de Bruin et al., 2007, pp. 938–956.
7. Montague, 2006.
8. See for example, Emerick, 2018, pp. 74–90.
9. Steinberg, 1991, pp. 17–20.
10. Written by Gerald Green and Directed by Martin Chomsky, premiered in the USA on NBC in April 1978 and later shown throughout the world.
11. Epstein, 1979.

Selected Bibliography

Anderson, John Robert, 1976. *Language, Memory, and Thought*, Hillsdale: Lawrence Erlbaum Associates.

Baumel-Schwartz, Judith Tydor, 2020a. "How will they ever take you seriously if you write about Veibers?", in: Judith Tydor Baumel-Schwart and Dalia Ofer (eds.), *Her Story, My Story? Writing about Women and the Holocaust*, Bern: Peter Lang Publishers, pp. 61–72.

Baumel-Schwartz, Judith Tydor, 2020b. "Ma Taasi Im Toar Behistoria ubli Teudat Horaa? Keitzad Hayiti Lehistoriyonit ulichokeret Medinat Yisrael" (What will you do with a degree in history and no teaching certificate? How I became a historian and Researcher of Israel Studies), in: Ofer Schiff and Avner Ben Amos (eds.), *Kavim Lidmuteinu: Lachkor et yisrael, Lichtov al atzmeinu (Profiles of Ourselves: Researching Israel, writing our stories)*, Sde Boqer: Machon Ben-Gurion and Yediot Aharonnot Sde Hemed, pp. 613–635.

Baumel-Schwartz, Judith Tydor, 2023, Forthcoming. "Remember, research, commemorate: The (re)making of a holocaust research institute", in: Zev Eleff and Saul Seidler-Feller (eds.), *Facing the Truths of History: Essays on Reception and Memory in Honor of Jacob J. Schacter* (Forthcoming).

Baumel-Schwartz, Judith Tydor, Refael Shmuel, 2021. *Researchers Remember: Research as an Arena of Memory Among Offspring of Holocaust Survivors, A Collected Volume of Academic Autobiographies*, Bern: Peter Lang Press.

De Bruin, Wandi Bruine, Andrew M. Parker, Baruch Fischhoff, 2007. "Individual Differences in Adult Decision-Making Competence", *Journal of Personality and Social Psychology*, 92:5, pp. 938–956.

Deitrich, Cindy, 2010. "Decision Making: Factors that Influence Decision Making, Heuristics Used, and Decision Outcomes", *Inquiries Journal*, 2:2, pp. 1–3.

Emerick, Christopher C., 2018. "Predestination and the Freedom of God", *Journal of Pentacostal Theology*, 27:1, pp. 74–90.

Epstein, Helen, 1979. *Children of the Holocaust: Conversations with Sons and Daughters of Survivors*, New York: Putnam.

Hirsch, Marianne, 1992. "Family Pictures: *Maus*, Mourning, and Post-Memory", *Discourse*, 15:2, pp. 3–29.

Montague, Read, 2006. *Your Brain Is (Almost) Perfect: How We Make Decisions*, New York: Plume.

Steinberg, Avraham, 1991. "Free Will Vs. Determinism in Bioethics: Comparative Philosophical and Jewish Perspectives", *ASSIA Jewish Medical Ethics*, 2:1, pp. 17–20.

Tseng, Julie, Poppenk, Jordan, 2020. "Brain Meta-State Transitions Demarcate Thoughts Across Task Contexts Exposing the Mental Noise of Trait Neuroticism", *Nature Communications*, 11. https://doi.org/10.1038/s41467-020-17255-9 accessed on May 7, 2020.

Chapter 4

Reflections on Postmemory – With Some Notes from Ireland and Greece

Richard Pine

Introduction

Other contributors to this volume have discussed extensively the definitions of postmemory. For the purposes of this chapter, therefore, I allude only briefly to the phenomenon (or condition) as defined by Marianne Hirsch:

> the relationship of the second generation to powerful, often traumatic, experiences that preceded their births, but that were nevertheless transmitted to them so deeply as to seem to constitute memories in their own right.[1]

Acknowledging that, in the writings of Hirsch, Stephen Frosh, and others, the theory of "postmemory" has been applied specifically to the Holocaust and its aftermath, I shall concentrate on other contexts to which the condition/phenomenon of "postmemory" may be applied: first, 20th-century Ireland and its "memory" of the "Great Famine" of 1845–1852 and, second, modern Greece in the aftermath of the "Anatolian Catastrophe" of 1922.[2]

I refer to postmemory as both a "phenomenon" and a "condition" because it seems to me that it can be regarded both as an "event", constituting a memory of a preceding trauma and as a state of mind which can be diagnosed and treated psychiatrically or therapeutically.

Taking Hirsch's definition as a given starting point, the theme of this essay is the evolution of oral culture into textual narrative – analogous, if you like, to the words spoken by a patient to their therapist, and thence transcribed into a narrative report of that encounter.

Two Personal Notes

England, Ireland, and Empire

Having been educated at an English public school and inheriting a strong sense of British empire from my family background, I have found it particularly challenging to study the work of post-colonial writers in places such as Africa, where the reaction to the British legacy has provoked cultural nationalisms. An example is Nigeria, where writers such as Chinweizu (*Towards the Decolonization of African Literature*, 1983) or Ngũgĩ wa Thiong'o (*Decolonizing the Mind: the politics of language in African literature*, 1986) have been particularly persuasive in both resistance to imperial legacies and articulating a new sense of identity.

This sense of "post-imperial guilt" affected me severely when, at the age of 18, I went to live in Ireland, a country which, until very recently, had long been dominated by my own. It is possible – if I may trespass on technical psychotherapy territory – that this, on my part, represents the "counter-transference" of that post-colonial *angst* into a post-imperial one.

Greece

In 2019, I was peripherally involved in the creation of a music drama, *Amíliti/ The Silent One*, by a Greek composer, Dimitra Trypani. This was a commissioned public work as part of the 2019 Paxos Festival. At the same time, it was an intensely private act of exorcism of a trauma which Trypani had carried within her as the fourth or fifth generation in her own family. The traumatic event constitutes the essence of the music drama: the burial, alive, of a girl who had dishonored her family by celebrating her sexual freedom.[3] The tension within the rehearsal room was severe; the traumatic energy released at its première in Paxos was at the same time electric and visceral. *Amíliti/ The Silent One* carried within it a "buried" (in every sense) story which had never been spoken, never been capable of articulation. The publication of the buried truth had been an act of the imagination on Trypani's part which was also a self-induced therapy, a release of a truth which had "generated", until it exploded onto a professional stage.

Trauma

As I shall discuss the condition of Greek collective memory in part of this essay, it's best to start with a basic Greek word: τραυμα [trauma] was the ancient Greek word for a *wound*, *damage*, or *disaster*; τραυματεία [traumateía] was a wounding and τραυματίας [traumatías] was a wounded man. Greek drama is replete with wounds: the maiming of Philoctetes, celebrated by Sophocles as an outcast (re-worked by Seamus Heaney in *The Cure at Troy* [1990] as a tension between public and private morality); or "The Limping Man" (as Lawrence Durrell entitled his screenplay for *Oedipus the King*), engendering the entire mythology and psychology of the "Oedipus Complex".

The connection between trauma-wound and memory was most effectively expressed by Czesław Miłosz in his 1980 Nobel speech: "It is possible that there is no other memory than the memory of wounds".[4] Miłosz cited the

Old Testament as an authority: "A book of the tribulations of Israel", but he also extended the "memory of wounds" beyond the Jewish victims of the Holocaust to "millions of Poles, Russians, Ukrainians, and prisoners of other nationalities".

Miłosz's occasion was one of rhetoric, and I do not believe he was entirely convinced that there can be no memory other than that of wounds. (A statement beginning with the words "I remember…" will alert a psychiatrist to his patient quite differently than the way a small child listens to his grandmother. The patient is likely to recall a trauma, whereas an elderly speaker may well be recalling a paradisal childhood of their own, rather than an occasion of wounding.) In his Nobel speech, Miłosz asked forgiveness for "my laying bare a memory like a wound", insisting that if the wounds are not remembered, they belong to a Europe "characterized by a refusal to remember […] a conspiracy of silence".

Giving a name to the unspoken, the repressed (what is repressed because it could not be named) is to admit it to the narrative of experience, and thus to articulate both the wound and the possibility of healing. A situation in which, as Miłosz puts it, the poet can "liberate himself from [the] remembrance" of events.

Orature to Literature

I introduce these ideas into my argument to highlight two factors in my essay: the sense of memory as the conduit and purveyor of both the pain and the lesion of wounds, and the sense of writing as the conduit and purveyor of faith, hope, and commitment. As Tilemachos Kotsias observes:

> Cynical as it may appear to say, people's misfortune, wars, emigration, the financial crisis and all the troubles of humanity are the finest nourishment for literature. Whichever way you look at it, literature is carnivorous: it seeks blood, and failing that it will satisfy itself with hardship and grief.[5]

Similarly, Luke Gibbons argues that "memory is not just a matter of retention or recollection but of finding the narrative forms that will do justice to this troubled inheritance".[6] Gibbons was writing specifically in relation to the Irish "Great Famine", but we can project this argument onto the way memory is adapted to either literary narration or oral culture as a means of transmitting both information and emotion from one generation to the next. This is vital to our understanding of the transmission of memory regarding the Irish "Great Famine".

John Waters sees the Famine as

> the most powerful metaphor of life in modern Ireland. It is present as a hidden motif in much of our literature and music, for all that the

creators of these works may deny its legitimacy. It casts a dark shadow over the way we live our lives.[7]

The poet Eavan Boland also saw the inherited memory of the Famine as a factor in the narrative of her poetry: "I am writing about an event I never witnessed [...] which nevertheless became *imaginatively* important to me".[8]

The development of orature into literature is merely one degree along the movement of speech to text. Imagination tends to demand a fiction as a form of witness to truth. And imagination is a vital ingredient or element in the articulation of trauma: not the exaggeration or distortion of a traumatic truth, but its development by means of the creative, and positive, strategy of the emotions which gives it a literary shape as poem, novel, drama, or memoir.

The *transposition* of the unspoken to the articulate, and then from the oral to the written testimony (which at that stage becomes *transcription*), is a process which, I argue, facilitates the meeting of fact and imagination at the same time as it enables a narrative to be created. The crucial point is whether imagination (we might call it "poetic license") is accepted if it changes the nature of truth rather than simply re-producing it in a new guise. *Metamorphosis* (the changing of shape or appearance) thus meets *metaphor* (the translation from one state, the unspoken or unwritten, to another, the text). If Kafka's Gregor Samsa remains Gregor Samsa after he has been metamorphosed into a gigantic insect, then the process of metamorphosis or transposition is an honest one. The "art" of literature is, therefore, to effect an honest metaphor, repositioning the narrative in the minds of auditors and readers in a way that is faithful to the original truth, and yet enhances it. We expect this not only of poetry, the novel, drama, or the memoir, but also for all texts which provide, or purport to constitute, an acceptable communal narrative such as a national credo or history, a "book of evidence". If a national narrative in any one of these genres is the aim of post-traumatic therapy then, I argue, the poet, dramatist, or novelist is a fit conduit for such narration.

Storytelling is more than the mere invention of fable: storytelling is the transmission of intimate and local knowledge and the wisdom that is derived from that knowledge, what to avoid and what to embrace, what to fear and what to cherish. It is cast in the form of a fable in order to increase its attraction and facilitate its transmission from speaker to auditor ("Once upon a time...."). A fable may be set in the form of an allegory, but it is true nonetheless. Whatever fiction the storyteller invents, it is derived from an experience, an "event", the truth of which is undeniable: as Liam O'Flaherty says in his novel *Famine*, "the queer, unholy wisdom begotten of hunger".[9]

As I have written elsewhere:

> All people tell their stories, as individuals and as societies; a dominant, outward-going nation will tell stories from a position of strength and

> confidence, and its public and private narratives will establish images and traditions of orthodoxy, success and rootedness; a colonised, subdued nation, however inhibited by its subjection, will tell stories of failure and embarrassment, and will create images of hope and despair which are future-oriented; thus nations tell these stories differently before and after freedom. [...] The place of writing moves from periphery to centre: writers also come to grief even while they are expressing joy. The force of freedom is sometimes greater than the writer's capacity to embrace it – the surprise and shock of the new.[10]

Freedom, as the result of revolution, in itself becomes a traumatic aspect of history.

We must, however, be mindful of the danger of allowing a "tradition" to replace history, of the imagination creating a genealogy of emotions which is not based in fact. As the Irish critic Seamus Deane observed of tradition,

> we are conscious that it is an invention, a narrative which ingeniously finds a way of connecting a selected series of historical figures or themes in such a way that the pattern or plot revealed to us becomes a conditioning factor in our reading of literary works.[11]

Deane warns that such a tradition may create "the ideological conviction that a community exists which must be recovered or restored".[12]

Two Europes

Miłosz identified "two Europes", in one of which we are in danger of forgetting, of ignoring, the reality of acts of "tyranny", "evil forces"; while in the other the poet's function is to bear witness, to give a language to the unspeakable because otherwise "whole zones of reality cease to exist simply because they have no name".

I refer here to an essay by Philip Sherard, entitled "The Other Mind of Europe", in which he argued that the Greek spirit had been air-brushed out of the European consciousness, to the detriment of its imagination. I join these two conceptions of a dualistic or two-speed Europe to indicate that this creative, positive strategy belongs to one Europe, while negative and dismissive strategies belong to another Europe.

John Waters believes that in the case of Ireland this is due (in part) to Ireland's perceived need to become "an advanced Western society"[13] – an impetus also plentifully evident in modern Greece, anxious to be accepted as part of "the West".[14] This could be read as a counterpoint to the contemporary (1847) idea that under Famine conditions "everything like shame was forgotten".[15] Ireland and Greece seem, in fact, to be connected by a ribbon of shame which both illuminates and occludes the post-trauma generations.

Ireland and the "Great Famine"

The "Great Famine" of 1845–1852 caused the deaths of approximately one million people and the emigration of another two million, out of a total population of eight million – a devastating loss of almost 40% of its people, and a concomitant diminution in the numbers of speakers of the Irish language, and a "disappearance" of many communities. At the time of the sesquicentenary of the Famine (1995–), it was argued that historians had previously concentrated on documentary evidence to the neglect of folklore and folk memory, possibly on the grounds that such memory was "emotive and therefore unacceptable to many historians".[16] As Cathal Portéir argues: "The echoes of those silenced voices which we have in folk memory are the nearest we can get to the experience of the poor of the 1840s and 1850s".[17] In 1956, Roger McHugh had already argued that, by means of such oral transmission, "hundreds of our people [...] still discuss the experiences of their ancestors in famine times".[18]

Ian McBride states unequivocally that "the remembrance of injustice and persecution, endurance and deliverance, has been fundamental to the shaping of modern Ireland".[19] The domination of the country – especially its culture and language – for centuries by a more powerful neighbor is a common experience for both Ireland and Greece.

The transmission of oral culture was facilitated by the establishment of the Irish Folklore Commission (in 1935) with the result that "150 years after the Famine, field-workers are still able to collect material from the living tradition".[20] Portéir's insistence on the living tradition underlines the fact that such memory is regarded as having been transmitted faithfully in a "vertical" fashion between generations, with a continuing vibrant relevance. Thus, he could claim that "most of the material quoted [in his 1995 collection *Famine Echoes*] comes from the children and grandchildren of the people who were eye-witnesses to the Famine".[21] It is, furthermore, important to realize that in many cases this was the testimony of "ordinary, often illiterate people"[22] – witnesses without recourse to the written narrative, and for whom orature was a central part of life.

In 1937, the Irish Folklore Commission promulgated a schools survey seeking this very type of memory: "Have the old people stories about the great famine of 1846–1847? [...] Great importance is attached to the *writing down* by the children of events which occurred locally during the famine years" (*my emphasis*). Thus, a literary narrative could be elucidated from an oral one. It was, in Roger McHugh's words, "making them real to the world at large".[23]

The concentration on the local and the particular is indicative of the realization that it may be relatively insignificant (in the global context) that a greater truth is to be found. As the Greek poet Odysseas Elytis wrote, "you will come to learn a great deal if you study the insignificant in depth".[24] To which we might add the view of his compatriot, the novelist Alexandros Papadiamandis: "the smaller the village, the bigger the evil".[25] The intimacy of the event can both illuminate and occlude what has actually happened.

Waters says: "not only are we [the Irish] reluctant to face the trauma of our own history – we are unwilling even to face the possibility that such an inhibited experience may exist in our collaborative consciousness".[26] The "creation" of memory is, in the eyes of some commentators, an act contrary to that of forgetting, by means of which the "buried" event can be restored. Waters insists that the Famine "must be talked about until we remember the things we never knew".[27]

Sinéad O'Connor's 1994 song "Famine" also addresses the question of whether the memory of the Famine is repressed; as critic David Lloyd observes, she "connects this with our deeply embedded habit of disavowing the personal and cultural damage that is in part the legacy of our colonial past",[28] thus emphasizing the need to re-examine that colonial past in order to escape from its inhibitions.[29]

This is also addressed by poet Nuala ní Dhomhnaill: "If [...] it takes seven generations for the overt behavior patterns caused by deep emotional trauma to be bred out of a population, how long must it take for the covert ones to leave us?"[30]

The "Famine echoes" project born of the sesquicentenary, and other cognate revisions of Irish history are, in fact, a form of therapy through which the anxieties of commentators like Waters can be assuaged: the act(s) of remembering reconstitute the experience, and thus make them contemporaneous; it is possibly this exorcism of historical memory which sits uneasily with the *locus standi* of Ireland in the so-called modern world.

Contemporary nationalists in Ireland alleged that the Famine could be regarded as a form of genocide: "a million and a half men, women and children were carefully, prudently and peacefully slain by the English government"; thus wrote John Mitchel in *The Last Conquest of Ireland (Perhaps)* in 1861.[31]

The fundamental nature of the change in Irish society was recognized at the time (1849–1852 in his *Irish Popular Superstitions*) by William Wilde, who saw the Famine itself and consequent emigration as factors in the elimination of both physical and cultural life. This, too, has consequences for the way Ireland regards itself in the modern world, since the loss of the Irish language and of orature led to a "disenchantment"[32] or loss of spirit – what we might call "Irishness", and which was hastened by the modernization of society and its worldview. Fundamental to this consideration is the role and power of storytelling which addresses both mythical topics of a universal nature, and local truths, all of which are transmitted effectively from generation to generation.

The Famine could thus be seen, in E Estyn Evans's words, as the end of "prehistoric times in Ireland",[33] or what Stuart McLean calls "the numinous geography evoked in the guise of popular belief".[34] A type of Irishness was diminished, if not eliminated. To put it more crudely, the spirituality of pagan, pre-Christian Ireland was obliterated. It is thus possible to view the recovery of Famine memory and of an Ireland preceding the "Great Famine" as a renaissance or restoration of an otherwise dead culture. As Dipesh Chakrabarty eloquently puts it, this type of re-experiencing of past memory "makes the present non-contemporaneous with itself".[35] Derek Hand, too, in discussing O'Flaherty's *Famine,* points out that the imagery and symbolic power of the famine become the means by which a displaced critique of the contemporary world can take place.[36] If, as Stuart McLean seems to argue, modern historiography has silenced "other ways of knowing", then the revisionism of Irish history through projects like the reclamation of "Famine memories" represents a redressing of imbalance toward the process of remembering for which Miłosz asks.

The Famine, like the Second World War and the "Anatolian Catastrophe", marked "a great historical divide".[37] It could be regarded as dividing a world in which remembrance was a vital (i.e. a living) part of cultural life from that in which we live today, in which it is too easy and convenient, in Miłosz's terms, to forget. This idea of "two Irelands" also characterizes the "two Europes" – to limit our discussion to the land mass in which these divisions occurred. The preceding world in which "I remember" is a point of celebration is divided from today's world in which "I remember" is a point of failure and remonstration. This, too, is true of the Holocaust and the "Anatolian Catastrophe" because the first memory is paradisal and the second is hellish: to Miłosz's "memory of wounds" we can therefore add "memory of loss" and its inversion, "loss of memory".

In her essay, "Irish Famine in Literature" Margaret Kelleher suggests that we might investigate analogies between the Irish Famine and the Holocaust. One of the novelists she discusses, Liam O'Flaherty, himself makes a similar connection to the expulsion of the Jews in his novel *Famine* (1937): "I'm afraid that something is going to happen in Ireland that will make our race wanderers on the face of the earth like the ancient Jews".[38] Kelleher indicates many works of modern Irish literature which either focus on, or allude to, the Famine: these include Somerville and Ross's *The Big House of Inver* (1925), Walter Macken's *The Silent People* (1962), John Banville's *Birchwood* (1973) and William Trevor's *Fools of Fortune* (1983); in poetry she includes Patrick Kavanagh's *The Great Hunger* (1942), Seamus Heaney's *Death of a Naturalist* (1966) and Eavan Boland's "The Making of an Irish Goddess" (1989); and also Tom Murphy's play *Famine* (1968).

O'Flaherty's *Famine* depicts not only the extermination of the life of the peasants but the hurt to their *dignity*. Kelly calls it "a saga of the unconquerable human spirit",[39] suggesting that the spirit of the Irish peasant can "rise above" the indignities of his or her life. That spirit is displayed in the declaration by one of his characters: "Why do we ever grumble at anything as long as we have our health and our eyes to see the sunbeams dancing on the river water?" and yet O'Flaherty is also forced to acknowledge that "the only holiday of the peasant [is] the furlough of approaching death".[40] O'Flaherty's novel is based on the belief that a peasant, whatever his or her condition, and whatever the circumstances, can espouse exclusively the concept of "freedom": "the freedom of the earth that bore you and the happiness and prosperity of those you love".[41]

O'Flaherty was writing *Famine* at the same period as the Irish Folklore Commission was soliciting narratives from descendants of the same people whom he was describing. The novel and the research project were cognate: both present the Irish peasant as a real – possibly even noble – human being, rather than a digit in history. This "resurrection" of the Irishness closest to the soil (also evident in O'Flaherty's next novel, *Land*), and O'Flaherty's ability to live back in that intimate association, the context to which he himself belonged, is a distinguishing mark of modern Irish fiction.

O'Flaherty's novel *Famine* and Murphy's play *Famine* have one chilling factor in common: the mercy-killing of those (mostly children) whose deaths from starvation would rob them of their dignity: in the novel a mother declares, having stifled her children "I had the right to put them out of their suffering".[42] In the text of the play, we are given this uncompromising stage direction: "*John comes out of darkness and exits. He has killed his wife and son*".[43]

In their literary works, O'Flaherty and Murphy re-imagined the visceral and psychological meaning of the Famine and thus re-presented it to a new audience-readership.

The "Anatolian Catastrophe"

In 2021, Greece celebrated the bicentenary of the opening of the war of independence from Ottoman (Turkish) rule. In 2022, it marked the centenary of its "Anatolian Catastrophe", an "event" (in terms of postmemory) of traumatic and long-lasting significance. The "Anatolian Catastrophe" was the culmination of a Greek aspiration, which amounted to national policy, to re-unite all Greek people within the structure of a modern state. The state itself was established and ratified in 1830 by an international treaty of superior powers, after a nine-year war of independence in which some, but only some, of the lands occupied by ethnic Greeks were liberated from the Ottoman Empire. Fourteen years later, It is commonly accepted that, fourteen years later, the Greek prime minister articulated the *Megáli Idéa* (or "Great Concept") of expanding the Greek territory to "embrace" those not yet included in the political state. In the period 1830 to 1918 Greece's borders did expand exponentially, with the adherence (*enosis* or union) firstly of the Ionian Islands in 1864 by virtue of international treaties and war, up to the end of the First World War. At that point, due to misunderstandings, misconceptions, and military mismanagement, an attempt was made to restore to Hellenism the key emotional, cultural, and spiritual centre: Constantinople (to this day Greece refuses to acknowledge the Turkish name of the city, Istanbul). The resulting military defeat led to the burning by the Turks of Smyrna (today Izmir), a city on the Turkish coast predominantly Greek in character, and the expulsion of 1.5 million ethnic Greeks to the Greek state from western Turkey ("Anatolia"), with a concomitant transfer of ethnic Turks from Greece to Turkey.

The effect of this expulsion was literally catastrophic, and its trauma continues to haunt modern Greece. The conquest of Constantinople by the Ottomans in 1453 had left Hellenism (that is, the "spirit" or "psyche" of the Greek mind) literally stateless, without a center, with no tangible identity other than its language. "Greece" did not, in fact, exist as a political state acceptable to western ideas of statecraft until 1830, and its identity was severely affected by the "Anatolian Catastrophe" which saw the extinction of the *Megáli Idéa* and, with it, the *raison d'être* of the Greek state. The long-term economic, social, and cultural repercussions of the defeat and the influx of refugees inflicted a psychic wound on the idea of "Greece".

The Greek critic Tilemachos Kotsias tells us:

> Greek literature has also concerned itself a great deal with lost homelands and ethnic cleansings, especially the expulsion of the Greeks and their uprooting from their ancestral homes. [...] Over the course of his more recent history (Greek Revolution, Balkan Wars etc.) the Greek has created within himself certain national antibodies which at the time were necessary for his own survival, but which continue to influence him today and obscure his judgement.[44]

The earliest account of the Catastrophe was Stratis Doukas' *A Prisoner of War's Story*, first published in 1929. It constitutes the story, as told to Doukas in 1928, of a soldier in the Anatolian campaign whose "narrative of testimony" becomes the essence of the book; Dimitris Tziovas credits Doukas with inaugurating a tradition of such testimony[45] which Doukas urged readers to collect as "valuable mosaics". The story is "a beautiful folk flower of oral discourse", which Doukas has enhanced by means of giving the narrative a sense of structure and unity and of dramatic climax.[46] In this way, the "oral discourse" becomes a form of literature.

Later accounts of the Catastrophe were George Theotokas' *Argo* (1933), Ilias Venezis' *Aeolia* (1943), Dido Sotiriou's *Farewell Anatolia* (1962) and, nearer our own time, *The Maze* by Panos Karnezis (2004). We should pay particular attention to Venezis' *Aeolia*, not least because, as an outsider, Lawrence Durrell's view of the novel and its subject-matter adds emphasis to the Greek storyline.[47]

Venezis, like Sotiriou, was a refugee from the Catastrophe. Eye-witness accounts (like those of the Irish Famine) were a vital element in the process of remembering, in creating a national narrative explaining the origins and effect of this culmination (and collapse) of the *Megáli Idéa*.

In his preface to the English translation of *Aeolia* Lawrence Durrell wrote:

> The tragedy of his expulsion from Anatolia still weighs heavily upon the heart of the modern Greek, whether he is a metropolitan or an exile from the bountiful plains and wooded mountains of Asia Minor. He cannot forget it. If he is an exile he returns again and again to Anatolia in his dreams: he broods upon it as Adam and Eve must have brooded upon the Garden of Eden after the Fall. [...] But it is more than the injustice, the cruelty, the madness of the whole episode which sticks in the mind of the modern Greek. It is also a sense of a lost richness, a lost peace of mind. [...] It has become a memory which he touches from time to time, like a man fingering a cicatrice.[48]

We must remember that *Aeolia* was written only 20 years after the "trauma", and that Durrell's introduction, written in 1947, was a tribute to the living testimony of its survivors. (Durrell, in Alexandria in the second world war, had published the poem *Anatolia* by his friend-in-exile, Elie Papadimitriou, a threnody for that trauma which she herself had witnessed.)[49]

The narrator of *Aeolia* is a girl whose voice (an authorial voice, naturally) saturates the reader's own mind from the opening pages ("The Discovery of the World") with the sacred atmosphere that binds men to the soil. The ensuing political and military crisis invades and dissipates that atmosphere, replacing it with darkness and despair. As a refugee, escaping from the Turkish advance, one character attributes brutality to the nature of man: "Surrounded by the throng of hunted people seeking refuge by the sea, she sensed that this was it, that the demon, their dark instinct, was roused, and she tried to comprehend it".[50]

The story ends with an old man in a refugee boat carrying away a bag of Anatolian soil "from our fields so we can plant a root of basil in our land of exile. To remind us...".[51] This image of memory as a metaphor becomes a trope of Greek literature and film, as exemplified in Tassos Boulmetis' 2003 film *A Touch of Spice* (originally Πολίτικη κουζίνα – meaning, literally, the Kitchen of the City [Constantinople]) in which the past lives of refugees (such as those from Anatolia) are recounted in tastes and aromas: "Our cuisine is tinged with politics. It's made by people who left their dinner unfinished somewhere else".

What is little appreciated outside Greece – and is seldom discussed in Greece itself – is the fact that the "Anatolian Catastrophe", as the invidious culmination of the policy and aspiration of the *Megáli Idéa*, precipitated decades of division in the Greek mind (1922 to at least 1974) which found expression (I use the word deliberately in the Freudian sense) in the dictatorships of 1935–1936 and 1967–1974, and the civil war which began covertly even during, and within, the resistance to the Nazis in the second world war and continued in open conflict from 1945 until 1948/1949. The

"Catastrophe" continues to raise the question of whether Greece "belongs" exclusively in the West or has other, reverberant associations.

Conclusion

The literary examples from Ireland and Greece which I have briefly discussed suggest, on one level, that the Irish and Greek peoples share a type of postmemory which was caused in each case by a different traumatic "event". Yet on another level, that of the rational, linear, historiographical, counter-intuitive, the psychological inference is absurd. Entire populations do not carry, as if in their DNA, a trauma transmitted faithfully from one generation to another. If they did, the world would be unsettled by angst-ridden peoples collectively seeking a therapy which they believe storytelling can provide.[52]

Yet we must ask, how in each case imaginative literature is being written out of a historical inherited sense of shame, sickness, and wounding. Does it exist solely in the minds of certain writers who are super-sensitive to certain rhythms and nuances in their own psyche which they wish to share with their compatriots?

Is it possible to live in a liminal world, on the threshold between, in the past, the positive and pre-traumatic experience, and at the same time in the present, the less positive – even negative – post-traumatic experience dominated by commodification and globalization? An "old" Europe and the present "Europe"? And is there available to us an imaginative strategy which will make it possible to live, even precariously, in that limen, that between-space?

My reflections on postmemory have concentrated on this role of the imagination as a therapeutic bearer of truths that might not be articulated, except by means of a liberating narrative which enables us to transcend the postmemory of trauma by imagining a possible future, even if we cannot heal or redeem it.[53]

Notes

1 "The Generation of Postmemory", *Poetics Today* 29/1 (2008); *my emphasis*. She also defines postmemory as "the relationship that later generations or distant contemporary witnesses bear to the personal, collective, and cultural trauma of others—to experiences they 'remember' or know only by means of stories, images, and behaviors": PMLA Presidential Address 2014: "Connective Histories in Vulnerable Times".

2 As we can appreciate from essays on Bosnia (Pierre Bayard), Cambodia (Soko Phay) and Armenia (Emmanuel Alloa), the term "postmemory" is not applied exclusively to the Holocaust (these essays are published in the *Journal of Literature and Trauma Studies*, volume 4 (2015), "Figurations of Postmemory", guest editors Emmanuel Alloa, Pierre Bayard, and Soko Phay. See also Simone Mitroiu (ed.), *Women's Narratives and the Postmemory of Displacement in Central and Eastern Europe*.

3 I discuss *Amíliti* in two essays in my *The Eye of the Xenos: Letters about Greece*.
4 https://www.nobelprize.org/prizes/literature/1980/milosz/lecture/. All subsequent quotations by Miłosz are from this source.
5 T. Kotsias, "Difference is Truly a Gift", in N. Lemos and E. Yannakakis (eds.), *Critical Times, Critical Thoughts*, p. 61; *my emphasis*.
6 L. Gibbons, "Doing Justice to the Past", in Tom Hayden (ed.), *Irish Hunger*, p. 269; *my emphasis*.
7 "Confronting the Ghosts of Our Past", in Tom Hayden (ed.), *Irish Hunger*, p. 28; *my emphasis*.
8 "Famine Roads", in Tom Hayden (ed.), *Irish Hunger*, p. 213; *my emphasis*.
9 L. O'Flaherty, *Famine*, p. 42.
10 R. Pine, *The Disappointed Bridge*, pp. xxiv–xxv.
11 S. Deane, "Heroic Styles: The Tradition of an Idea" in *Small World*, p. 134.
12 Ibid., p. 142. We must also beware of the close connection between *tradition* and *treason* or *betrayal*, both of which derive from the Latin verb *tradere*. As Jack M Balkin tells us, a tradition may have its opposite or alternative, a contratradition, which it suppresses in order to establish "the hegemony of a particular way of thinking [...] The overt, respectable tradition", Balkin says, "depends upon the forgetting of its submerged, less respectable opposite": "Tradition, Betrayal and the Politics of Deconstruction".
13 J. Waters, "Confronting the Ghosts of Our Past", p. 27.
14 See my discussion of the statement by Kostas Karamanlis "We belong to the West" in my *The Eye of the Xenos*.
15 William Carleton, in his novel *The Black Prophet*, quoted in Tom Hayden, *Irish Hunger*, p. 25.
16 Cathal Pórtéir, "Folk Memory and the Famine" in his *Famine Echoes*, p. 4.
17 C. Pórtéir, "Folk Memory and the Famine", p. 12. See also Cathal Pórtéir (ed.), *The Great Irish Famine* [Thomas Davis Lecture Series].
18 R. McHugh, "The Famine in Irish oral tradition", in R. Dudley Edwards and T. Desmond Williams (eds.), *The Great Famine*, p. 391.
19 McBride, introduction to *History and Memory in Modern Ireland*, p. 5.
20 C. Pórtéir, *Famine Echoes*, p. 13.
21 Ibid., p. 13; see Pórtéir's p. 11 for his discussion of the "parallel" and "vertical" methods of transmission of oral testimony.
22 Ibid., p. 16.
23 R. McHugh, "The Famine in Irish Oral Tradition", p. 391.
24 Odysseas Elytis, "Axion Esti", in *Collected Poems* trans. J. Carson and N. Sarris, p. 127.
25 A. Papadiamandis, "The Fey Folk", *The Boundless Garden*, p. 241.
26 "Confronting the Ghosts of Our Past", p. 27.
27 Ibid. Seamus Heaney saluted Patrick Kavanagh's *The Great Hunger* not merely for its insistence on the presence of the peasant in Irish history, but for "raising the inhibited energies of a subculture to the power of a cultural resource": *Preoccupations*, p. 116.
28 "The Memory of Hunger" in Tom Hayden (ed.), *Irish Hunger*, p. 32.
29 Luke Gibbons also refers to "the painful negotiation of popular memory in cultures encumbered with the ordeal of colonisation": "Doing Justice to the Past", p. 260.
30 "A Ghostly Alhambra" in Tom Hayden (ed.), *Irish Hunger*, p. 69.
31 Quoted by Niall Ó Ciosáin, "Famine Memory" in McBride, p. 107. Much more recently, the English historian AJP Taylor went so far as to draw a parallel with the Holocaust: reviewing Cecil Woodham Smith's *The Great Hunger* under the headline "Genocide", he stated that in the 1840s "all Ireland was a Belsen"

[...] The English [...] had killed two million Irish people": quoted in James S Donnelly Jr., "The Great Famine and its Interpreters, Old and New" in Tom Hayden, *Irish Hunger*, p.119; it is notable that the numbers of the dead vary from one historical source to another.
32 I am adopting the term "disenchantment" employed by Stuart McLean in his study *The Event and Its Terrors*.
33 E. Estyn Evans, *Irish Folk Ways*, p. 282.
34 S. McLean, *The Event and Its Terrors*, p. 5.
35 D. Chakrabarty, *Provincializing Europe*, p. 63.
36 D. Hand, *A History of the Irish Novel*, p. 176.
37 G. Zimmermann, *The Irish Storyteller*, p. 274.
38 Liam O'Flaherty, *Famine*, p. 129.
39 A. A. Kelly, *Liam O'Flaherty the Storyteller*, p. 127.
40 O'Flaherty, *Famine*, pp. 32, 117.
41 Ibid., p. 172.
42 O'Flaherty, *Famine*, p. 430.
43 Tom Murphy, *Famine*, p.86.
44 T. Kotsias, "Difference is Truly a Gift".
45 In his "Introduction" (p. ix) to *A Prisoner of War's Story* (1999 translation by Petro Alexiou).
46 Ibid., pp. xiii, 54.
47 I discuss this more fully in "War, Agón and the Greek Literary Imagination".
48 L. Durrell, "Preface" to I. Venezis, *Aeolia* trans. E. D. Scott-Kilvert, pp. v-vi.
49 Papadimitriou's *Anatolia* is reprinted in R. Pine and V. Konidari (eds.), *Borders and Borderlands*.
50 Ibid., p. 244.
51 Ibid., p. 259.
52 I note that "epigenetic memory" in relation to DNA is currently being explored by, among others, Natan PF Kellermann ("Epigenetic transmission of holocaust trauma: Can nightmares be inherited").
53 I am indebted to Emilie Pine, Director of the Irish Memory Studies Research Network for commenting on this essay.

Bibliography

Alloa, Emmanuel et al. (eds.), 2015, "Figurations of Postmemory", *Journal of Literature and Trauma Studies* 4, 1–2.

Balkin, Jack N., 1990, "Tradition, Betrayal and the Politics of Deconstruction", A Yale University Faculty Scholarship Paper. https://digitalcommons.law.yale.edu/fss_papers/283/

Boland, Eavan, 2000, "Famine Roads", in Tom Hayden (ed.), *Irish Hunger: Personal Reflections on the Legacy of the Famine*, Boulder, CO: Roberts Rinehart.

Chakrabarty, Dipesh, 2000, *Provincializing Europe: Postcolonial Thought and Historical Difference*, Princeton, NJ: Princeton University Press.

Chinweizu et al., 1983, *Toward the decolonization of African literature*, Washington, DC: Howard University Press.

Deane, Seamus, 2021, *Small World: Ireland 1798–2018*, Cambridge: Cambridge University Press.

Donnelly, James S. Jr., 2000, "The Great Famine and Its Interpreters, Old and New", in Tom Hayden (ed.), *Irish Hunger: Personal Reflections on the Legacy of the Famine*, Boulder, CO: Roberts Rinehart, 117–133.

Doukas, Stratis, 1999, *A Prisoner of War's Story* trans. Petro Alexiou, Birmingham: Centre for Byzantine, Ottoman & Greek Studies, University of Birmingham.
Edwards, R. Dudley and T. Desmond Williams (eds.), 1994, *The Great Famine: Studies in Irish History 1845–52*, Dublin: Lilliput Press.
Elytis, Odysseas, 2004, *Collected Poems* trans. J Carson and N Sarris, Baltimore, MD: Johns Hopkins University Press.
Estyn Evans, E., 1967, *Irish Folk Ways*, London: Routledge and Kegan Paul.
Gibbons, Luke, 2011, "Doing Justice to the Past", in Tom Hayden (ed.), *Irish Hunger: Personal Reflections on the Legacy of the Famine*, Boulder, CO: Roberts Rinehart, 250–262.
Hand, Derek, 2011, *A History of the Irish Novel*, Cambridge: Cambridge University Press.
Hayden, Tom (ed.), 1998, *Irish Hunger: Personal Reflections on the Legacy of the Famine*, Boulder, CO: Roberts Rinehart.
Heaney, Seamus, 1980, *Preoccupations: Selected Prose 1968–1978*, London: Faber and Faber.
———, 1990, *The Cure at Troy: A Version of Sophocles'*, Philoctetes, London: Faber and Faber.
Hirsch, Marianne, 2008, "The Generation of Postmemory", *Poetics Today* 29/1, 103–128.
Kavanagh, Patrick and Tom MacIntyre, 1988, *The Great Hunger: Poem into Play*, Gigginstown: Lilliput Press.
Kelleher, Margaret, 1998, "Irish Famine in Literature", in C. Portéir (ed.), *The Great Irish Famine* [Thomas Davis Lecture Series], Cork: Mercier Press, 232–247.
Kellermann, N. P. F., 2013, "Epigenetic transmission of holocaust trauma: Can nightmares be inherited", *Israel Journal of Psychiatry and Related Sciences* 38/1, 33–39.
Kelly, A. A., 1976, *Liam O'Flaherty the Storyteller*, New York: Barnes & Noble.
Kotsias, Tilemachos, 2015, "Difference is Truly a Gift", in N. Lemos and E. Yannakakis (eds.), *Critical Times, Critical Thoughts: Contemporary Greek Writers Discuss Facts and Fiction*, Newcastle-upon-Tyne: Cambridge Scholars, 53–62.
Lloyd, David, 1988, "The Memory of Hunger", in Tom Hayden (ed.), *Irish Hunger: Personal Reflections on the Legacy of the Famine*, Boulder, CO: Roberts Rinehart, 32–47.
McBride, Ian (ed.), 2001, *History and Memory in Modern Ireland*, Cambridge: Cambridge University Press.
McHugh, Roger, 1994, "The Famine in Irish Oral Tradition", in Edwards and Williams (eds.), *The Great Famine: Studies in Irish history 1845–52*, Dublin: Lilliput Press, 391-436.
McLean, Stuart, 2004, *The Event and Its Terrors: Ireland, Famine, Modernity*, Stanford, CA: Stanford University Press.
Miłosz, Czesław, "Nobel Lecture" at https://www.nobelprize.org/prizes/literature/1980/milosz/lecture/
Mitroiu, Simone (ed.), 2018, *Women's Narratives and the Postmemory of Displacement in Central and Eastern Europe*, London: Palgrave Macmillan.
Murphy, Tom, 1984, *Famine*, Dublin: Gallery Press.

Ní Dhomhnaill, Nuala, 1998, "A Ghostly Alhambra", in Tom Hayden (ed.), *Irish Hunger: Personal Reflections on the Legacy of the Famine*, Boulder, CO: Roberts Rinehart, 68–78.

Ó Casáin, Niall, 2001, "Famine Memory", in Ian McBride (ed.), *History and Memory in Modern Ireland*, Cambridge: Cambridge University Press, 95–117.

Ó Cathaoir, Brendan (ed.), 1995, *The Great Irish Famine* [Thomas Davis Lecture Series], Cork: Mercier Press.

——— (ed.), 1999, *Famine Diary*, Dublin: Irish Academic Press.

O'Flaherty, Liam, 1937, *Famine*, New York: Random House.

Papadiamandis, Alexandros, 2007, *The Boundless Garden: Selected Stories* volume 1, Evia, Greece: Denise Harvey.

Pine, Richard, 2015, *The Disappointed Bridge: Ireland and the Post-Colonial World*, Newcastle-upon-Tyne: Cambridge Scholars.

———, 2021, (ed. with Vera Konidari), *Borders and Borderlands: Explorations in Identity, Exile and Translation*, Newcastle-upon-Tyne: Cambridge Scholars.

———, 2021, (with Vera Konidari), *The Eye of the Xenos: Letters about Greece*, Newcastle-upon-Tyne: Cambridge Scholars.

———, 2021, *The Quality of Life: Essays on Cultural Politics 1978–2018*, Newcastle-upon-Tyne: Cambridge Scholars.

———, 2008 "War, *Agón* and the Greek Literary Imagination" in R. Pine and E. Patten (eds.), *Literatures of War* Necastle-upon-Tyne. Cambridge Scholars, 72–89.

Portéir, Cathal (ed.), 1995, *Famine Echoes*, Dublin: Gill and Macmillan.

———, (ed.), 1995, *The Great Irish Famine* [Thomas Davis Lecture Series], Cork: Mercier Press.

Venezis, Ilias, 1949, *Aeolia* trans. E D Scott-Kilvert, London: William Campion, 1949.

Waters, John, 1988, "Confronting the Ghosts of Our Past", in Tom Hayden (ed.), *Irish Hunger: Personal Reflections on the Legacy of the Famine*, Boulder, CO: Roberts Rinehart.

wa Thiong'o, Ngũgĩ, 1986, *Decolonizing the Mind: The Politics of Language in African Literature*, London: James Currey.

Zimmermann, Georges Denis, 2001, *The Irish Storyteller*, Dublin: Four Courts Press.

Chapter 5

Traumatic Childhood and Growing Up in the Shadow of Trauma

When Post-Trauma Meets Postmemory: The Story of David, a Holocaust Survivor

Maia Jessica Shoham

The term *postmemory* refers to the deep connection between Holocaust survivors and their families. It is a structure of intergenerational and transgenerational transmission of traumatic knowledge and experience.

The survivors' traumatic memories are transferred to their children and the following generation through selective silences, related stories, and more. This traumatic experience is passed down in the family and etched into their minds. Its importance lies in it being a memory and testament to the survivors' unthinkable traumatic mental events.[1]

While true memory is experienced by the person and recalled during the recollection processes, postmemory belongs to another specific person and is passed on to a close one after it is over. It is an unbearably harsh memory that the person who experienced it cannot contain, and therefore, two people are needed to contain it.

In defining the term postmemory, Hirsch chose to include the term *post* because of its ambiguity: Although it relates to an event that has ended, it is a perpetual memory that lives on in future generations through intergenerational transference.[2]

The second generation was born into a family environment emersed in trauma. Overwhelming and alien trauma materials were implanted in them from birth, becoming an integral part of them. Hoffman termed parental trauma materials *shadows* that subsist in the children's psychic lives, with a similar shape and fabric to the original trauma, but still distinguishable.[3] Gampel called the Holocaust's negative effects on the second generation, *radioactive fallout*.[4] According to her, trauma has the power to spread and infect and is passed down through the generations. The individual stands helpless against this penetration. Hirsch argued that at times, the intensity of the second generation's postmemory may be so powerful that it overshadows and barely allows narratives and experiences unlike their parents' trauma to exist.[5]

Although the second generation did not live through the Holocaust, its members live with its effects, and it is understandable that they are often preoccupied with Holocaust-related content. Unlike survivors endeavoring

DOI: 10.4324/9781003274650-6

to survive, some of their children can digest their parents' inconceivable traumas and create a transformation through active creativity such as sculpture, poetry, and painting. Thus, the trauma becomes thinkable data. The transformation process occurs thanks to their deep identification and ongoing internal work.[6] That is what Hirsch refers to as postmemorial work.

This idea seems to be inspired by the container-contained model by Bion (1897–1979). This is a case of massive and chronic trauma, and the second generation constitutes an inverted container for their parents.[7] They contain and gradually process trauma materials that their parents cannot bear.

Frosh distinguished between postmemory as a form of *traumatic identification*, and postmemorial work as a form of *working through*.[8] The following generation is subject to the tyranny of their parents' memories, which in their experience, become their own. These memories dictate their comportment. This type of postmemory does not allow traumas to be processed and a life existence that recreates these traumas appears in its place. In contrast, in postmemorial work as a form of what Freud (1856–1939) termed *working through*, the second generation manages to experience and think about their parents' traumas.[9] They find a way to absorb postmemory and transform it so that the past's ghosts or shadows of trauma loosen their grip.

In this case study, I will discuss a post-traumatic Holocaust survivor who was separated from his family at a young age. He could not contain the unbearable traumatic separation, which was beyond his psychological powers. The patient later reconnected with his mother in Israel and lived with her until she died at an advanced age. His mother did not share her wartime past. Instead, she lived in depressed silence. My patient's mother's trauma was a postmemory for him and affected him unconsciously, along with the post-trauma he suffered from due to his own experiences.

Case Study—David (Fictitious Name)

I worked weekly with David many years ago, during my internship as a clinical psychologist. His treatment lasted four years. During the intake interview, David described his difficulty sleeping and his limited ability to function, resulting from his many anxieties. He said he never watched television or answered the phone, he never went far from home, and he was so nervous that he would physically pull on his teeth until they fell out. "My nerves are eating me up. I have a broken, incessant record playing inside." He said that all his symptoms began when he was taken from his mother.

David entered our sessions limping and wide eyed. During this initial therapy period, he repeatedly told me his story, keeping to the same details and expressions that he provided during intake.

His story occurred between the ages of 6.5 and 11: He was taken from his family, smuggled by boat with other children to Israel, and placed on a kibbutz until he was later reunited with his mother, also in Israel. During the sessions, David would express suffering and cry, however I found it difficult to relate to his pain because of his repetitive and rigid way of speaking. He either ignored my questions or answered them curtly. Whenever I tried to understand and connect by mirroring his feelings, he would become suspicious. He asked to shorten the sessions and became concerned about confidentiality. I realized that he was experiencing my attempts to understand him as intrusive and that he needed me to listen to him repeating his narrative precisely as it was.

A few months passed and David shared that whenever he woke up, he would tell himself his story, as if telling himself a bedtime story. We discussed his repetitive narrative as an attempt to create a shell for himself, to form experiences of order, continuity, control, and security. I learned that his reconstructions (as he called his repetitive narrative) also occurred during the day and I understood that they had become a refuge to which he fled, and where he would stay. I told him that this refuge was making it difficult to meet external reality. In response, David talked about the terrifying and unpredictable world that he lived in, and how he survived it through avoidance. David started bringing me copies of his medical records and asked to see me every other week. I expressed my confusion. David explained that his sessions with me were very important to him, and he wanted to spread them out in order to prolong his treatment and postpone the end.

David was anxious about our parting. His anxiety was contagious and flared up in me, as I was in my first trimester and knew that we would have to part ways for a while when I gave birth. I experienced him regressing and feeling helpless; I suggested he consult with a psychiatrist. David was terrified by the suggestion: "If I do, it means I am crazy." During one session, after months of discussing it as much as possible, he asked if I thought he should see a psychiatrist. When I suggested considering it, he cried out in pain and jumped to his feet: "I'm not crazy...if you don't want me, I will get up and go." I asked him to sit down and told him I did not want him to leave. He appeared to feel that I wanted to get rid of him, so I told him that our talks were central to treatment, and psychiatric treatment could be a calming addition. David started crying, seemed relieved, and for the first time, noticed the painting behind me of two children walking hand in hand. He agreed to see the psychiatrist and asked me to accompany him to his first appointment.

In this segment, we can see how trauma filled every part of David's psyche. His recurring story was a frozen and static traumatic imprint that he lived in. And so, despite his advanced age, he continued to be a child who had been separated from his mother, lonely and helplessly facing a frightening world. I had many questions at this time: How could one turn a traumatic impression into a living memory so that it becomes a *mental action*? How are new events and memories from the rest of a person's life woven into the mind after the traumatic fault? These questions came to me due to the experience of emptiness that characterized his treatment at this stage, making me wonder whether movement and mental development were possible for David in our therapeutic relationship.

David was able to build a life after the trauma occurred. He married and started a family. Yet he was obsessed with his story of being separated from his family. It appeared that the people in his life did not have emotional access to him because of his intense post-trauma. To him, life around him was a shadow of life, and those close to him were living through the shadows of trauma through him.

During this period, my presence resembled the presence he experienced with his mother: I listened in silence. His mother, being a Holocaust survivor, was most likely post-traumatic, and for her own reasons, unable to narrate her past. His psyche seemed to demand from me to be that way for him, perhaps as it had demanded it from his mother.

David clung stubbornly to the narrative of disconnect, which for him was a valuable part of his life; a collection of traumatic memories that he repeated obsessively and perpetually, thereby tormenting himself. I was surprised to notice elements of pleasure and gratification. I think they stemmed from the compulsive preservation of his memories as forms of belonging: It was if he had an internal restraining order preventing him from adding details and recalling them. David was torn from his family at a young age, and his only remaining personal belongings were his memories, which he zealously safeguarded.

Post-Traumatic Memories as Restricting David's Family from Processing His Postmemory

David was fixated on his traumatic memories. It took time until he felt safe enough with me to lower his defenses slightly. Then, in my presence, he began to recall details that were beyond the sphere of his frozen reconstruction. His narrative expanded, and he started to ask questions. Recalling is the first step in a vital mental process. When it begins, a small internal space is created for new thoughts and feelings.

When I returned from seven months of maternity leave, we continued therapy and David began to recall other memories. He was the sixth of ten children, and as a child, he saw his mother pregnant most of the time. Perhaps my having been pregnant and busy with my own needs felt familiar enough from his past. This memory was therefore permitted to enter his rigid internal structure. In our first session, David shared that during our break, he had come to the clinic at our regular time. He would walk his regular route from home, wait outside for the right time, reconstruct his story, and then return home. I reflected to him how difficult it had been for him to tolerate the break from therapy, which was reminiscent of being separated from his mother. This led to a lengthy discussion about waiting for his mother, which he had experienced as eternal and impossible, and about their reunion in Israel.

David said that after he returned to his mother, he never left her again. His siblings were scattered among various kibbutzim. He married and started a family, and they lived in a small caravan in his mother's backyard. David could never hold down a job. He was repeatedly dismissed because of outbursts of rage and his unsatisfactory pace of work. He spent most days in his mother's house, where they would sit in the living room together and cry. David repeatedly told her the story of being taken from her. According to him, his mother was not a verbal woman, and she never had a job or learned Hebrew. When I asked what his mother went through during the war and how she experienced being separated from him, he replied that he did not know, and he had never asked. After his mother died, he moved into her house with his family.

I realized that his mother's silence had prevented her from being a real presence. I am surprised that although David talked often about her, she remained a vague and empty image. I assumed she had been mentally broken and had never recovered.

This was a shared tragedy. Although they lived together and lived long lives, they both remained in grief and melancholy over fault and absence (Freud, 1917). The absence was so totally etched in them that it blocked the possibility of having a living relationship. There was no repair. Until his mother died, it seemed they were both compulsively engaged in continually recreating the day they were reunited, with him repeating to her all he had gone through after they had been separated.

I understood this as a damaged connection between two deeply hurt and broken, post-traumatic psyches who were stuck in the dark pit of separation. Possibly, the mother felt herself as not existing, and perhaps she also felt guilty and silenced. As such, she silently listened to her son's reconstructions and cried for him, for her absence from his life, and for what she had experienced. The horror of absence and psychic deadness was etched in David's soul and were deepened by her grating silence. On top of David's own trauma, his mother's undigested traumatic experience in relation to her crumbling life and self-disintegration was imprinted and fused into his experience of absence and even of mental deadness.

His mother's absence and the void he experienced as an unbearable pit in his psyche were filled by his post-trauma; that is, by his intrusive memories of his traumatic experiences.

David existed in a split world: Although he lived with his wife and children, he was self-absorbed, rarely talked to them, and was sensitive to sounds from the outside world. But he also lived with his mother, sitting and reconstructing his story with her for hours on end.

Both his repetitive inner narrative in the presence of his family and his repetitive spoken monologue in the presence of his mother constituted empty words that filled spaces and blocked anxiety and unbearable feelings. His repetitive narrative constituted noncommunicative content that prevented understanding, connections, and closeness with himself and others.

Therapy as Partly Unraveling David's Mother's Postmemory That Was Imprinted on His Post-Traumatic Memories

As I mentioned, on my return from maternity leave, additional content was allowed in—some referencing himself and his children, some referencing our own relationship. I think that my interest in him and his family helped him think about himself and his relationship with them. Sometimes he surprised me by answering a question I asked before I took maternity leave. About a year after we began therapy again, David shared, "I remember you asked me if I was angry with her," meaning his mother, "and I said no, but this week I am angry.... When I was sent away, I could still taste milk on my lips...I hardly ever spoke, I loved her, I was tied to her apron strings..." David was now wondering how "For 65 years I have kept reconstructing the same thing, like a broken record, and suddenly it's being recreated differently in me. I've started asking why I, not my siblings, was sent away. Was I a bother to her?"

David was starting to have new thoughts, insights, and uncomfortable feelings about his life: "What have I ever done in life? I married, had children and that's it.... I haven't really lived life.... and it is already over." Later: "How did I not have therapy earlier? I used to lash out at people and they would run away from me." David then started arriving two hours early for our sessions and waiting outside my room. I could feel him becoming more demanding, and we discussed his immense need. He shared that he had never told his story to his children because he was afraid to burden them. A few sessions later, he told me that he decided to tell them his story and it had been a meaningful experience that had brought them closer.

David also decided to visit the kibbutz he was sent to as a child when he arrived in Israel. He returned energized and told me that everything was still there. I was impressed by his actions and I told him as much. Suddenly, he remembered playing in the woods with his friends when he got a splinter in his foot. He noted that he had always remembered himself as lonely, and he was surprised to realize that he had friends to play with. We talked about the fact that his broken record (as he called his reconstructions) was inaccurate: This memory had raised new content (of togetherness and play) and with it, new emotions.

David's therapy continued to progress, and he shared some thoughts with me: "I want to be here...but sometimes I think that because I keep repeating myself, you will get tired of me. I want you to know, I'll understand and stop coming." The childhood danger of being sent away had surfaced again when he sensed the end of my internship. In response, I shared when therapy would end, and he replied that henceforth, his thoughts would be occupied with our parting.

David was fixated on why his mother had sent him away, rather than his older siblings. To my surprise, he added that he had tried to tell his mother what he had gone through in her absence, but felt she was self-absorbed and did not understand. I responded that his mother had been busy picking up the pieces from the war and had therefore found it hard to contain him. To this, he responded, "But I'm not mad at Mom, because no one can take her place." At the time, I was pregnant again with identical twins and the night before our session, I had an upsetting dream: I was holding my babies, one in each arm and someone was forcing me to decide between them and send one away. I awoke in terror and felt terrible guilt over having to make the impossible choice. Our session was that morning, and I was still feeling the nightmare's impact. I realized that although my dream was from my inner world and was related to my pregnancy, it also connected me to David's deep pain and to the distress his mother possibly felt following the choice she was forced to make.

In the following sessions, our discussion of his mother expanded, and I found myself giving David fragments of the feelings and thoughts I had in my nightmare, as if lending the words to his mother. David had shrouded himself with feelings of loss and sorrow. He realized that his mother had been sad and depressed. As new thoughts regarding his mother and their relationship developed, I noticed David was beginning to talk more about his daughters, and about wanting to be with them more regularly.

Six months of therapy remained, and David's depression was worsening. Detached from people, he rarely left home. He shared that he had read an article that had shocked him, about a mother who had crushed her baby while breastfeeding. He expanded further and added that doctors' mistakes can also kill. I responded that he had dared to become attached to me and was now feeling threatened. In response, David recalled asking his mother why she had cut him off, and how she had cried, saying with remorse that if his father had been alive, she would not have sent him away. I was moved to hear his mother's touching response.

David caught pneumonia and was depressed by the high doses of medication he was taking. I suggested that his depression and illness could be related to our separation. From that point on, we moved back and forth between his separation from his mother and our imminent separation; between his time on the kibbutz, where he was offered an adoptive mother, and the option he now had of seeing another therapist. David was trying very hard to fend off the reality of the end, and I was concerned about his severe depression. Whenever I raised the option of a new therapist, he reacted with pain and opposition. He said he had no choice—his body and mind would not allow him to try someone new; he was doomed to remain lonely, like on the kibbutz, and as he would be after me. I felt powerless, unable to stay with him, and admit that our parting was registering within him as a death.

One day, he told me how he had rejected his kibbutz adoptive mother. He addressed me as if I were that adoptive mother: "No matter what you give me, I will always want my mother." I responded, "There is no one like a mother, but when you are so attached to her, it is difficult to form a relationship with anyone else, and then you remain very lonely." As our time to part approached, David became increasingly confused, and often spoke to me as if I were his mother or adoptive mother.

Suffering from recurrent pneumonia, and still heavily medicated, David was exhausted and engrossed in our parting. I felt like I was abandoning him. Killing him. I did not know how to soften the blow. Nothing was helping. David sensed my difficulty and said,

> At least it was in stages. I remember asking you two years ago how long we would have...what enters my mind is etched there. I have no barriers with you. I handed you my record and now you have it... How can I start all over again?

We discussed his experiences of loyalty compared with the betrayal he had felt when he was asked by the kibbutz to meet his adoptive parents. David surprised me and said that he had met with his kibbutz adoptive parents only once, and their home had been uninviting. At the same time, he said that he had been looking at the other therapists at the clinic, but he did not believe that any of them could help him.

During our final session, David said that for the last month he had been looking around the room and waiting room and trying to burn my face to his memory, or as he called it, to his record. "I won't forget you. When I reconstruct my memories, I notice that you are in them...as if I now have two records." David added that he always found parting difficult and elaborated: "With you it is different because you ask how I feel and how I will be, and I also ask what will happen to me when I stop seeing you." I responded that I, too, often thought about him, and added that "I recently asked myself why I insist on sending you to another therapist." David nodded: "And what was your answer?" I explained that parting was hard for me, too, and that I was probably trying to alleviate my feelings of guilt and sadness by knowing he has a good therapist, and would not be lonely. David replied that he had no desire to see another therapist. To that, I responded that I understood and accepted this; that I knew he would be fine: He had his wife, children, and grandchildren who loved and valued him.

Seven months after therapy ended, David called and asked how I was before requesting my permission to begin therapy at the clinic with someone else. I was happy he was willing to move on and encouraged him to act on his decision.

Discussion

This case study describes post-trauma and postmemory processing work done in therapy, with the patient's trauma and his mother's trauma that was imprinted in it.

These were transferred to me through projective identification during the therapeutic relationship we formed. This gradually allowed some movement to open up an inner space. Processing his traumatic impressions and turning them into memories enabled David to observe, rethink, and understand them. As a result of processing the trauma, David felt a vital desire to visit places in his past and become closer to his family. Thus, his outer and inner worlds became more accessible to him, and he became more accessible to his close ones.

When David began therapy, he was trapped in a kind of unconscious traumatic capsule of frozen materials. He appeared encased in the rigid armor of reconstruction that embodied a pseudo-experience of security. According to Tustin (1913–1990), this allowed the protection and demarcation of the self and the world.[10] While treating him, I was exposed to a deep and uncommunicative trauma experience that was dominating all avenues of David's life; trauma that blocked the possibility of meeting a narrative different from his trauma story; one that left no room for vital mentality and relationships. The processes of projective identification became ineffective. Instead of promoting communication, they became the kind that preserves and ingrains trauma. His family seemed to have lost hope of reaching him.

A powerful transfer of trauma occurred during therapy, when at the beginning I was required to be an extension of his mother—silent and attentive to his story. It took a long time before I could gradually and carefully give back small parts of the emotional experiences I had during his therapy. Simultaneously, David developed an increasing ability to take back materials from his own story. That is, his ability to internalize began to improve, as did his ability to think new thoughts regarding himself and his mother.

During therapy, through transference and countertransference processes, I experienced part of the traumatic effects to David's psyche.

In addition, with the help of the nightmare I had, I could feel from within my own inner world, some of what the mother had experienced while she was separated from David.

My nightmare had resembled the experience of detachment between David and his mother and allowed me to deeply identify with their experiences. It helped me to process the shock of being torn away and to offer David a few integrative, processed fragments resulting from my work on the trauma in my psyche and in his. I believe this shared and disturbing experience allowed David to start thinking about what his mother had experienced during the war. These initial buds of separation contributed to the distinction between his traumatic memories and his mother's postmemory.

David's inner world was made up of layers of his own traumas and of his damaged environment. David experienced many traumas during the war, and he absorbed his mother's trauma when they were reunited. David lived with her most of his life, but failed to go through a processing process. They both seemed to freeze very early in time—he as a child, and she as a mother. Thus, his life came to a halt and was fraught with failure, conflict, and disease, mirroring his internal world.

His mother experienced traumatic events during the war that were never processed or told. Her experiences were never processed, and this created within her a traumatic lacuna that was etched deep within David. It was passed on by intergenerational transference and became his postmemory, which he reconstructed with me in therapy by transference and countertransference.

David's act of waiting for his mother until she died constituted an intergenerational transference of his mother's act of waiting for another fate. Although he had waited for his mother for four agonizing years, his mother's act of waiting was also implanted in him as if it were his own, along with the feelings, memories, and traumatic effects connected to the experience of waiting. Finding it hard to move forward, his mother waited for a lost world, and lived a lifeless existence, while he became someone who was waiting all his life for his mother, despite being reunited with her. In treatment, David's postmemory was conveyed to me by processes of identification, transference, and countertransference. He acted out the wait for his mother by waiting for two hours before our sessions; by coming to the clinic on my maternity leave; and by objecting to considering a new therapist to take my place. In my estimation, all of these were what prompted the nightmare I had.

David's ability to project onto me the difficult moments etched in his mind enabled some of the processing of his postmemory. In addition, my ability to identify with his projections, such as answering in his mother's name, and going through the areas of pain, anguish, guilt, and abandonment, calmed him and promoted movement. When some of his projected feelings could be returned to him, I was able to again be David's therapist who existed in the present.

Whenever I identified deeply with David's mother, I felt as if I were in psychotic transference. I became a mediating conduit narrating David's mother for him. These moments enabled David and me to hear and connect to experiences that had previously not been experienced.

David's ability during therapy to go beyond the boundaries of his traumatic capsule—Visiting the kibbutz he had lived on as a child, as well as other developments—exposed him to an environment that had not been reconstructed or paralyzed. Thus, it became revealed that his family was less haunted than he was and was able to contain his postmemory and traumatic experiences.

Toward the end of treatment, David's distress worsened, and he found himself truly struggling to survive. The movement between what was happening in the room and the original trauma—and processing between these two events—made it possible for the introverted mother figure to gain depth. The introverted mother figure and their relationship were at the core of his trauma, and by separating further from this figure, he weakened the trauma's clutch. Therefore, David began to remember, dream, think, and face reality.

Finally, David's ability to contact me seven months after we parted ways to request my support to begin new therapy was evidence of the intensification of the vital movement within him. David was able to stop waiting for the therapist he had left, and to consider working with a new therapist; that is, to move from being consumed by perpetual waiting, and become someone who can resume his life and move on.

Notes

1 Hirsch, 2008.
2 Hirsch, 2012.
3 Hoffman, 2005.
4 Gampel, 2005.
5 Hirsch, 2008.
6 Ibid.
7 Miller, 1983.
8 Frosh, 2019.
9 Freud, 1917.
10 Tustin, 1980, 1986.

Bibliography

Bion, Wilfred Ruprecht, 2018a. "Development of Schizophrenic Thought", in *Second Thoughts* (1967). New York, London: Routledge. (Original work published 1956).

Bion, Wilfred Ruprecht, 2018b. "A Theory of Thinking", in *Second Thoughts* (1967). New York, London: Routledge. (Original work published 1962).

Freud, Sigmund, 1917. "Trauer und Melancholie" [Mourning and Melancholia], in *Internationale Zeitschrift für Ärztliche Psychoanalyse* [*International Journal for Medical Psychoanalysis*]. Leipzig and Vienna: Hugo Heller. Vol. 4, No. 6, pp. 288–301. Retrieved August 12, 2014.

Freud, Sigmund, 1937. "Analysis Terminable and Interminable", in *International Journal of Psycho-Analysis*, Vol. 18, pp. 373–405.

Frosh, Stephen, 2019. "Postmemory", in *The American Journal of Psychoanalysis*, Vol. 79, pp. 156–173.

Gampel, Yolanda, 2005. *Ces parents qui vivent à travers moi: Les enfants des guerres* [Those Parents Who Live Through Me]. Paris: Fayard.

Hirsch, Marianne, 2008. "The Generation of Postmemory", in *Poetics Today* Vol. 29, No. 1, pp. 103–128.

Hirsch, Marianne, 2012. *The Generation of Postmemory: Writing and Visual Culture After the Holocaust.* New York: Columbia University Press.

Hoffman, Eva, 2005. *After Such Knowledge. Memory, History, and the Legacy of the Holocaust.* London: Vintage.

Miller, Alice, 1983. *The Drama of the Gifted Child.* London: Virago.

Tustin, Francis, 1980. "Autistic Objects", in *International Review of Psycho-Analysis* Vol. 7, pp. 27–40.

Tustin, Francis, 1986. *Autistic Barriers in Neurotic Patients.* London: Routledge.

Chapter 6

From Stone Tomb to Flourishing Vineyard

Moving from Silent Testimony to Living Creativity in "Creating Memory", a Bibliotherapy Initiative for Third Generation Holocaust Survivors

Bella Sagi

Introduction

For many years, Holocaust survivors and their testimonies constituted a main research focus regarding the Holocaust and its nationwide memory. Much historical research was based on testimonies, some written, but most living, recorded, and subsequently also videotaped, in order to preserve the truth of the events with all their details, facts, and intolerable contents.[1] At present, much narrative research is addressing the types of testimonies heard, and sometimes incapable of being heard, and the obliterating force of trauma.[2] Many other research fields, such as psychoanalysis, literature, cinema, and culture, deal with memory of the Holocaust through existing testimonies, and the manner in which this memory is represented in language, which seems at times unfeasible.[3]

Satner (1992) makes the claim that the testimonies were aimed at structuring history and memory via personal narratives that come together to form a national narrative, where the legitimate chosen narrative was one that encompasses Holocaust and revival, forming a distance from the real pain of the trauma.[4] This narrative served as a dissociative defense mechanism against direct contact with the trauma, but at the cost of disconnection, of replacing processing of the mourning with "fetishist" fixation on a single story, and ultimately creating a pathological process that in Freud's terms can be termed "melancholia".[5] In this way, we bequeath to the second, third, and soon fourth generations, a dissociation with regard to the Holocaust as a collective historical event, as well as its consequences of emotional disconnection and estrangement.[6]

The challenge that confronts us at present is to enable the processing of mourning that has become fixed in place, to give renewed life to a calcified narrative, and to offer an alternative to the familiar narrative that has become "sanctified". The question at present is how to transform the story of the survivors from something that happened "over there", in the words of

DOI: 10.4324/9781003274650-7

Momik, David Grossman's protagonist in "See under: Love" (1986), to the here and now, with no intergenerational transference of the trauma.

For many years, survivor testimonies were a major channel for memory of the Holocaust. Moreover, even the survivors felt that they bore the burden of disproving the world's doubts regarding the historical events, perceived as existing outside human experience.[7] Subsequently, the debate concerning allowing those who had not been "there" to speak the Holocaust, write about it, and write it, exceeded the boundaries of a literary issue, and was defined as an ethical and moral debate,[8] conceptualized as the Holocaust representation crisis.

Conspicuously, literary criticism of Holocaust literature is rarely based on aesthetic criteria alone. Rather, it addresses ethical problems that arise, and first and foremost the question of the truth. Wardi (1986)[9] emphasizes that it is not enough to check the historical aspects of events described in the literary work, and it is no less important to understand the psychological validity of the characters. Not only must the "truthfulness" of the camps' physical description be stressed, but rather the credible reflection of particular people's behavior versus the Nazi extermination machine, without flattening them into roles (survivor, victim, and Nazi). This flattening, which stems from the aggressor-victim discourse, prevents any contact with the "grey zones" of the Holocaust, forming a fixation on identification stemming from a division into "good" and "evil".[10] The "grey zone" is a concept through which Primo Levi (1919–1987), in his autobiographical book,[11] related to experiences in which aggressor and victim became morally confused. This "zone" is one of complexity, human guilt, and painful identification with a unique traumatic experience, one that is naturally hard for us to occupy. Sanyal claims that reading, understanding, and representing a one-time event such as the death camps encounters the limits of human thought ("the thinkable") and of human discourse ("the sayable").

True to its nature, guilt is passed on. Sanyal emphasizes that second-generation survivors received their guilt feelings as an integral part of memory of the Holocaust, both the survivor guilt of their parents and their own guilt as unable to save their parents from the past and to serve as a suitable replacement, a satisfactory "memorial candle", to that lost by them.[12] This process generated the primary conflict with regard to memory of the Holocaust and its cultural representation: On the one hand, the Holocaust itself became a sanctified event and, as such, no one who had not experienced it could take a legitimate part in the discourse about it. On the other, the guilt-wrecked second generation could not bear any contact with their parents' shattering pain and tried to find ways to protect their own souls from the threatening intergenerational trauma, therefore, responding by a dissociative process that included disconnecting entire parts of their soul.[13] This conflict also reproduces the main dialectic of mental trauma, from denying the terrible deeds to the desire to declare them aloud, from silence to shouting.[14]

In the world of literature and culture, a vibrant debate has been raging since the 1980s regarding the options of Holocaust representation by the second generation, and today also by the third generation. This debate always begins with questions about the legitimacy and limits of representation.[15] For example, David Grossman's book *See under: Love* (1986) created a storm, particularly surrounding Grossman's brave choice not to be satisfied only with the perspective of the child Momik, a second-generation survivor, but rather to create a fantastic course where Shlomik, the older author, enters the "White Room", the image chosen by Shlomik to describe the Holocaust itself. This course is supported by a journey in time to the camp, where Shlomik meets his grandfather, Anshel Wasserman, who within that fantastic world cannot die, and Nigel, the camp commander, the Nazi. Shlomik enters a space where a dialogue occurs between the parties, one that is only possible due to a fantastic course in which a victory is attained over death. Thus, the narrator is not just a second-generation child, but he transfers the second-generation child to the Holocaust itself through the fantastic narrative.[16] Grossman won great acclaim for this literary work, but it also attracted intense criticism that was basically ethical rather than literary, for daring to enter the sacred space of the Holocaust despite not having experienced it himself, and not from the objective and scientific stance of a historian.[17]

I suggest approaching this debate from another angle. Maintaining the sanctified space resulted in its "immobilization". Personal narratives were transformed into a national narrative, where the legitimate chosen narrative was one that encompasses Holocaust and revival, that retains a distance from contact with the real pain of the trauma.[18] This narrative served as a cultural defense mechanism, but it was a fairly initial defense mechanism based on principles of division and disconnection, and thus, one that prevented engagement in processing, in mourning. This resulted in pathological mourning, or in Freud's terms "melancholia".[19] Mourning and melancholia (depression) are similar in the emotional processes surrounding the loss, but in melancholia there is another component that does not exist in mourning – self-inflicted damage to one's sense of esteem that leads to intense impoverishment of the self. Therefore, the pathological fixation on one immobile narrative is an unconscious attempt to adhere to that part of the self that experienced the trauma, and not to truly part with it.[20]

This same fixation represents the difficulty of trauma survivors, who feel that their existence is split between the eternal presence of the traumatic memory and the concrete presence of the real world. They normally cannot and do not even wish to merge the two worlds, and therefore the traumatic memory remains immobile and timeless.[21] Moreover, the intensity of these terrifying events does not allow their integration in one's regular narrative memory. Many times, they are preserved as a "frozen picture" that cannot be assimilated in one's life story.[22]

A similar mental process may take place on the national level, thus bequeathing to members of the second, third, and soon also fourth generation, a dissociation regarding the Holocaust as a collective historical event and its consequences, emotional disconnection, and estrangement.[23] Studies show that post-trauma symptoms are also transmitted inter-generationally, to one's children's children, and recent studies demonstrate the psychological price paid by young members of the third generation in the form of post-traumatic symptoms, anxiety, and attachment difficulties.[24]

Attempts to form live contact with the "frozen" areas have generated many meaningful processes in the educational, psychoanalytic, and cultural spheres. Shoshana Felman[25] speaks about her complex endeavors to introduce her students as witnesses to literary texts on the Holocaust, and ultimately to testimonies of Holocaust survivors. Subsequently, a pedagogy of memory evolved, accentuating processes of empathy and encouraging emotional connection with survivors' testimonies and the sharing of feelings, in contrast to the remote historical perspective from which the Holocaust is taught within the existing educational system, nearly always only in history class.[26] The same empathy is perceived as very significant for novice teachers when wishing to learn more, and later to teach, about the Holocaust, as an emotion that promotes active and creative processes and that liberates from the frozen fixation of the trauma.

The "Creating Memory" Program

In this chapter, I will discuss the attempt made to deal with this issue in an Israeli program called "Creating memory",[27] operating among young third and fourth-generation survivors of the Holocaust. The research participants were partly grandchildren and great-grandchildren of Holocaust survivors and partly fit the national chronological definition of third- and fourth-generation survivors. Previous studies found no difference in the perception of the Holocaust as a national Jewish cultural and historical constitutive traumatic experience between family members of Holocaust survivors and those who have no direct connection to the Holocaust but live in Israel and belong to the Jewish people.[28]

The initiative, which began in 2019, is based upon a program that encourages and inspires a renewed encounter with personal stories that constitute part of the testimonial tapestry of national memory, internal and intrapsychic processing of this encounter, and consequent production of literary works. Hence, via a bibliotherapy methodology, they attempt to transform the "there and then" into a "here and now". In their perception, the therapeutic force of the writing and creative process advances the processing of mourning, which mandates contact with the pain but also facilitates life.

The purpose of the study accompanying the program was to examine the writing processes and products of the program participants, young Israelis of the third and fourth generation of the Holocaust, and to conclude what can be learned about the role of this and similar programs regarding the possibility of connecting contemporary young people to the memory of the Holocaust. It also dealt with what one can learn about their ability as a culture and as a nation to form a personal, living, and changing narrative. Moreover, since the program includes bibliotherapy processes, as a bibliotherapist who investigates the encounter between trauma and language it was important for me to understand the role of writing in these processes, what explicit themes are addressed by the young participants, and what world of metaphors and images reflects the more implicit parts of the psychological process in the creative encounter with the world of trauma.[29]

The research method was a narrative qualitative method that combines methodological tools from the field of qualitative research, using a model for narrative analysis of written texts that is based on a matrix of parts and whole, content and form,[30] and tools from the field of literary interpretation that include thematic analysis, metaphors and images, identification of the speaker in the text, and the direction of the plot.[31]

In the program's first year (2019), some 20 workshops were held throughout the country. About 100 young people in their early 1920s, studying at yeshiva, midrasha (religious educational institutions for young men and women), and various academic settings, participated in the workshops. At the end of the program, a collection of texts written by the participants was published, with their consent (40 texts were collected and analyzed in the study).

Findings

When analyzing the texts, three leading themes were found to reflect the options available to young people when they encounter the memory of the Holocaust. These options clearly exist on a continuum that relates to issues of identity and memory, and they are formed as opposed to an internal occupation with proximity and distance. The national symbols of Holocaust memory are confronted by estrangement and disconnection, mental resistance manifested in various forms in the texts. The opportunity for personal writing is challenged by another, closer space. At one end of the identity and memory continuum are texts that demonstrate an entanglement with the past, an adherence to memories that are not my own. On the other end of the identity continuum is the command to "remember" that maintains a connection between objects. It offers not an entanglement but rather a separateness. This position of separateness is reached thanks to the process of observation, which is capable of moving between different witnessing options, between memory modes.[32] The observation facilitates creative processes and growth.

On an unconscious level, the metaphors and images found maintain the same world of relations between disconnection and connection, between an engulfing experience of terror and catastrophe, and the possibility of rescue and growth.

"Adhering to Memories That Were Not My Own": Entanglement

The writers, young people in their 1920s, deal with their connection to the Holocaust. Some are third-generation survivors, and some have a nation-based connection, although the Holocaust is clearly part of their identity. One of the writers refers to a clear legacy he received from his mother, a second-generation survivor, the legacy of remembering, to which he relates as the 614th religious commandment: "It is a 'different commandment to remember'. A rooted 'remember'. A family 'remember'. It is not only a commandment to 'remember' that which was, but a 'remember' of – who are you? 'Remember that you are a third generation Holocaust survivor', you wrote to me" (text no. 38). The understanding that it is important to remember appears obvious; it is part of the ceremony, part of socialization in Israel, but the writer understands something new here, an invitation to recognize the memory as part of himself, as a component of his own identity. A large group of writers place themselves along this sequence, and consequently ask: To whom does this memory belong?

One of the participants describes an experience of becoming entangled in memories, and writes in the first person: "I remember when I was in the Holocaust/... The same feelings arise in me/And longing for the days that/ And pain for the opportunities that/Which in fact never were" and she concludes "Entering and adhering to memories that were not my own" (text no. 4). She describes the contact with these memories as a contact devoid of defenses; she is willing to become entangled with these memories and to let them exist within her, as part of herself and of her inner emotional world. This contact with no limits of the self and with no defenses seems dangerous, it includes something of the unhealthy entanglement that reconstructs pathological family patterns, called "enmeshment trauma".

Another writer describes a memory of reaching a room where she had to change her clothes to a uniform, perhaps the camp uniform or maybe some other uniform. This experience is described entirely in the first person in full identification with the harsh dehumanizing experience: "At night/I itched from the fabric/I yearned to return to my own bed/To my nightgown" (text no. 20), and in another text, the writer describes her nocturnal fear of falling asleep, when her mother promises her that the Holocaust will not occur again, but she finds it hard to believe: "In my pillow barbed wire/And my throat is constricted/And I remind myself/That mothers/Of other children/ Also promised them/Before they fell asleep/Before a war/And stroked with soft hands" (text no. 17).

In many texts, the identity of the self is reflected in the topic the writer is addressing, and this can be identified by recurrences of the phrase "I" in the text, as much as 6–7 times in a 10–15 line poem. The "self" sought is one that connects the writer's present with the past of the Holocaust, and with an "other" through which this past is experienced and with whom it is possible to identify: "How I was separated from my friends/How I saw my home for the last time/How my mother was taken away in a train from which she never returned" (text no. 4). Sometimes the other is revealed in a symbol embraced by the writer, for instance one writer describes a visit to the Auschwitz Museum and standing before the shoe display at the museum. She writes about how she chose to focus on one special shoe: "One red shoe that symbolizes for me one story of one woman from among a million stories of shoes; a shoe that symbolizes an entire life" (text no. 31).

The intermixing of the memories, which merges with the intermixing of identities between the generations, is enhanced by the metonymical representation of the Holocaust through bodily scars. The psychological scars are manifested in the physical scars: "And maternal love?/Remains in the scars. Look for it among grandma's wrinkles" (text no. 29). A major element in the occupation with the remembering body in the texts is the hands, the symbolism of the numbers on the arms, the helplessness expressed by the phrase "powerless" (in Hebrew *ozlat yad*, i.e., powerless hands), and the aging body reflected in the wrinkled hand: "It has been years since I saw them/The hands in the market pulling a cart/That tell a story even though their mouth remains sealed" (text n. 18) or a text entitled "Hands" that speaks about the hands from different angles: "Surrendering hands and face to the wall/Hands that no one will ever know/Hands squeezing a trigger/Hands praying in the strangling cells", and further on: "Hands on which a number was carved/Those same hands were once soft" (text no. 33).

"Trying to Remember/To Experience/To Feel a Connection": Disconnection

At the same time, there is a distance and a sense of estrangement versus the national symbols of the Holocaust, as evident in quite a few texts that deal with Holocaust Day and the sounding of the (memorial) siren. The writers describe their sense of resistance when they are required to be with the memory of the Holocaust at a particular moment, because it is necessary, because the siren has sounded, and because there is a ceremony: "Come on, think sad thoughts. /Think about Grandpa David and Grandma Henya. How he saved her. How they were heroes. /About Schindler's List, The Boy in the Striped Pajamas, The Pianist. /About where was God." (text no. 24) or "Trying to concentrate. /Trying to feel. /Trying to demonstrate to myself things that others went through. Love, Identification, connection" and further in the text "Quiet again. /Snow. White. /A blank page. A flicker of something vague. /Ending" (text no. 26). The choice of short sentences and short lines, in a structure that resembles a list, demonstrates the writer's disconnection, the difficulty of forming within himself the feelings he longs for.

Another text describes the 60 seconds of the siren's sounding as a span of time that the writer takes apart, generating the few seconds in which he allows himself to encounter something of the Holocaust within himself: "Now you think as hard as you can, strain your mind. Have to see the sights, and the terrible horrors… And then the sound of the siren ends. /And what remains?" (text no. 29).

The writers, notably with courageous honesty, demonstrate the struggle of third-generation survivors to feel something in connection with the national symbolism of Memorial Day for Holocaust and Bravery. Some feel slightly guilty at "not succeeding", some describe an experience of disconnection and even guilt: "Hey! Focus, concentrate, at least think about Grandma, she was from the second generation, that's much closer, trying trying, but its so hard, and why can't it be done on a chair?... And the emptiness takes hold and fills me with other things, and then the sound of the siren ends once more, and maybe by next time I will learn, how to stand when the siren sounds for other people" (text no. 34).

The attempt to feel connected requires effort, it's inconvenient, it doesn't "fit their plans". One conspicuous text in this context is "Holocaust now", which voices this resistance: "Why Holocaust now/When there is so much to think about… Why Holocaust now/When everything is flourishing/When we've only just gained liberty/And there's wind and sea and smiles… Why Holocaust now/And how does it concern me" (text no. 11). The agonizing experience surrounding the desire to connect and the difficulty is reflected by another writer: "Siren./Trying to remember to experience/To feel a connection/To imagine lament cry pray/Fog./Can't remember" (text no. 2). She describes trying to form a continuity from separate pictures of grandma as a child and another picture of a train, but no continuity is formed, showing that the disconnection experienced by the writers is not personal, is not only theirs, because they are "that generation" or because "they don't feel like it". Fragmentary disconnection is a feature of post-traumatic memory that is comprised of broken fragments, this writer remains bereft of a story. If there is no story it is very hard to remember anything, and it is even harder to feel.

The "no-story" is a constitutive experience of second and third-generation Holocaust survivors who grew up within an enormous silence, as described by Shlomik, David Grossman's protagonist in his book "See under: Love" (1986), the option of talking about "that" or about the "over there" that overshadowed his childhood begins with a process of believing that "about what happened there only the dry facts should be written, otherwise – I have no right to address that wound" (ibid., p. 95) but ends with a statement that a different language is needed: "…Almost poetry is needed" (ibid., p. 95). Regular language is insufficient for the psychological movement intended to melt icebergs, poetry is needed, and maybe from the poetry new possibilities of creating a story, feeling, and remembering can be born.

"A Child Peers Through the Keyhole": Connecting Through Gazes

The third theme is in a different point on the continuity from entanglement to disconnection. As I see it, this theme represents the possibility suggested by the "Creating memory" program, which is that of observation; however, observation of memories that "are not my own" or of silenced stories is not simple and risk-free observation, so most of the writers describe it as an opportunity to take a peek, a quick glance, and perhaps the glance will arouse the libido and lead to creative work. Peeking through the keyhole is also a normal fantasy of children at the oedipal stage, according to Freud, and there is something in the locked room or in the parents' "white room" that generates a deluding confusion; there is something unknown there, a secret, darkness, and excitement, but there is also anxiety, guilt, and loneliness. The imagination activated in this situation is powerful, libidinally charged, and it leads to creativity.[33]

One of the writers describes her attempt to situate herself versus the memories of the Holocaust, whether entering the "castle of mourning" or remaining outside: "Slipping between fence and alley/Standing and peeking into windows" (text no. 18). She tries to find her way in this symbolic world of Holocaust memories and finds the solution of the momentary gaze, remains outside "facing the castle gathering memories" but is stimulated sensorily and experientially: "and I heard and I smelled odors".

Freud describes melancholia as an open wound, the libido retreating from the lost object retreats into the self; this is a constant shadow of the loss, and the search for it becomes an intergenerational search. In a text entitled "Memorial candle" another participant writes: "A child peers through the keyhole/ Observes the bent back/Of another child with an aching body/Reconstructing his father's Hannukah menorah" (text no. 5). As stated, this experience of the momentary gaze at the chain of previous generations, the peeking through the keyhole, is a conspicuous theme in a large part of the texts I analyzed in the study. The writers describe a momentary peeking that reveals an unexpected picture, a surprising and sometimes even intimidating reflection.

Another participant writes:

> After the flood he took the illuminating stone that shines like an enchanted crystal ball/Hoping that a dancing herd of elephants would be reflected from it through the eye of a needle,/But instead he saw thousands of big, long-lashed eyes of frightened children.

Hence, this momentary peek can also come at a cost and the question we should address, regarding the future of Holocaust memory among the younger generations, is how to form a real connection and a readiness to approach the pain while taking care to avoid intergenerational transference of the trauma.

"After the Flood": Images and Metaphors in the Texts

The necessary caution can be demonstrated by focusing on the images and metaphors in many of the texts. In writing that deals with trauma there is often a discrepancy between the explicit and the implicit, between themes and topics that deal with contents, for instance with coping and building a life after a constitutive trauma, and images and metaphors that constitute a bridge to the unconscious, through which the trauma is expressed in a vibrant, visual, and sensory manner.[34] The intergenerational transference of the search for an emotional connection, for integration, is also intergenerational transference of the trauma, and it is reflected in the images and metaphors in many of the texts written by the program's participants. The metaphorical and image world of the writers is a world of catastrophe, as evident for instance in some of the prominent examples: images from the story of the flood, depths, "if the water had receded", and also a stone tomb, fog, the mark of Cain, a sealed mouth, hands that remember, poppies that remember the blood, all the space, a pillow of barbed wire, the cry of stones, a frothing stream of water, the big fire, the broken vessel, a locked garden, abominable earth, billows of smoke, my dove in the clefts of ashes.

Versus this inner world of images there is an external, fixated world of images that arouses estrangement, distance, and resistance. One of the participants writes of the siren sounding occasion: "Come on, think sad thoughts... About Schindler's List, The Boy in the Striped Pajamas, The Pianist" (text no. 24). She tries to feel connected to the external ritualism through empty images that have no personal meaning for her but remains unconnected to them. "Emptiness, a terrible feeling, like a bird imprisoned in the wide world" (text no. 34). One participant writes about his experience of standing while the siren sounds, while another reacts to this requirement with what might even be grasped as rage: "So I remembered the journey, and loathsome Poland/The camps, and the fences, and the pain of the generations... and what use was that?" (text no. 29).

The overused images and the empty metaphors eliminate the connecting and therapeutic value of the metaphor. Studies found that the use of metaphors and images in processing trauma allows emotional distance from the painful event but without emotional disconnection, rather on the contrary in a way that involves the listener and therefore the witness to the trauma in the grave events,[35] but for this purpose there is need for emotional immersion in the metaphor, it must be transformed from general to personal, from national to private; in Dana Amir's (2018) words, moving between the different modes of the trauma-related language.

Amir[36] suggests four types of trauma-related language modes. One of them, the metaphorical witnessing mode, represents the possibility of recovery from the trauma. This mode relates to areas within the witnessing narrative in which the internal witness function is present, namely, they encompass motion between the first and third person of the experience, between the experiencing body and the observing, reflective body. Nevertheless, Amir stresses that in the term metaphorical language she does not mean language that is full of metaphors but rather language that observes, that establishes an observation point regarding its object of reference without losing its live connection to this object, since it exists based on analogies. The same observation point expressed in the theme of looking through the keyhole allows a more reserved approach to the traumatic zone.

The traumatic lacuna is a "frozen" area, a space where the trauma exists separately forever. However, "the recovering element to which the metaphorical mode is related refers to the very ability to create movement that 'thaws' the frozen areas and releases the traumatic substances from the territory-of-returning to the territory-of-thinking".[37] Namely, the possibility that those who write at "Creating memory" encounters will form a live connection with themselves through these memories that are not their own, rehabilitates and liberates the "frozen" area. This process releases the catch in time and the experience of the Holocaust as an eternal event that exists outside time.[38]

On the individual level, it is possible to relate to this process as a bibliotherapy process, in which a deep creative encounter with a meaningful text and with the writing and creative processes facilitated by this encounter generate mental motion of a therapeutic nature.[39] But beyond the individual level, beyond the specific attempts of these young third-generation Holocaust survivors, to create something that derives from the memory of the Holocaust in their life, to deal with the role of the trauma in shaping their personal identity, the national question remains. Can those processes that were so meaningful on the individual level be translated to the national level as well?

My assumption is that yes, the forces of creation, integration, and connection to the trauma are forces that can and even should be channeled into processes similar to the "Creating memory" program, which enable an encounter with the trauma through parts of the mind dedicated to creation, growth, and development. Winnicott (1896–1971) refers to the sources of creativity and to its vitalness as something that causes a person, more than anything else, to feel that life is worth living. He says that living uncreatively is as though they are entrapped in the creativity of someone else or of a machine.[40] Namely, future coping with memory of the Holocaust on the national level requires an element of creativity, one that will release us from frozen traumatic areas, which were probably what Winnicott meant by his concept of a "machine", facilitating humaneness, meaning, and hope.

This type of solution is reflected in one of the texts. The text deals with the frightening, threatening, bewitching encounter with the "shining stone", the stone retained from the catastrophe of the flood. After peeking into the nightmarish world of the stone ("thousands of big, long-lashed eyes of/ Frightened children/Until he would yell out in his dream shattered words from the depths", text no. 1), the writer concludes with the creative solution she found: "And buried the stone deep in the ground/And heaped a mound and planted on it/A vineyard".

The poetic solution to coping with the memory of the Holocaust is one of continuity and growth. The vineyard hints, of course, at the People of Israel, as in Prophet Isaiah's vineyard parable (Isaiah 5:1–7), but the poetic solution also offers us the possibility of mental and physical contact with the earth, from whence we came, where all began, and all will end. The earth is the same earth, it contains the illuminating stone that indicates the great rescue after the great calamity ("after the flood"), and that is where the vineyard takes root. From a place of disconnection, estrangement, and silence, from a stone buried as in a tomb, the vineyard is formed, a living, growing, fruit-producing place.

Conclusion: From Silent Witnesses to Active Creators

Recent studies have found that the shift from the common attitude to teaching Jewish history, which focuses on empathetic understanding, to the pedagogic attitude of engaged witnessing, is promoting more meaningful pedagogical processes regarding Holocaust memory, particularly among the younger generation[41]; this is evident from the current study as well.

The engagement of the young participators in the "Creating memory" program is engagement through observation, through intrinsic connection, and through creativity manifested in writing. In this manner, they are transformed from **silent witnesses** of a single story that conceals the survivor generation's trauma as a stone buried in a tomb, uncommunicative and silent, into **active creators.** Through writing, as when tilling the land, the active creators touch these memories (not their own), peek at these stories (also not their own), hold them in their hand as a clod of earth, crumble and resuscitate them. In this way, oxygen enters the frozen areas, movement begins, and recovery begins. This is exactly what poet Yehuda Amichai (1924–2000) refers to, and I will end with his words that summarize the findings and the conclusions concisely and lyrically: "…doubts and loves/ Dig up the world/Like a mole, a plow. /And a whisper will be heard in the place/Where the ruined/House once stood" ("The place where we are right"/ Yehuda Amichai).

Notes

1 Cohen, 2007.
2 Laub & Felman, 1992.
3 Amir, 2012.
4 Santner, 1992.

5 Ball, 2006.
6 Lacapra, 2001.
7 Lang, 1992.
8 White, 1992.
9 Wardi, 1986.
10 Sanyal, 2002.
11 Levi, 1958.
12 Hirsch, 2012.
13 Ball, 2006.
14 Herman, 1992.
15 Friedlander, 1992.
16 Sagi, 2004.
17 Morahg, 1999.
18 Santner, 1992.
19 Ball, 2006.
20 Fraud, 1925.
21 Amir, 2012.
22 van der Kolk & van der Hart, 1995.
23 Lacapra, 1992.
24 Scharf, 2007.
25 Felman, 1991.
26 Naishtat Bornstein & Naveh, 2017.
27 Bigman & Hershkowitz, 2019.
28 Lazar, Litvak-Hirsch & Chaitin, 2008.
29 Sagi, 2021.
30 Lieblich, Tuval-Mashiach, & Zilber, 2010.
31 Elkad-Lehman & Greensfeld, 2011.
32 Amir, 2018.
33 Eaden, 2012.
34 Sagi, 2021.
35 Sagi, 2021; Lakoff & Johnson, 1980.
36 Amir, 2018.
37 Amir, 2014, p. 24.
38 Atarya, 2014.
39 Simchon, 2013.
40 Winnicott, 1989.
41 Gubkin, 2015.

Bibliography

Amichai, Yehuda, 1963. *Poems 1948–1962*. Tel-Aviv: Shoken [Hebrew].

Amir, Dana, 2012. "The inner witness", *International Journal of Psychoanalysis*, Vol. 93, pp. 879–896.

Amir, Dana, 2018. *Bearing Witness to the Witness: A Psychoanalytic Perspective on Four Modes of Traumatic Testimony*. London & New York: Routledge Publishers.

Ataria, Yochai, 2014. "Traumatic memories as black holes: A qualitative-phenomenological approach", *Qualitative Psychology*, Vol. 1, pp. 123–140.

Ball, Karyn, 2006. "Holocaust memory and the inhuman: Traumatic repetition between Freud and de Man", *Canadian Review of Comparative Literature*, September–December, Vol. 33–34, pp. 365–388.

Bigman, Efrat, & Hershkowitz, Martin, 2019. *Creating Memory 5*. Jerusalem: Self-published.
Cohen, Boaz, 2007. "World conference on holocaust studies and heroism in our time, Jerusalem, 1947': The Yishuv's initial coping with holocaust studies and its commemoration", *Cathedra*, Vol. 125, pp. 99–118 [Hebrew].
Eaden, Claudia, 2012. *The Other Side of the Image: Following Freud and Lacan*. Tel Aviv: Resling [Hebrew].
Elkad-Lehman, Ilana, & Greensfeld, Haya, 2011. "Intertextuality as an interpretative method in qualitative research", *Narrative Inquiry*, Vol. 21 (2), pp. 258–275.
Felman, Shoshana, 1991. "Education and crisis: Or the vicissitudes of teaching", *American Imago*, Vol. 48(1), pp. 13–73.
Freud, Sigmund, 1925. "Mourning and Melancholia", *The Standard Edition of the Complete Psychological Works of Sigmund Freud*, London: Hogarth Press, pp. 152–170.
Friedlander, Saul, 1992. *Probing the limits of representation*. Cambridge, MA: Harvard UP.
Grossman, David, 1986. *See under: Love*. Bnei-Brak: Kibbutz Meuhad Pub. [Hebrew].
Gubkin, Liora, 2015. "From empathetic understanding to engaged witnessing: Encountering trauma in the Holocaust classroom", *Teaching Theology & Religion*, Vol. 18 (2), pp. 103–120.
Herman, Judith, 1992. "Complex PTSD: A syndrome in survivors of prolonged and repeated trauma", *Journal of Traumatic Stress*, Vol. 5 (3), pp. 377–391.
Hirsch, Mariann, 2012. *The generation of postmemory: Writing and visual culture after the Holocaust*. New York: Columbia UP.
Lacapra, Dominick, 2001. *Writing history, writing trauma*. Baltimore, MD: The Johns Hopkins UP, pp. 181–219.
Lakoff, George, & Johnson, Mark, 1980. *Metaphors we live by*. London: Sage.
Lang, Berel, 1992. "The representation of limits", in *Probing the limits of representation*, S. Friedlander (ed.), Cambridge, MA: Harvard UP, pp. 300–317.
Laub, Dori, & Felman, Shoshana, eds., 1992. *Testimony – Crises of writing in literature, psychoanalysis and history*. London: Routledge.
Lazar, Alon, Litvak-Hirsch, Tal, & Chaitin, Julia, 2008. "Between culture and family: Jewish-Israeli young adults' relation to the Holocaust as a cultural trauma", *Traumatology*, Vol. 14 (4), pp. 93–102.
Levi, Primo, 1958. *If this is a man and the truce*. London: Abacus.
Lieblich, Amia, Tuval-Mashiach, Rivka, & Zilber, Tamar, 1998. *Narrative research*. Thousand Oaks, CA: Sage.
Morahg, Gilad, 1999. "Israel's new literature of the Holocaust: The case of David Grossman's See Under Love", *Modern Fiction Studies*, Vol. 45 (2), pp. 457–479.
Naishtat Bornstein, Lilach, & Naveh, Eyal, 2017. "From empathy to critical reflection: The use of testimonies in the training of Holocaust educators", *Journal of International Social Studies*, Vol. 8 (1), pp. 4–36.
Sagi, Bella, 2004. *The victory over death: Fantastic realism in the representation of collective historical trauma*. M.A. Dissertation, Jerusalem: The Hebrew University.
Sagi, Bella, 2021. "Only when it's written here": Personal writing as testimony in the aftermath of childhood sexual abuse", *Journal of Poetry Therapy*, Vol. 34 (3), pp. 150–163.

Santner, Eric, 1992. "History beyond the pleasure principle: Some thoughts on the representation of trauma", S. Friedlander (ed.), *Probing the limits of representation: Nazism and the final solution*. Cambridge: Harvard UP, pp. 143–154.

Sanyal, Debarati, 2002. "A Soccer match in Auschwitz: Passing culpability in Holocaust criticism", *Representations*, Vol. 79, pp. 1–27.

Scharf, Miri, 2007. "Long-term effects of trauma: Psychological functioning of the second and third generation of Holocaust survivors", *Development and Psychopathology*, Vol. 19, pp. 603–622.

Simchon, Michal, 2013. "Words from the brink of the chasm", *International Journal of Narrative Therapy and Community Work*, Vol. 3, pp. 1–7.

van der Kolk, Bessel, & van der Hart, Onno, 1995. "The intrusive past: The flexibility of memory and the engraving of trauma", C. Caruth (ed.), *Trauma: Explorations in memory*. Baltimore, MD: The Johns Hopkins University Press, pp. 158–182.

Wardi, Charlotte, 1986. *Le Genocide dans la fiction Romanesque histoire et representation*. Paris: Presses universitaires de France.

White, Hayden, 1992. "Historical emplotment and the problem of truth", S. Friedlander (ed.), *Probing the limits of representation*. Cambridge, MA: Harvard UP, pp. 37–53.

Winnicott, Donald, Woods, 1989. *Playing and reality*. London & New York: Routledge.

Chapter 7

Never Forget – The Net Will Remember

Connective Memory as a Form of Postmemory in the Age of Digital Platforms

Oshri Bar-Gil

Introduction

My grandmother, Savta Hannah, was a Holocaust survivor. Although we did not discuss it often, I heard some shocking stories about the selection process, trains, and the impossible daily life in the camps from her. The subject came up occasionally, and I even visited Poland and Eastern Europe twice. But my grandmother's death took me and my family down a new path of Holocaust memory and immersion in the story of her experiences. A handwritten note she left behind, sandwiched between shopping lists and phone numbers, concisely summarized the transit places she was sent to, and gave us a glimpse into the possibility of experiencing her tumultuous journey of survival during World War II in a new way.

Her personal and material memories resurfaced as parts of a collective memory reservoir, not only in museums and remembrance sites that provide collective memory forms, but also in online repositories that have texts and photographs which have been uploaded to the web, enabling us to see them for the first time.

The emergence of databases and search engines has connected this memory with an endless number of links between memory fragments. They once belonged to living people, but are now viewed, related, edited, and curated by the search engines, genealogy websites, and social networks that surround us.

What are the effects of Holocaust connective postmemory? It helps us to share knowledge that was previously difficult to access and understand. That's how, with the help of Big Data, we, the third generation, can discover names, faces, places, and records that our parents didn't have. It helps us uncover new dimensions of the survivor's journey. New discoveries and crossings created by new network technologies have supported our family in finding missing relatives, as well as discrepancies in other memories. These would have remained undiscovered if databases didn't have the digitization and AI capabilities they do now.

DOI: 10.4324/9781003274650-8

88 Oshri Bar-Gil

This chapter will flow through our story of the third-generation revelation of my grandma's story, which reveals how "connective" memory algorithms and databases shape our personal memory in a new way – the postmemory of the Platform Age. I will start by describing the changes in memory patterns that follow technological affordances. The second part of the chapter will use my family's story to illustrate the transition from personal to the collective, mediated by the connected society – the connective postmemory. The chapter will conclude by trying to imagine what the next phases in the transition of memory might be.

The Memory of Savta Hanna

Let me start the story with the "Thestalh" in Figure 17, as my grandmother, Hanna, used to call this type of notes. When my grandmother, Hanna, died, we found this note in one of her notebooks, written between shopping lists and phone numbers. It seems that she was trying to recall and conserve her biological memory by writing it down on paper. This list, written in Hebrew, specifies places she had been at on certain dates. This could be referred to as a transition from biological to "material" memory (Figures 17).[1]

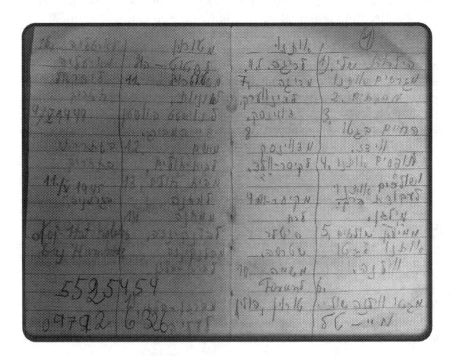

Figure 17 The list that started our journey.

Figure 18 Map location of our virtual journey based on the stations mentioned in her notes.

This note sent us on a journey that involved physical, archival, and virtual research, to better understand her war journey. The earlier generation (second generation from the Holocaust) that received the note, used archives and museums to understand her journey. At certain point in time, they even used digital archive services. However, the third generation tapped into the net and mined the digitally connected global memory. While researching other subjects, such as memory and agency in the late information age, I understood that it's not only a personal story but a story about Holocaust memory in general, or might I say – the postmemory of the Holocaust in its connective phase. The question of how we can "remember" what the earlier generations did not know is the focus of this chapter. I would like to claim that what enables us to remember this way is the shift to connective social memory in general, and in Holocaust memory in particular. But is connective memory even memory? Or is it a "postmemory", as the other chapters in this book suggest?

Let me start my answer by describing the shift toward connective memory.

The Shift to Connective Memory: From Collective to Mediated Memory

French sociologist Maurice Halbwachs coined the term "collective memory" to explain how individual memory is influenced by collective social memory.[2] Halbwachs points out that it is impossible to separate internal personal and external collective memories.[3] As a follow-up to Halbwachs, Alison Landsberg expands her theory by referring to it as "prosthetic memory".[4] Through tangible objects, consumers can sensitively and physically experience events from the past that are not part of their personal memories, or those of their reference groups. The Holocaust Museum in Washington gives even those who did not experience the Holocaust, or who are not members of the groups that have a collective memory of the persecution, a chance to experience this "prosthetic" memory. Therefore, Landsberg suggests that prosthetic memory may "transfer" memories and can cause changes in existing behaviors and perceptions. It is due to the construction and mediation through material means and memory enterprises, such as museums, that it is possible to collectively understand personal memory through the experience of "sites of memory".[5]

The work of Jose Van Dijck adopts Landsberg's view but emphasizes the importance of looking from the opposite direction as well – exploring not only how external, prosthetic memory constructs internal, personal memory, but how public and personal memory simultaneously shape each other.[6] Van Dijck claims that memories are not only contained in our minds or externally in culture, but that they are interrelated in a complex way. The social construction of memory by media or objects results in a "mediated" memory, which is not only found in our minds, external objects, or in technology, but also in the relationships between them.[7]

Throughout history, humans have used external objects to preserve memory for long periods of time. If you are an older reader who lived before the digital age, you may recall "memory boxes" in which a variety of objects were stored: documents, albums, letters, pictures, notes, diaries, audio and video tapes, and other types of memories. For memory researchers, these boxes serve as repositories of memory aids, which store knowledge and past experiences, and facilitate the creation of future memories. Van Dijk describes this phenomenon as "mediated memories".[8] Some suggest thinking of these memory aids simply as "media", which is merely an extension of our ability to perceive. Photography, television, and radio are examples of visual extensions, while turntables and other musical devices are examples of auditory extensions.[9] Memory media enable long-term access to memory by allowing recollection at a later time. The process of accessing memory through media can remediate memory, even for individuals who have no firsthand experience of it. Accordingly, it is clear that memory and perception are closely connected and mediated by the media, so an extension of perceptual abilities is an extension of memory abilities.[10]

Material objects of memory can change, disappear, or get lost. Unlike material objects, which are designed to reproduce memory faithfully, human memory works differently. It filters, shapes, forgets, and censors information.[11] Its purpose is to create an environment in which the individuals can function at their best.[12]

The use of material objects for memory expansion has been a central part of man's war on oblivion throughout history, utilizing technologies and media that have evolved over time. With the use of literature, personal diaries, static and video cameras, documentation, and constant surveillance by technology platforms, our details are preserved with great "care" and accuracy. This is our very own personal "Funes the Memorious", which never forgets any detail or memory. As Borges describes him: "... I am afraid he was not too gifted to think. To think means to forget differences, to generalize, to undress. In Funes' overcrowded world there were only details, almost immediate".[13] Borges' story reveals that the excess information resulting from disabling the filters which we use to forget, reduce, and focus. Memories can significantly impair our ability to comprehend, draw conclusions, make decisions, and conduct ourselves autonomously in society. Human memory is not a neutral or indifferent document of events, but an active response to them. The French philosopher Michel de Certeau argued that memory answers more than it records.[14] Due to the otherness of impression memory, the individual constantly seeks to revive the past and understand it to guide his current activities.

The objects that preserve collective memory convert human experience into memories and act as a means of preserving personal and interpersonal continuity. Paradoxically, the digital accuracy and lack of temporal narratives that characterize it can sometimes impair continuity and can cause a change in a person's relationship to their memories. In light of this observation about memory, it is worth asking what impact technology has on its use: how do these changes affect the memory of the Holocaust and how might these changes affect future generations?

Technologically-Mediated Memory

We can describe modern prosthetic memory, provided by the web, as continuously generating and transferring memory data from one place to another. This memory differs from the "memory of experience" that Landsberg discusses, since it drastically affects the subject's position by virtue of the experiences created at the various sites of memory. The key question in this context is how biological memory differs from the digitally extended and mediated memories. It's not only as simple to assert that the net "saves" our memories.

The processing of this multiplicity of data in an incessant algorithm changes the meaning of memory to individuals, but how does it affect society? The Scottish sociologist and memory researcher Andrew Hoskins suggested the term "connective memory" to describe it.[15]

The Affordances to Connective Memory

The technology is not new, nor is its use for a more adapted human behavior. The French philosopher Bernard Stiegler sees these tools as a type of prosthetic and human aid. According to him, unlike the familiar term "prosthesis", the purpose is not to repair or complete what needs repair, but to increase human capabilities in new ways.[16] He describes the dependence created between human beings and their prosthetic devices as a continuation of evolution in other ways – "epiphylogenesis".[17]

The term "affordances" is used by psychologist James Gibson to describe the "new possibilities for action" that environmental change opens up.[18] There are two potential sources of affordances: "supply", the technology which presents something new itself, and "demand", the social changes that increase or legitimize certain modes of use. Even if these capabilities are not realized, they can have implications and effects on users, following the very possibility and opportunity that shapes user beliefs and perceptions regarding reality, and their positions within it.[19] I will now describe the technological changes that these affordances have produced for memory.

In tandem with the proliferation of digital memory and the expansion of connections between them through social networks, the number of people participating in shaping global memory by searching, accessing, reading, and participating in its construction has increased significantly. It seems that very little content has remained stable or unchanged by the users of the various systems. Through the weakened "institutional gatekeepers" of memories, a wider approach has been created to the questions of whom, what, and how to remember in a collective memory that is constantly changing, connecting, and being added to.[20] This is another aspect of the connective memory phenomena.

Known as shared memory, it is characterized by a combination of immediacy, volume, and a wide range of digital information woven into databases that are the frequently updated information infrastructures according to which both machines and people function. As a result, the information comes from users who upload, tag, edit, and share digital information in an unprecedented fashion. Since the information is digital and stored in a centralized location, it can easily be scanned, searched, retrieved, manipulated, modified, and transferred, regarding both the information that the user produces and that which he retrieves.[21]

The affordances embodied in connective memory expand the scope of memory externalization on several levels: both in the quantity and volume of memory, and in the rate of penetration of products into the market. Those changes are in variety – the multiplicity of digital content types stored and the links between them; velocity – cloud-based digital memory has become faster, to the extent that it is sometimes faster than users' local digital memories; and trust – digital memory is storing more sensitive information.[22]

To process information in such quantities requires novel ways of analyzing and presenting it. In recent decades, there have been developments in the ability to use machine learning algorithms. In addition to their enhanced usefulness, these algorithms are unique in that their performance improves as the amount of data they receive increases. Thus, as the amount of information grows, the ability to use it will also increase.[23]

The Cloud Affordances for Memory

Advances in the world of cloud computing, improvements in algorithms (AI) which assist in image recognition, the ability to store data in large quantities (Big Data), increasing network speeds, and more powerful end devices are advancing the access to new Holocaust memory through technological affordance. The purpose of this section is to examine the possibilities arising from technological advances and social norms that have developed following the introduction of cloud computing as a new type of external-technological memory, and how it is used by users' connective memory services. The purpose of this is to explain how these mediate memory processes in new ways.

The ease, convenience, and availability of retinal retrieval culminate in phenomena highlighted by the transition to the digital age: the proliferation of the Internet and the multitude of the domains occupied by it.[24] The increasing externalization and digitization of memory means it is no longer stored in tangible objects.[25] This allows, and indeed almost compels, a quick "sharing" of memory and decisions with other actors.[26] Sharing can be done through social networks or even by using Google search engine. The psychologist Adrian Ward describes the connection between personal memory and a "cloud" memory this way: "We have become accustomed to the constant presence of the Internet in our lives, and we download, use, and lend pieces of information from our minds to the cloud of information on the Internet".[27]

The cloud contains everything and follows its user everywhere, but exists nowhere. It enables and represents the change in perception of memory as containing digital, mobile information, allowing direct access to shared memory beyond the sum of its individual components, regardless of their particular physical location. In addition to connecting to the information cloud permanently through a variety of end devices, this allows for further changes to the digitally extended memory through autonomy and independence in processing the information, utilizing the tools available in the Internet cloud, such as search engines. Since the transition of the digital memory to the cloud, it has affected a range of areas of practice and life; they become more quantitative, more measurable, and can thus be preserved by digital memory. Moreover, there is a growing complexity in how digital memories connect with each other through a variety of different sources and databases.[28]

Users are increasingly reliant on and affected by these affordances. In turn, this affects their behaviors, beliefs, and choices by algorithmically meditating their memories for them, leading to the concept of connective memory.

From Digitally Mediated Memories to Connective Memory

Hoskins borrowed Landsberg's definition of prosthetic and mediated memory to the late information and social network age. By using the concept of connective memory, he is connecting the collective to digital memories and the flood of information they produce.

Connective memory has two key features. The first is the participation of the masses – editing, copying, sharing, sending, and responding, further expanding the ecology of digital memory. Second, connective memory is dispersed and abundant, but, following various algorithmic processes, it can be retrieved for immediate analysis, filtering, and searching. As media researcher Anat Ben-David points out, the change began with digital objects stored in Internet archives, which became moving elements in the always-changing digital network.[29]

In addition, I believe that using the network's memory services maintains a collaborative relationship with personal memory and becomes, for us, a shared, prosthetic digital and multidisciplinary memory. The example I'll use is in collaborative navigation software – the "memory" of each user regarding the past section of travel translates into a "shared memory" of traffic rates and geographical locations, which enables them and others who have not yet traveled this section to choose their path forward.

I might add that the memories mediated by human agents and by material objects deplete in a natural way and leave us with replicas, particularly those represented by digital objects. This fact infers that the mediational weight of connective memory will only grow in the future, which raises the question of what our role in preserving this kind of memory will be.

What is the Role of the Human in the Connective Memory?

While "non-human actors", as Latour calls them, can affect shared memory, they are still limited in their ability to "create" memories in a way that is suitable for human consumption.[30] Their spontaneous ability is limited and therefore they need actual human users to create a reliable shared memory. Thus, people are required to create "memories" by collecting data, such as taking photos and writing emails to produce data that can be processed by algorithms. The people involved in manufacturing and preserving memory can thus be viewed as the "ghosts in the machine" that produce the shared memory pool.

The innovation of the period is reflected in the fact that once the information is created, Non-human actors can use it and materially affect the shared memory by editing, accessing, and retrieving it. In addition, memory mediation mechanisms used on digital platforms also affect the global mode of oblivion, which occurs when the memory is out of reach or unavailable through the memory retrieval services offered, for example, by Google, or if it isn't cataloged or appears in the wrong context.

A combination of Hoskins, Landsberg, and Stiegler's theories can explain only part of the way in which human memory expands. A concerning realization is that the volume of virtual activity undertaken by users in the information space increases relative to their activity in the real world. The second significant question is to be found in asking what happens when a key entity like a corporation controls these memory processes.

A surprising phenomenon of the late information age is the intensity of desire displayed by network users to participate in the creation, as opposed to the simple consumption, of information.[31] A significant portion of this phenomenon is aggressively marketed to users by technology companies, who view the creation of information by users as a direct source of profit, as a direct consequence of the increased consumption of their services, or indirectly, as a result of the sale of ancillary services or information. As algorithms are developed, more and more information can be analyzed, making it possible to draw conclusions from the vast databases within the shared memory. This benefits both the connective memory, and the ability to create and influence it.

People's motivations to participate can be explained through de Certeau's understanding of human aspiration: that is, to be understood. We can better understand the user motivation to become the spirit of the shared memory machine by recognizing their aspirations to make their mark in the construction of discourse and the shared connective pool of memory, regardless of whether the repository is managed by foreign algorithms owned by economic corporations. This is especially true if this desire can be achieved in a simple and easy manner, such as by broadcasting their position, tracking a travel route on Waze application, or by viewing the ratings of restaurants where they are presently eating. According to the findings, another reason for participating in the construction of the shared memory pool is that it allows one to be understood for oneself. Sullivan refers to this as "consensual self-validation".[32]

Memory as a Means to Power and Control

In George Orwell's dystopian novel 1984, he wrote: "He who rules the past rules the present, and he who rules the present rules the future".[33] As Orwell points out, this is true not only for society, but also for individuals. In an economic-political sense, global shared memory, managed as a black box, creates a complex loyalty problem for platform service users outsourcing memory processes. When mapping the interests of various actors, it becomes clear that despite users trusting them to faithfully preserve their memories ("controls the past") and understand decisions in both virtual and real spaces for them ("controls the present"), platforms such as Google have economic interests that motivate their actions ("controls the future"), such as gaining views on advertisements or encouraging the purchase of products that are sponsored by Google.[34] Thus, the shared memory services that Google offers its users have the potential to affect people at a personal and social level. What impact will this have on Holocaust remembrance?

The Personal Story of a Memory – Materially Mediated to Digital and Connective Memory

The different stages of the collective memory mediation sketched above correlate with the changes in the remaining memory from the Holocaust, and the stories of survivors and families search for validation of their memories. After the Holocaust, because of various political and external reasons, it took some time for its memory to be institutionalized and commemorated. Zvi Bernhardt characterized this period, beginning with the liberation of the survivors and ending in the early 1950s with the closure of the DP (Displaced persons) camps, as the period in which most of the survivors settled in their various countries of immigration. This period included the frantic search for family members and friends who survived, as well as the commemoration of Holocaust victims.

The first archived material memory about my grandmother's story that we could find was the Page of Testimony, about the death of her family members, filed in Yad Vashem (see Figure 19 below).

It is important to note that the collection of the Pages of Testimony – begun in the mid-1950s – was not seen as a way to gather information, but as a means of commemoration. As stated in Martyrs' and Heroes Remembrance (Yad Vashem) Law (1953):

> The task of Yad Vashem is to gather in the homeland, material regarding all those members of the Jewish people who laid down their lives, who fought and rebelled against the Nazi enemy and his collaborators, and to perpetuate their memory and that of the communities, organizations, and institutions which were destroyed because they were Jewish.

As can be seen in this early Pages of Testimony in Figure 19 below, this endeavor was accomplished by listening to a daily radio broadcast in Israel – "Hamador Lehipus Krovim" ("the search for relatives program").[35]

From Material to Digital Memory

The next, digital, phase was carried out later. By 2000 Yad Vashem had an extensive and ever-expanding database of names and fates, which went online in 2004.[36] Once testimonies were indexed, we discovered that Savta Hanna gave two testimonies, more than 30 years apart, as can be seen in the victims' data base (Figures 19–22).

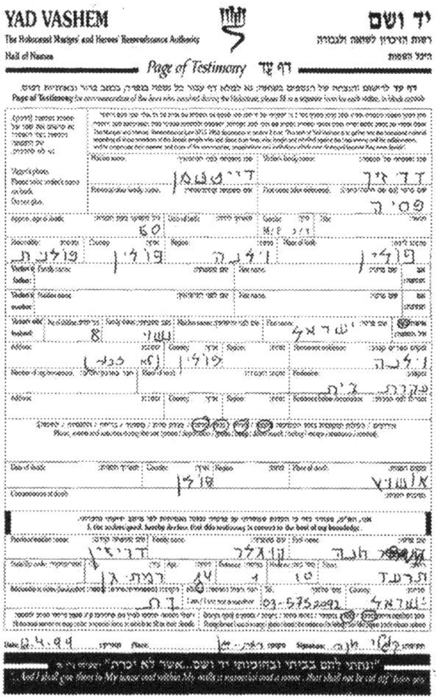

Never Forget – The Net Will Remember 97

Figure 19 The first page of testimony.

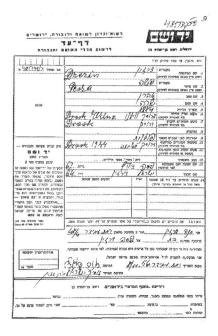

Figure 20 The second page of testimony.

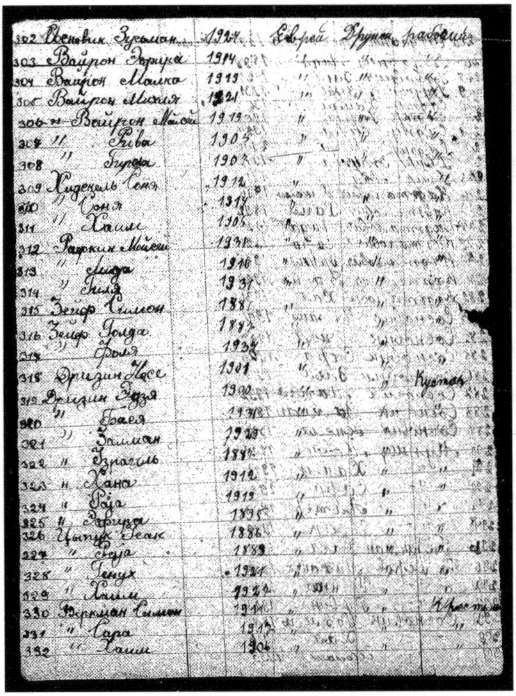

98   Oshri Bar-Gil

Figure 21 List of people from Drujsk who were murdered. Automatically linked by the Yad Vashem algorithms.

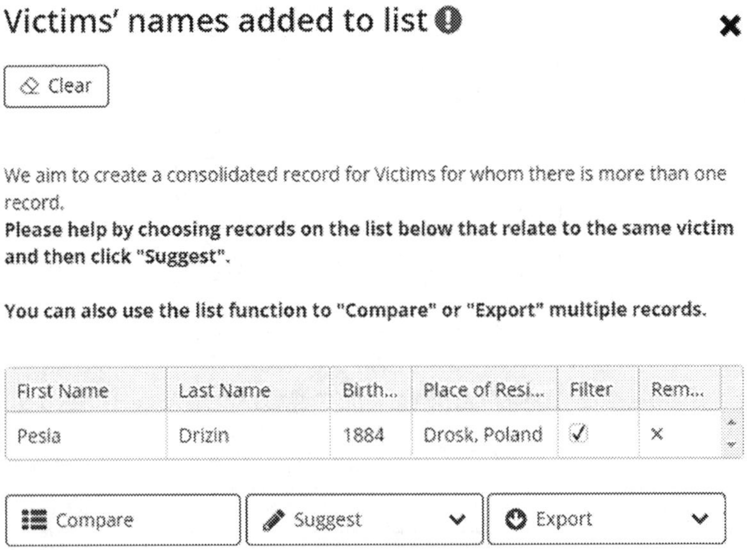

Victims' names added to list ⓘ   ✕

[⌫ Clear]

We aim to create a consolidated record for Victims for whom there is more than one record.
Please help by choosing records on the list below that relate to the same victim and then click "Suggest".

You can also use the list function to "Compare" or "Export" multiple records.

First Name	Last Name	Birth...	Place of Resi...	Filter	Rem...
Pesia	Drizin	1884	Drosk, Poland	✓	✕

[≡ Compare ⌄]   [✎ Suggest ⌄]   [⊙ Export ⌄]

Figure 22 Consolidation suggestion at the Yad Vashem archive. The human needs to connect the dots for the machine.

From Digital Memory to Big Data and Connective Memory

Sometimes digital memory takes the form of multiple databases connected together. When databases hold an extensive volume of data, curate a variety of information from different sources and types (audio, video, location based, etc.), and accumulate at an ever-growing velocity, we get "big data", as Mayer-Schonberger calls it.[37]

As digital abilities grew over time, the Yad Vashem archive improved and the archive is now connected to other databases through a series of sophisticated algorithms, which leads to the larger mediating role of algorithms in memory. In our case, it offered a list taken from a Russian archive listing people from Druysk who were murdered (see Figure 21). Previously, we hadn't known that this archive existed, and we don't speak or read Russian, but the algorithms connected us with this piece of archival memory.

This digital archive allows me to stress another important aspect of the change in memory: the difference in the perception of timelines. In digital memory, our perception of time is broken, and we see objects simultaneously in a database. It is interesting to know that the names and details are almost identical, but we as human beings had to check the database to know that they were referring to the same people. This also correlates with the role of human beings in the connective memory machine (see Figure 22).

Even while writing this chapter, the algorithms made more connections to newer documents and pieces of memories, and I received a number of alerts regarding new people that search the genealogy tree I made in one of the websites (Figure 23).

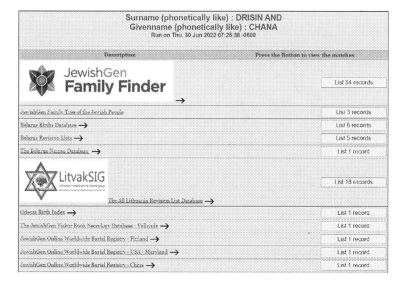

Figure 23 Screenshot of connected archives search from Jewishgen.org website. Each line is a search in records found in different databases.

Once information is digital and online, algorithms and search engines can index it and make it accessible. As accessibility rises, new memory discoveries become possible. In my story, this is represented by the "Druya memorial book". The desire to remember the Jewish communities that were destroyed during the Nazi regime spawned a vast and rich library of memorial books for communities that examine community life from as many angles as possible – the town and Kehilla life, as well as events that happened to the Kehilla members during the war.[38]

The Druya memorial book, "Sefer Ha-Kehillot", was written in 1973, and so it skipped the older generation's curiosity. We only learned this story about Savta Hanna in 2018, after it was digitalized and put online in 2017.[39] This shows the connective memory attributes that stem from free access and search engine optimization.

In considering Wikipedia as a repository of collective memory, commemoration through memory forming and sharing activities play a crucial role in the collective memory processes involved and illustrate the transition to connective memory.[40] Some of the Wikipedia pages we visited included more than 50 different editors, resulting in a variety of articles and talk pages. These articles used the editors to make a novel memory, connecting archives, historical facts, photos, and other sources in constant debate and ever-changing articles, shaping the connective memories of the Holocaust.

As these memories are formed, they have a profound emotional effect on the user. As a result of the memory connections made, they are able to validate the memory experience they gained using the connected digital consensus. The American psychoanalyst Harry Stack Sullivan, one of the founders of the relational school, calls this "consensual validation"[41]. We have experienced this validation several times when pieces of memory that were transferred to us orally or by handwritten note were confirmed through various documents and official testimonies found online. The strongest effect was when it included elements like photos and detailed descriptions. Examples including death marches during the evacuation of camps, transitioning ghettos mentioned in Wikipedia, or other descriptions that now offer the "official stamp" of belonging to the collective memory. In the past, this service was provided by the archive, but I claim that today it is undertaken by Wikipedia.

Linking and indexing are not new. Connective memory is characterized by being dispersed but algorithmically processed. At the same time, it exists through the participation of the masses editing, sharing, connecting, and responding. Who are the masses that shape the connective memory of the Holocaust? I would argue that, while the older generations job was collecting those memories, the next generation must undertake the fusion of those memories and carry out the "connective" job by linking them.

What Lays Ahead? What Will the Next Changes in Holocaust Memory Look Like?

It seems that new affordances will continue to mediate our collective and personal memory of the Holocaust in new ways. These might include the growing involvement of algorithms in memory mediation, but this involvement might have a downside, moving us further from the memory by expanding the mediation space too much.

As an example, let me illustrate this idea using the debate about coloring Holocaust images. The fierce debate began with *Auschwitz Untold: in Colour*, made by Channel 4.[42] The documentary colorized original Auschwitz photos and footage to a truly stunning effect. The carefully applied color gave the painfully familiar scenes a contemporary resonance. Some critics claim that this was impossible to deny. The director, David Shulman, argued in an interview conducted by the Jerusalem Post: "The colorization of a black-and-white archive is one aspect of making this history more accessible to a younger and wider audience. The effect is quite shocking, and the color seems to give more humanity to the people. The footage may be from over seven decades ago, but the story is certainly relevant to today's reality".[43]

Figure 24 Savta Hanna and I.

While it can be seen as a great achievement that enables better immersion in the memory from a technological perspective, it begs the question of where the line between mediation and moderation of memories and history is.

New connections can be made by advancements in technology and the digitization and connection of new databases. Large parts are mediated by the net and "remembered" by the connective memory agents that mediate (and modulate and moderate) this memory to us as human beings. Immersive technologies such as VR and image coloring might help us experience the memory better. But the quality of this memory and the ways in which it helps us to remember, are up to us.

As for me, I'll always cherish my unmediated memories with Savta Hanna and keep on searching for new ones (Figure 24). My generation and me will have these, but the next generation will have no choice.

This is only one family story, and it is one which was contributed to by many family members, but I think it is also the story of the memory of the Holocaust in the third decade of the 21st century.

Notes

1 For a full list of places and events see the Appendix. For the maps of locations mentioned see Figure 18.
2 Halbwachs, 1992, pp. 168–171.
3 Ibid. p. 3.
4 Landsberg, 2004.
5 In a personal conversation that took place in the Memory Studies Association conference at Madrid (26/6/2019), Landsberg stated that she believes that the main sites where personal memories are produced by social influence are physical sites, whereas virtual memories are not as effective in constructing the subject's attitudes and motivations. This is due to the lack of sufficient immersion in the experience, so she estimates we will see a significant improvement once this is solved digitally.
6 van Dijck, 2007.
7 Belk, 2013, p. 477.
8 van Dijck, (n 5): pp. 1–3.
9 Marshall McLuhan and Quentin Fiore, 1967.
10 van Dijck, (n 5): pp. 15–16.
11 Paul Atkinson and Richie Barker, 2020.
12 van Dijck, (n 5): p. 152.
13 Borges, 2000, p. 108.
14 de Certeau, 1984.
15 Hoskins, 2017, pp. 62–84.
16 Stiegler, 1998, pp. 152–153.
17 Ibid. p. 135.
18 Gibson, 1979.
19 Landers and Marin, 2021, pp. 235–240.
20 Selwyn, 2019.
21 Kansteiner, 2017, pp. 85–127; Hoskins, (n 14).
22 Frischmann and Selinger, 2018.

23 McAfee and Brynjolfsson, 2017.
24 Ward, 2011; Turkle, 2011, p. 28.
25 Negroponte, 1996.
26 Agger, 2015.
27 Ward, (n 23).
28 Aydin, González and Verbeek, 2018; Clowes, 2015, p. 261; Hoskins, (n 14); Kansteiner and Hoskins, (n 20); Van Dijck, Thomas Poell and Martijn de Waal, 2018.
29 Ben-David, 2021.
30 Latour, 2005.
31 Castells, 2010; Shirky, 2011.
32 Sullivan, 1950, p. 317.
33 Orwell, 1984, p.143.
34 Zuboff, 2018.
35 Bernhardt, 2020.
36 Ibid.
37 Mayer-Schönberger and Cukier, 2013.
38 See http://www.jewishgen.org/yizkor.
39 Neustadt, 1973.
40 Ferron and Massa, 2014, p. 22.
41 Sullivan, (n 31); Bromberg, 1980, p. 237.
42 *Auschwitz Untold: In Colour*, 2020.
43 Gal, 2020.

Bibliography

Agger, Ben. 2015. *Oversharing: Presentations of Self in the Internet Age*. New York: Routledge.
Atkinson, Paul, and Richie Barker. 2020. "'Hey Alexa, What Did I Forget?': Networked Devices, Internet Search and the Delegation of Human Memory." *Convergence*. https://doi.org/10.1177/1354856520925740.
Auschwitz Untold: In Colour. 2020. Accessed January 9, 2022. https://www.channel4.com/programmes/auschwitz-untold-in-colour.
Aydin, Ciano, Margoth González Woge, and Peter-Paul Verbeek. 2018. "Technological Environmentality: Conceptualizing Technology as a Mediating Milieu." *Philosophy & Technology*, April. https://doi.org/10.1007/s13347-018-0309-3.
Belk, Russell. 2013. "Extended Self in a Digital World." *Journal of Consumer Research* 40 (3): 477–500. https://doi.org/10.1086/671052.
Ben-David, Anat. 2021. "Critical Web Archive Research." Daniel Gomes, Elena Demidova, Jane Winters, and Thomas Risse (eds.), *The Past Web: Exploring Web Archives*, 181–188. Cham: Springer International Publishing. https://doi.org/10.1007/978-3-030-63291-5_14.
Bernhardt, Zvi. 2020. "Yad Vashem and Holocaust Victim's Search for Family." In *Tracing and Documenting Nazi Victims Past and Present*, 173–182. De Gruyter Oldenbourg. https://doi.org/10.1515/9783110665376-010.
Borges, Jorge Luis. 2000. *Fictions*. London, UK: Penguin.
Bromberg, P. 2014. "Sullivan as Pragmatic Visionary: Operationalist and OperRelationalist." *Contemporary Psychoanalysis* 50: 509–530.

Castells, Manuel. 2010. *End of Millennium*. 2nd ed., with New preface. Information Age, v. 3. Oxford ; Malden, MA: Blackwell Publishers.

de Certeau, Michel. 1984. *The Practice of Everyday Life*. Los Angeles, CA: University of California Press.

Clowes, Robert. 2015. "Thinking in the Cloud: The Cognitive Incorporation of Cloud-Based Technology." *Philosophy & Technology* 28 (2): 261–296. https://doi.org/10.1007/s13347-014-0153-z.

Dijck, José van. 2007. *Mediated Memories in the Digital Age*. Stanford, CA: Stanford University Press.

Ferron, Michela, and Paolo Massa. 2014. "Beyond the Encyclopedia: Collective Memories in Wikipedia." *Memory Studies* 7 (1): 22–45. https://doi.org/10.1177/1750698013490590.

Frischmann, Brett, and Evan Selinger. 2018. *Re-Engineering Humanity*. Cambridge ; New York: Cambridge University Press.

Gal, Hannah. 2020. "New Documentary Colorizes Images from Auschwitz for First Time." *The Jerusalem Post | JPost.Com*, January 27, 2020. https://www.jpost.com/diaspora/antisemitism/new-documentary-colourizes-images-from-auschwitz-for-the-first-time-615539.

Gibson, James J. 1979. *The Ecological Approach to Visual Perception*. New York: Psychology Press.

Halbwachs, Maurice. (1925) 1992. *On Collective Memory*. Translated by Lewis A. Coser. Chicago, IL: The University of Chicago Press.

Hoskins, Andrew. 2017. "Memory of the Multitude: The End of Collective Memory." Andrew Hoskins (ed.), *Digital Memory Studies: Media Pasts in Transition*. London: Routledge.

Kansteiner, Wulf. 2017. "The Holocaust in the 21st Century : Digital Anxiety, Transnational Cosmopolitanism, and Never Again Genocide without Memory." Andrew Hoskins (ed.), *Digital Memory Studies: Media Pasts in Transition*, 110–140. Routledge. https://doi.org/10.4324/9781315637235-5.

Landers, Richard N., and Sebastian Marin. 2021. "Theory and Technology in Organizational Psychology: A Review of Technology Integration Paradigms and Their Effects on the Validity of Theory." *Annual Review of Organizational Psychology and Organizational Behavior* 8 (1): 235–258. https://doi.org/10.1146/annurev-orgpsych-012420-060843.

Landsberg, Alison. 2004. *Prosthetic Memory: The Transformation of American Remembrance in the Age of Mass Culture*. New York: Columbia University Press.

Latour, Bruno. 2005. *Reassembling the Social: An Introduction to Actor-Network-Theory*. Clarendon Lectures in Management Studies. Oxford ; New York: Oxford University Press.

Mayer-Schönberger, Viktor, and Kenneth Cukier. 2013. *Big Data: A Revolution That Will Transform How We Live, Work, and Think*. Boston, NY: Houghton Mifflin Harcourt.

McAfee, Andrew, and Erik Brynjolfsson. 2017. *Machine, Platform, Crowd: Harnessing Our Digital Future*. New York: W. W. Norton & Company.

McLuhan, Marshall, and Quentin Fiore. 1967. *The Medium Is the Massage*. New York: Random House.

Negroponte, Nicholas. 1996. *Being Digital*. New York: Vintage Books.

Neustadt, Mordechai. 1973. *Sefer Druyah u-ḳehilot Miyor, Droisḳ, ye-Leʼonpol. Yotsʼe Druyah yeha-sevivah be-Yiśrael.* http://archive.org/details/nybc313750.
Orwell, George. 1949. *1984.* London: Secker & Warburg.
Selwyn, Neil. 2019. *What Is Digital Sociology?* Cambridge ; Medford, MA: Polity Press.
Shirky, Clay. 2011. *Cognitive Surplus: How Technology Makes Consumers into Collaborators.* Reprint edition. New York: Penguin Books.
Stiegler, Bernard. 1998. *Technics and Time: The Fault of Epimetheus.* Stanford, CA: Stanford University Press.
Sullivan, Harry Stack. 1950. "The Illusion of Personal Individuality." *Psychiatry: Journal for the Study of Interpersonal Processes* 13: 317–332.
Turkle, Sherry. 2011. "The Tethered Self: Technology Reinvents Intimacy and Solitude." *Continuing Higher Education Review* 75: 28–31.
Van Dijck, José, Thomas Poell, and Martijn de Waal. 2018. *The Platform Society: Public Values in a Connective World.* New York: Oxford University Press.
Ward, Adrian F. 2013. "One with the Cloud: Why People Mistake the Internet's Knowledge for Their Own," https://dash.harvard.edu/handle/1/11004901.
Zuboff, Shoshana. 2018. *The Age of Surveillance Capitalism: The Fight for a Human Future at the New Frontier of Power.* New York: Public Affairs.

Appendix

List of Places and Events Mentioned and Their Connective Memory Fingerprint

Number	Place/event	Main Connective memory
1	Druysk	Google maps: tinyurl.com/5n8ph44w The Druya archive: http://www.eilatgordinlevitan.com/druya/druya.html Book of Druya (Online): https://www.yiddishbookcenter.org/collections/yizkor-books/yzk-nybc313750/neustadt-mordechai-sefer-druyah-u-kehilot-miyor-droisk-ve-le-onpol
2	Vidzy Ghetto	Vidzy ghetto google photos: https://tinyurl.com/2p86yuvh Wikipedia: https://tinyurl.com/ydcpdu2j
3	Miligen work camp (close to Kaunas)	
4	Vilnus ghetto, Rudninky 10 st. next to The Epstein gymnasium	The Gymansium certificates: https://www.jmuseum.lt/en/news/i/634/ Google streetview: https://tinyurl.com/3xrp83n5 Yad Vashem: https://www.yadvashem.org/yv/en/exhibitions/vilna/during/ghetto_establishment.asp Wikipedia: https://en.wikipedia.org/wiki/Vilna_Ghetto
5	Riga	Holocaust Encyclopedia: https://encyclopedia.ushmm.org/content/en/article/riga
6	Dvinsk ghetto	Wikipedia: https://en.wikipedia.org/wiki/Daugavpils_Ghetto
7	Kaiserwald concentration camp – Working at the air plane factory	Wikipedia: https://en.wikipedia.org/wiki/Kaiserwald_concentration_camp VEF factory: https://en.wikipedia.org/wiki/VEF

8	Excavation to Turowo	
9	Stuthof Camp	Wikipedia, arolsen archives, Holocaust encyclopedia
10	To Neuengamme camp by boats	Wikipedia: https://en.wikipedia.org/wiki/Neuengamme_concentration_camp Holocaust encyclopedia: https://encyclopedia.ushmm.org/content/en/article/neuengamme JewishGen: https://www.jewishgen.org/forgottencamps/camps/neuengammeeng.html
11	Blankenese Camp (other side of Hamburg)	wikipedia: https://en.wikipedia.org/wiki/Neuengamme_concentration_camp#Evacuations,_death_marches,_and_the_bombings_of_Cap_Arcona
12	Evacuation to Bergen Belsen. Liberation	Wikipedia: https://en.wikipedia.org/wiki/Bergen-Belsen_concentration_camp Holocaust encyclopedia: https://encyclopedia.ushmm.org/content/en/article/bergen-belsen
13	Displacement From Germany to Italy – Castel Gondolfo	JCPA: https://jcpa.org/article/jewish-displaced-persons-in-postwar-italy-1945-1951/ Wikipedia: https://en.wikipedia.org/wiki/Rescue_of_Jews_by_Catholics_during_the_Holocaust
14	Immigration From Bari to Israel with ship "Campidoglio"	Ship archive: https://www.wrecksite.eu/wreck.aspx?148381

Part II

Postmemorial work in Literature and Art

Chapter 8

Letting the Monster In? Illustrating the Holocaust in Contemporary Israeli Children's Picture Books

Erga Heller

Introduction, or Children's Picture Books as Collective Postmemory Representations

This chapter focuses on contemporary visual representations of the Holocaust in Israeli children's books, and especially on the question of the presence or absence of visual illustrations of horrifying aspects, as a representation of Shoah postmemory. It examines how horror and monstrosity are handled in the illustrations and compares between the norms of written and visual narrative.

In young adult graphic novels about the Holocaust, the graphic interpretation is used to build a visual knowledge of the Holocaust, to transmit the violent history by its visualization, and to encourage the readers to commit themselves to memory.[1] But the readers of picture books and readers of young adult graphic novels are two very different categories. Even if the illustrations employ a similar artistic language, the audience's ability to interpret it and relate it to history differs enormously, as does the appropriate degree of exposure to violent contexts.

Representing trauma in Holocaust literature for very young readers is long known as a controversial issue.[2] Since the 1990s, Holocaust representation in children's literature has been perceived as an important educational issue that must be approached without causing trauma in young readers.[3] New literary works for children about War, the Holocaust, or terror attacks help construct empathy toward victims and minorities, and promote moral discussions.[4]

Within Israeli culture, however, the narrative of the Holocaust, verbal and visual, is also a major part of the discourse of national identity. In Israel, fiction is a seminal way of discussing the Holocaust with children. As a result, more than 30 new Hebrew children's books about the Holocaust or the Second World War have been published over the last 20 years (2000–2020), and about the same number of books for children about these subjects, including graphic novels, have been translated into Hebrew. These are in addition to the hundreds of children's books about the Shoah available to young Israeli readers, published locally or translated into Hebrew.

DOI: 10.4324/9781003274650-10

Hebrew Shoah books for young readers follow the governing norm in children's literature which requires a "happy ending" closure. The happy ending is not compatible with the Israeli collective memory of the Second World War and the Holocaust, and prohibits plots containing trauma, extreme monstrosity, orphaning, and the loss of faith.[5]

The Shift of Contemporary Israeli Picture Books about the Shoah

Most of the original fictional works on the Shoah written for children and young adult in Hebrew during the two last decades are picture books for young readers (three- to eight-year-olds). These works were written by survivors or professional authors, or by younger authors who chronologically belong to the age group of the second or third generation, even if they are not direct descendants of Shoah survivors. Jewish-Israeli identity is heavily based on Israel's being a safe haven for Jews from persecutions, or as the Israeli Independence Proclamation Scroll words it, "to be masters of their own fate".

Under these circumstances, education becomes an important vehicle in molding a society that sees itself as a surviving collective. Teaching about the Holocaust is mandated by the Israeli Ministry of Education from kindergarten to high school, and the bulk of new children's books on the Shoah swiftly finds its way to the Hebrew language and literature curriculum, and to school libraries.

Most children's Shoah literature in Hebrew in the past two decades deals with biographical narratives told from new perspectives. Some have a child-like narrator who is unaware of the full consequences of the atrocity they describe, others are narrated by inanimate objects such as toys and dolls.[6] The texts often present their plots as fictional, hiding their biographical or historical nature from the young readers. This informative meta-text often appears only on the back cover, or in an appendix, and in some cases, is only mentioned in book reviews or interviews. These metatextual forms are obviously inaccessible to three- to eight-year-old readers, hence the "authentic" readers are unaware that they are reading historical narratives.[7]

Contemporary Israeli children's books about the Shoah address a new generation of readers who were born three generations or more after the Jewish victims of the Third Reich. Despite the time that has passed, there is an audience for new books. Nowadays, few of the books are actually written by the survivors, yet they are published into a literary atmosphere in which writing for children about the Holocaust is acceptable, and there is a choice of genres, including fiction, which in many ways is the opposite of survivor testimonials and other autobiographical forms such as diaries. The illustrations in these books reflect a modified historical visualization in contrast to less fictive forms.

An important stage in the literary freedom of telling a war story was marked by the work of the Israeli children's author Uri Orlev (b. 1931, Poland), himself a Holocaust survivor. Orlev established a vivid fictional way of writing a fantasy about fears and war, although in *The Thing in the Dark* (1976) he referred to a Middle Eastern war (1973) and not to the Second World War.

Only in the 21st century has Orlev's approach been developed by the new generation of authors, such as Hadas Leibovich (b. 1971), into a fantasy, instead of memories or autobiographical testimony. Leibovich is not a second/third generation author. Yet her children's picture book represents a short episode of a blind Jewish man who was a distant relative of hers: her grandmother's uncle, who did not survive the Holocaust. In Leibovich's *Brooms Dancing in Winter* (*Metatim Rokdim BaHoref*, 2020), Alice, a young Jewish girl, accompanies her blind father to his workplace in a brush factory under a borrowed identity, when Nazis appear without warning to seize the Jews in the factory. The manner in which little Alice describes the raid, hiding for hours in a tiny broom cabinet, and watching the brooms' joyful dances, transfers her fears, as well as those of the young readers, to the realm of fantasy. Leibovich's solution of replacing the traumatic experience with an uncanny one as a fantastic daydream, and its surrealist visual interpretation by the illustrator Noa Paran, enable the young audience to relate to Alice's story without being threatened by it.

Writing for children about the Holocaust often crosses generic boundaries, weaving biography, autobiography, fiction, and fantasy.[8] Contemporary Hebrew children's literature and its illustrations are no exception, although this weaving came relatively late in comparison to children's Holocaust literature in English. Children's Holocaust literature in Israel in the new millennium exemplifies this trend well. Leibovich's *Brooms Dancing in Winter* is the latest example and the most distinct so far. Prior to Leibovich's picture book, there were books like *A Hug of Love* (*Hibuk shel Ahava*) by Gila Mazliah-Liberman in 2015, or *Bear and Fred* (*Hadubi shel Fred*) by Iris Argaman (b. 1967) in 2016. Both authors were interested in the theme of childhood throughout the Holocaust, but their motivation was different. Mazliah-Liberman is an educational psychologist who was in charge of the subject of Holocaust in preschool education, while Argaman is a professional writer.

A Hug of Love is told by an old toy horse, a Shoah survivor, to the other toys in the kindergarten; *Bear and Fred* is narrated from the point of view of Fred's teddy bear. Using toys as narrators, audience, and frame of reference allows the creation of a fantastic plot, which reduces the level of horror for the young reader/auditor.[9]

Visualizing History, Portraying Postmemory

Most of the studies on children's Holocaust literature focus on the narrative and historical content while neglecting the field of visual narrative.[10] Yet, in view of the fact that young readers rely to a great degree on the non-verbal in order to understand the verbal narrative,[11] the paucity of research on the topic is surprising. More specifically, in trauma and atrocity literature, the illustrations serve as mediators of violent historical memories, and their presence is critical to the holistic experience of the reading child, further emphasizing the lacuna in the research literature.

One of the central visual symbols of Holocaust illustrations is the "Yellow Star". Although it is not a unique characteristic of Hebrew books, it has become something of a recurring visual attribute there by literally coloring the pages of many picture books in yellow, using the color to symbolize the Holocaust.

The first Hebrew picture book about the Shoah that was printed in Israel on bright yellow pages was Batsheva Dagan's *Chika the Dog in the Ghetto* (*Chika HaKalba BaGehtto*) in 1992.[12] Dagan (b. 1925) is a Polish-born Israeli author and children's psychologist, a Holocaust survivor. Her picture book, *Chika the Dog in the Ghetto,* tells the story of five-year-old Mikasch and his beloved dog Chika. Mikasch's parents explain to him that they must give their dog to a family friend outside the ghetto who will care for him throughout the War's duration because the Nazis have decreed that Jews are not allowed to have pets. Mikasch worries about Chika during the weeks in hiding, and they are happily reunited when the War ends.

In the 21st century, the book was selected to be a part of the Hebrew language and literature curriculum for elementary schools, and this may explain why the bright yellow background was chosen to its new edition. In Nazi-occupied lands, Jews were required to wear a yellow Star of David with the word *Jude*, but the actual star is illustrated in the yellow-paged book only once, when Mikasch's father sneaks out of the ghetto to deliver Chika into the family friend's custody. Of course, sneaking out of the ghetto with a Yellow Star is not realistic, but the illustrator, Avi Katz, uses it to emphasize his Jewishness in a hostile environment. Yet its rays, so to speak, are spread over every page of the book, so there is no need for the actual article of clothing. Thus, the connotation of yellow is constructed as the color of Jewish persecution in the Holocaust, and the postmemory of young readers is re-written visually. Yellow Stars denote Jews, adults as well as children, but the illustrations in Hebrew children's books about the Shoah contain a double meaning. Yellow is used also to connote light, as a metaphor for Sabbath and the Jewish holidays, or for hope. In *Chika the Dog in the Ghetto* yellow is used to mark the Jewish home and Jewish holidays: light yellow and beige tints surround the Hanukkah lamp at Mikasch's home in the opening illustrated scene. Candles are illustrated in the opening pages of other picture books on the Shoah as well, revealing the characters' Jewish identity from a secure domestic perspective, as shown in Yael Albert's illustrations to Tamar Meir's *Francesco Tirelli's Ice Cream Shop* that was published in 2017. Based on true events, the story is told from the point of view of little Peter from Budapest. He, his family, and other Jews hide at the back of the Tirelli's ice cream shop throughout the War. In *Francesco Tirelli's Ice*

Cream Shop (*Hanut HaGlida shel Francesco Tirelli*) yellow is used widely, to describe the joyful side of life before, during, and after the Holocaust: ice cream scoops, chandeliers, and also yellow stars.

The most distinctive use of yellow following Katz's illustrations for *Chika the Dog in the Ghetto* is found in later picture books such as *Kaleidoscope*, written by Chava Nissimov (b. 1939) and published in 2015, and *Bear and Fred*, written by Iris Argaman and published in 2016. Like *Chika the Dog in the Ghetto*, *Kaleidoscope* is also dominated by bright yellow, since hope and light, symbolized by light yellow – are the narrative's main themes. Like Orlev and Dagan, Nissimov is also a Polish-born Israeli author and a Holocaust survivor.

Kaleidoscope tells the story of five-year-old Eva, who was placed with a Polish family during the War. Although *Kaleidoscope* is based on Nissimov's autobiography, some facts were changed to fit children's literature norms, like the happy reunion with her mother that ends both the verbal and the visual narratives (the author's mother survived the Holocaust, but she and her daughter – the author – did not live together after the War). Kineret Gilder's illustrations for *Kaleidoscope* are based on two significant colors: black and yellow. In Gilder's visual narrative, yellow is used to identify Jews by the Yellow Star, but yellowish stars illuminate the heroine's daydreams and memories as well as her real survival path through the War, for her hair is colored blond (the same tint of bright yellow is used throughout the book). Yellow is used to amplify non-visual qualities as well, such as the smell and taste of an orange that Eva eats, as well as the security and freedom that Eva feels upon arrival in Palestine (pre-State Israel), where the warm yellow sands contrast with her voyage on the stormy seas.

The emotional possibilities of the same color – yellow – nurture new visual awareness in the young readers, encouraging them toward an ad-hoc understanding of the strange new situation. Hence, they may feel insecure or as if they were being chased like the child protagonist.

The visual identification that Gilder suggests in the illustrations to *Kaleidoscope* by her dichotomous uses of yellow, blocks much of the potential monstrosity from reaching young readers, thus creating a more secure postmemory. The yellow sands at the end of the story in Israel take up a much larger area than the little Yellow Stars. Thus, Gilder's pictorial interpretation adopts a collective Israeli visual conception of the Shoah of what is suited to young readers. At the same time, it strengthens the national credo of regeneration and growth, which appears verbally in the Israeli Proclamation of Independence and in the Bible. The final illustration of the yellow sand echoes God's promise to Abraham: "I will multiply thy seed as the stars of the heaven, and as the sand which is upon the sea shore" (Genesis 22 17, KJV). The biblical allusion connects the personal story to national history, setting up a postmemory that melds the personal into the collective.

Bear and Fred (or *HaDubi shel Fred*) by Iris Argaman is another biographical fiction in the form of a children's picture book. In 2016, Iris Argaman adapted the story of a Shoah survivor, Fred Lessing, who was forced to leave his parental home in Delft with only his teddy bear for comfort. Argaman uses the same literary device as Gila Mazliah-Liberman used earlier in her 2015 picture book *A Hug of Love* (or *Hibuk shel Ahava*), having the toy (Bear/toy horse) narrate the story. Bear's understanding of the War is as restricted as that of a child, and his fears are limited to a childlike world: how long should they hide, what will happen if they part, will they ever reunite with Fred's family, and so forth. In the inevitable happy end, Fred and Bear reunite with Fred's parents, and Bear and Fred stay together forever. (In the real world, as Argaman writes in the afterword, Fred gave Bear to Yad Vashem, the Shoah Memorial Museum.)

Bear and Fred also uses yellow as a thematic device. Although the book is based on a true story, and the actual beige-tinted Bear may be seen at a Yad Vashem exhibition and remembered by visitors, its illustrator, Avi Ofer, works deliberately against this artistic restriction, and does so in a way that responds to the collective visual memory of the Shoah, which is marked by yellow. Ofer inverts Bear's and Fred's color scheme: beige-tinted Bear becomes golden-yellowish, and Fred and his world during the Holocaust are depicted in Bear's original greyish-beige tone. Bear's color corresponds with the Yellow Star as an attribute of Fred's Jewish identity, and it acts as a symbol of hope for the end of the War. Ofer's shade of yellow is more muted than that of Katz and Gilder, perhaps because of the inevitable comparison with the actual historical artifact (i.e., the toy); but he uses the color in the same way that Katz and Gilder use bright yellow in their books. The strategic use of yellow in these children's books channels postmemory from a symbol of persecution in a dark past to a lighted, hopeful present, one that is faithful to the norms of children's literature yet is not untrue to history. Although the illustrated yellowish Bear is different from the authentic toy, its visualization enables the readers to identify the marked color – yellow – with the antisemitic persecution and genocide. By using a closed yellowish tint – maybe even unconsciously – the illustrators re-iconize the Yellow Star and unify its cultural conception by the new generation of young readers. In that way, they interrupt with the automatic procession of contemporary cultural visual interpretations of yellow.

Re-Taking the Picture of War and the Paradox Tuning Postmemory

Illustrating picture books about the Holocaust enables the illustrators to modify or to re-touch common pictures of the War, whether they were truly captured by cameras or established as such in the collective memory. The foremost motivation to change a historical document is to keep the norms of children's literature, which are to avoid extreme visual content, such as massacres, bodies of dead children, or deep despair. These books may be said to mediate the postmemory of the Shoah in these young readers. But here, a paradox re-emerges within the illustrations: one of the purposes of illustration in children's books is to demonstrate what cannot be said in words, and the pictures in picture books cannot be silenced. The illustrations tell a story in a clear voice, but as we shall see, it is not always a clear voice of a war or of the War.

The literary norms, by their nature, contradict the essence of visual documentation and memory of the Holocaust, collective as well as private. If the illustrations were to maintain historical accuracy, they would be inappropriate for children, their intended audience; yet if the illustrations follow the norms of children's literature they may miss their original purpose. This paradox is usually solved by following the generic expectations, shielding children from such extreme content, as of course it should be. This generic self-restriction is also part of the construction of postmemory. And even though the contemporary plots illuminate a unique experience, they explore it with a childish knowledge that enables them to avoid a negative and threatening existence, while the visual narrative is not always linked to that childish knowledge. On the one hand, the illustrator is restricted by literary norms and by cultural taboos, but on the other hand, the illustrators are free to suggest a historic bridged view.[13] They can depict authentic views, reconstruct historic pictures. But since they are a part of the children's literature system, they cannot depict extreme violence in their illustrations for children. They have to protect the readers as a part of that literary unwritten pact. So how can they show the past without the Past? And do all illustrators act alike?

First, we should note that this situation does not necessarily affect the quality of the illustrations, rather it forces the illustrators to suggest alternate solutions, as we have seen; nor does it interfere with the verbal contents, since the authors are obligated to the same norms as the illustrators and thus do not detail the monstrosity of the Holocaust in picture books for young readers.

One common device that illustrators use, as demonstrated above, is the distinctive yellow palate that connects central Holocaust attributes such as the Yellow Star to other connotations linked to the State of Israel. And although most contemporary Israeli Holocaust books do indeed refer to, or are based on, a yellowish scale, all depict dark colors or black that anamorphically illustrate the atrocity of war or a specific Nazi threat in a particular scene, because of the mandatory characteristics of the children's literature norms. Another common strategy is the use of reconstructed photographs. For example, the autobiographical picture book, *Why Joshua's Name Is Joshua* (or *Lama leNaphatli Korim Naphtali,* 2009), written by Alona Frankel (b. 1937), a Polish-born prolific Israeli children's author and illustrator and Holocaust survivor, is based on a photo album. *Why Joshua's*

Name Is Joshua is part of an educational series for toddlers, but visually and content-wise it differs from the other cheerful and colorful books in the series, in which very young readers became familiar with the joyful toddler Joshua and his loving mother. But *Why Joshua* contains darkened illustrations that are not common in toddlers' books, nor in Frankel's other books. The illustrations in *Why Joshua* reveal another sort of book within the book – a photo album – that contains reproductions of old black-and-white photographs alongside faked, illustrated ones. Joshua's mother tells him about a different time when the world was unfair and unequal. Through the family photo album, Joshua learns about the history of his family and discovers that he is named after his mother's grandfather. Frankel offers the very young readers a softened version of the Shoah in a way that is adapted to their age and understanding. The photos in the album include only smiling faces, and the dangerous world is only implied by the dark background with sharp lines behind the photo album. However, because Frankel's visual interpretation is based on colors, lines, and geometric forms more than on authentic photograph from the War, it exposes an ambivalence at the heart of the illustrations: the photo album serves as a device to see the past, yet the "inside story" can be both real, because it is based on authentic photographs, and unreal, because it is based on an animated book within an animated book. This double vision exemplifies the semiotic paradox or the psychological refusal and denial mechanism inherent in the creation not only of children's Holocaust literature, but in the very idea of postmemory.

Ariela Kalvaria Friedman's *There was a Castle* (*Haya Sham Armon*), published in 2011, was written by a second-generation author, is addressed to juvenile readers, and tells the author's mother's story. It forms another sort of a photo album. The book's illustrator, Maria Givner, adapted Kalvaria Friedman's family album into a visually ambivalent narrative. Using a collage technique, Givner combines manipulated (i.e. colored) photographs based on Kalvaria Friedan's black-and-white photographs of the period to present ordinary Jewish life in Poland, and added rough drawings in black and white to depict the War and the heroine's encounters with the Nazis. She embedded the manipulated photos in vintage frames, as in an authentic old album. By creating illustrations that masquerade as authentic historical documents, Givner visually narrates a colorful and optimistic version of the Shoah. And as in the illustrations of Katz, Gilder, and Ofer, she adds yellow to her re-touched photos. Like them, she uses the same tint of yellow for the Yellow Star, for rural Poland's sunrays, and for an Israeli sunset. Givner's visual interpretation emphasizes the limits of the Shoah illustration for children – the solid barriers against atrocity, the optimistic desire for a happy ending that require a "manipulated" authenticity.

As with other strategies and devices in recent Holocaust literature for young readers in Israel, the production of fake-authentic pictures of the Holocaust may be considered part of a larger trend to "re-color" the protagonists' worlds in the Shoah. This new perception undoubtedly affects the contemporary visualization of postmemory, enabling new generations of young readers to find some hope in the darkness of collective visual memory. Yet the emotional effect that is suggested by the dark and light color schemes may cause distress and create a sense of instability in the readers; thus, an unliteral and highly sensitive reading is achieved without any visual and verbal mentions of detailed atrocities. In addition, by using those special color schemes the illustrators drive the readers into a cultural and personal consciousness that is receptive to the authentic visual world that was created by the Nazis and threatened former Jewish generations.

Conclusions and Summary

As a result of the new attitudes of the Israeli education system toward Holocaust education, a large number of Hebrew fictional picture books about the Holocaust have been published during the last two decades, in the hope that they will be included in the curricular and ex-curricular texts lists, as indeed happens. Yet, alongside the aesthetic, historical, and moral motives for publishing the new Shoah stories for young readers, one cannot deny another motivation: a commercial one. The new texts' commercial value does not impair their literary value but impacts their ending and visual design. Hence, it plays a role in the postmemory scene.

Most of the picture books produced in Israel at the beginning of the 21st century are written by professional writers who are Holocaust survivors or members of the Second Generation of Holocaust descendants. The survivor generation includes Orlev, Dagan, Nissimov, and Frankel; the extended family circle includes authors as Leibovich, Meir, and Tal-Kopelman. They use the personal narrative as the basis for the plot of the picture book while abbreviating the original ending or changing some of the authentic biographical events to match the norms of plot ending to the norms of children's literature. The stories focus on a child of a similar age to the readers, and his or her experiences and wellbeing are adapted and re-told in a manner that will not harm a young child's perception, understanding, and above all – wellbeing.

Another group of books were written by professional authors who have no familial connection to the Holocaust, but the story that they narrate is a biographical story of a real survivor (for example: Argaman). These stories, too, are adapted for the young readers, according to the norms of children's literature. The literary result of these two different types of authors is similar, and that suggests the appearance of a new pattern of postmemorial Holocaust writing for children in 21st-century Israel.

As for the illustrators, since all of them are professional illustrators, the common characteristics that emerge from their work, especially the color choices, are significant for the visual-cultural implications of the texts.

The combination of a marked, yellow-based scale and manipulated or re-touched photographs in the children's books examined are characteristic of contemporary Israeli Shoah children's literature. It has developed as a literary response to the collective visual memory of the Shoah, although it is reminiscent of dangerous over-nationalistic tendencies. Hebrew children's literature transmits the Israeli collective memory of the Shoah without detailing specific historical artifacts or sights, unless they are an integral part of the narrative and not damaging to the readers, as in the case of the Yellow Stars, Judaic artifacts, and children's toys.

Distressing scenes and historical atrocities are elided or at most hinted at in 21st-century Hebrew children's literature. Visually, collective memory is shifted to include positive elements, and the voice of the personal narrative is strengthened. The articulation of postmemory is constrained on the one hand by the certainty that the young readers will be exposed to harsher views of the Holocaust later in life, as part of the educational system's sustaining of collective memory, and on the other, by the limitations of the generic norms of children's literature. No detailed Nazi monstrosity is depicted, no monsters are allowed in the visual construction of the postmemory of the Holocaust in Hebrew, which begins as a mild

Acknowledgments

The author wishes to thank authors Iris Argaman and Tamar Meir, and editors Dorit Zeltner and Yotam Shwimmer for their answers and assistance. Thanks to Hakibbutz Hameuchad – Sifriat Poalim Publishing House, Keter Publishing House, Tal-May Publishing House, and Zeltner Publishing House.

Notes

1 Aarons, 2020, p. 10.
2 Shavit, 1988; 2005; Bosmajian, 2002; Kertzer, 2002; Kokkola, 2003; Sacerdoti, 2016.
3 Kidd, 2005, p. 121; Rudin, 2021, p. 158.
4 Baer, 2000; Majaro, 2014; Giambastiani, 2020; Ulanowicz, 2013, p. 31; Wójcik-Dudek, 2020, p. 24.
5 Sarig, 2019.
6 Van Tuyl, 2015.
7 Only three exceptions were found within this literary corpus, all illustrated by the authors (Frankel, 2009; Shakine, 2020; Tal-Kopelman, 2014). Although Shakine's Hebrew graphic novel is suitable for young readers, her English edition is addressed to young adults. This difference is due to the importance of Holocaust education in Israel and to collective knowledge about Jewish history during WWII. The two versions of Shakine's autobiography are identical but their front matter is different, and the different designs point out different readers; The Hebrew blue-and-yellow book cover addresses young readers while the darker colored version in English addresses young adults.

8 Kokkola, 2003, p. 84.
9 Lassner and Cohen, 2014.
10 Walter and March, 1993; Lezzi, 2009.
11 Schwarcz, 1982; Schwarcz and Schwarcz, 1991; Nikolajeva and Scott, 2000; Nikolajeva and Scott, 2013.
12 Dagan's book was translated into six languages: English in 1993; Russian in 2000; German in 2008; and Polish in 2012, with the original illustrations, which were replaced with a restrained color scale of beige and light blue by Aleksandra Cieślak in 2018. Translations to French and Italian appeared in 2018, with illustrations from the Polish edition. Only the English, Russian, German and the first Polish edition keep the original yellowish design and Katz's illustrations. Other translations published by the Państwowe Muzeum Auschwitz-Birkenau show a yellowish Chika on the front cover only (without the hero, the little Jewish boy Mikasch, and without the Ghetto surroundings) by the Polish illustrator Aleksandra Cieślak.
13 Rudin, 2021, p. 183.

Bibliography

Aarons, Victoria, 2020. "'Sometimes Your Memories Are Not Your Own': The Graphic Turn and the Future of Holocaust Representation", in *Humanities*, Vol. 9, No, 4, p. 136. https://doi.org/10.3390/h9040136

Argaman, Iris, 2016. *HaDubi Shel Fred* (Illustrations: Avi Ofer). Bnei Brak: HaKibuzt HaMeuhad. [In Hebrew]

Argaman, Iris, 2020. *Bear and Fred* (Illustrations: Avi Ofer). New York: Amazon Crossing Kids.

Baer, Elizabeth R., 2000. "A New Algorithm in Evil: Children's Literature in a Post-Holocaust World", in *The Lion and the Unicorn*, Vol. 24, No. 3, pp. 378–401. https://doi.org/10.1353/uni.2000.0026

Bosmajian, Hamida, 2002. *Sparing the Child: Grief and the Unspeakable in Youth Literature about Nazism and the Holocaust*. New York: Routledge.

Dagan, Batsheva, 1992. *Chika Hakalba baGehtto* (Illustrator: Avi Katz). Lohamei Hageta'ot: Moreshet.

Dagan, Batsheva, 1993. *Chika the Dog in the Ghetto* (Illustrator: Avi Katz). Cleveland: Kay Tee.

Frankel, Alona, 2009. *Lama leNaphatli Korim Naphtali* [*Why Joshua's Name Is Joshua*]. Ben Shemen: Modan. [in Hebrew]

Giambastiani, Verbena, 2020. "Children's Literature and the Holocaust", in *Genealogy*, Vol. 4, No. 1, p. 24. https://doi.org/10.3390/genealogy4010024

Kalvaria-Friedman, Ariela, 2011. Haya Sham Armon [*There was a Castle*] (illustrations: Maria Givner). Tel Aviv: Gvanim. [in Hebrew]

Kertzer, Adrienne, 2001. *My Mother's Voice: Children, literature, and the Holocaust*. Peterborough: Broadview Press.

Kidd, Kenneth B., 2005. "'A' is for Auschwitz: Psychoanalysis, Trauma Theory, and the Children's Literature of Atrocity", in *Children's Literature*, Vol. 33, No. 1, pp. 120–149.

Kokkola, Lydia, 2003. *Representing the Holocaust in Children's Literature*. New York: Routledge.

Lassner, P., and Cohen, D. M., 2014. "Magical Transports and Transformations: The Lessons of Children's Holocaust Fiction", in *Studies in American Jewish Literature*, Vol. 33, No. 2, pp. 167–185.

Leibovich, Hadas, 2020. *Metatim Rokdim BaHoref* [*Brooms' Dancing in the Winter*] (Illustrations: Noa Paran). Tel Aviv: Zeltner Publishing. [in Hebrew]

Lezzi, Eva, 2009. "Representations of the Shoah in Picture Books for Young Children: An Intercultural Comparison", in *European Judaism*, Vol. 42, No. 1, pp. 31–50.

Majaro, Nadine, 2014. "Looking for Ideology in Children's Fiction Regarding the Holocaust", in *New Review of Children's Literature and Librarianship*, Vol. 20, No. 1, pp. 1–14. https://doi.org/10.1080/13614541.2014.863637

Mazliah-Liberman, Gila, 2015. *Hibuk shel Ahava* [*A Hug of Love*] (Illustrations: Danny Kerman). Tel Aviv: Yesod Publishing. [in Hebrew]

Meir, Tamar, 2017. *Hanut HaGlida shel Francesco Tirelli's* (Illustrator: Yael Albert). Jerusalem: Keter. [in Hebrew]

Meir, Tamar, 2021. *Francesco Tirelli's Ice Cream Shop* (Illustrator: Yael Albert). Minneapolis: Kar-Ben Publishing.

Nikolajeva, Maria, and Scott, Carole, 2000. 'The Dynamics of Picturebook Communication", in *Children's Literature in Education*, Vol. 31, No. 4, pp. 225–239.

Nikolajeva, Maria, and Scott, Carole, 2013 [2000]. *How Picturebooks Work*. New York: Routledge.

Nissimoc, Chava, 2015. *Kaleidoscope* (Illustrator: Kineret Gilder). Tel Aviv: Tal May. [in Hebrew]

Orlev, Uri, 1976. *Hayat HaHoshech* [*The Thing in the Dark*] (Illustrations: Milka Cizik). Am Oved. [in Hebrew

Rudin, Shai, 2021. "Language, Poetics, and Ideology in Holocaust Literature for Hebrew-Speaking Children", in *Children's Literature,* Vol. 49, pp. 157–188. https://doi.org/10.1353/chl.2021.0010

Sacerdoti, Yaacoba, 2016. "A Badge of Complexity: Israeli Holocaust Books for Children", in *Journal of Children's Literature*, Vol. 42, No. 1, pp. 5–18.

Sarig, Roni, 2019. "Under Empty Skies: The Absence of God and Parental Replacement in Israeli Children's Literature on the Jewish Holocaust", in *Children's Literature Association Quarterly*, Vol. 44, No. 3, pp. 271–289.

Schwarcz, Joseph H., 1982. *Ways of the Illustrator: Visual Communication in Children's Literature*. Chicago: American Library Association.

Schwarcz, Joseph, and Schwarcz, Chava, 1991. *The Picture Book Comes of Age*. Chicago: American Library Association.

Shakine, Esther, 2008. *HaMasa shel Tika*. Tel Aviv: Schocken. [in Hebrew]

Shakine, Esther, 2020. *Exodus: A Graphic Novel*. Munich: Hirmer.

Shavit, Zohar, 1988. "Die Darstellung des Nationalsozialismus und des Holocaust in der deutschen und israelischen Kinder-und Jugendliteratur", in Malte Dahrendorf and Zohar Shavit (eds.), *Die Darstellung des Dritten Reiches im Kinder-und Jugendbuch.* Frankfurt a. M.: Dipa-Verlag, pp. 11–42.

Shavit, Zohar, 2005. *A Past Without Shadow: Constructing the Past in German Books for Children: Vol. 1st English ed.* New York: Routledge.

Tal-Kopelman, Judy, 2003. *HaMegera Hashlishit shel Saba*. Tel Aviv: Yediot Books. [in Hebrew]

Tal-Kopelman, Judy, 2014. *Grandpa's Third Drawer: Unlocking Holocaust Memories*. Philadelphia: Jewish Publication Society.

Ulanowicz, Anastasia, 2013. *Second-Generation Memory and Contemporary Children's Literature: Ghost Images*. New York: Routledge.

Van Tuyl, Joclyn, 2015. "Dolls in Holocaust Children's Literature: From Identification to Manipulation", in *Children's Literature Association Quarterly*, Vol. 40, No. 1, pp. 24–38.

Walter, Virginia A., and March, Susan F., 1993. "Juvenile Picture Books about the Holocaust: Extending the Definitions of Children's Literature", in *Publishing Research Quarterly*, Vol. 9, No. 3, pp. 36–51.

Wójcik-Dudek, Małgorzata, 2020. *Reading (in) the Holocaust: Practices of Postmemory in Recent Polish Literature for Children and Young Adults*. Bern: Peter Lang.

Chapter 9

"Where's the Little Girl? What Little Girl? Was There Ever a Little Girl?"[1]

From Narrative Memory to Emotional Postmemory in Nava Semel's Book *And the Rat Laughed*

Naama Reshef

A traumatic memory is frequently a silent memory. The trauma victim is subject to a complex and intense set of pressures that precludes him or her from giving verbal representation to the memory seared within, sentencing it to silence.[2] The traumatic story is encoded beneath the threshold of consciousness in a psychological crypt that suppresses the story but which, simultaneously, preserves it within its vitality and reverberating emotional power, thus consuming the self from within.[3]

The Israeli author Nava Semel (1954–2017), one of the first to write about the influence of the Holocaust's trauma on members of the second generation, addresses the issue of silent memory in her book **And the Rat Laughed** (2001).[4] In this chapter, I will examine Semel's perception of the inability of narrative memory to carry the memory and replace the silence. I will also highlight the emotional memory and poetic sphere within which it exists as an alternative proposed by Semel to what the narrative is unable to tell.

On the Impossibility of Narrative Memory of Trauma

The story of **And the Rat Laughed** begins with the attempt of an "old woman", as she is called throughout the book, to tell her granddaughter about her experiences during the Shoah. Various reasons prevent her from laying her memory bare in the form of a coherent narrative: fear of being criticized by those around her, and of the toxic story's impact on her close family,[5] feelings of terror and pain that accompany the story,[6] and the concern that the listeners, and indeed even she herself, would distort and misinterpret the original trauma.[7] Another problem the old woman encounters is the difficulty to condense the original traumatic experience that transcends

DOI: 10.4324/9781003274650-11

the bounds of imagination and understanding into a template of words – the recognized language and accepted representation:

> Darkness. This is where the story reaches an impasse. The old woman is finding it difficult to explain darkness to someone for whom it has an obvious meaning, part of the day-and-night cycle [...] At this point in her storyline, she is inclined to give up trying. Her darkness is not about a lack of light nor even a contrast with light. It's a subcutaneous substance that has mass and weight and has managed to defy the laws of nature and work its way through every barrier in the human body. [...] her darkness would not lend itself to reformulations.
>
> (pp. 19–20)[8]

The grandmother eventually tells her granddaughter the story, but rather than telling the entire story with clarity, succeeds only in conveying hazy fragments – "a shell of the story" (p. 47) – a girl, father, mother, pit, darkness, a rat, and a figure called Stefan. The narrative story fails, the dry factual events of the traumatic experience cannot be conveyed to the next generations, and it seems as if the memory has been buried forever.

The Relay Race of Remembrance

Moments before the granddaughter leaves, the old woman, seemingly in a flash of internal intuition, asks to tell her a fictional story. The granddaughter is indignant. Stories are sugar-coated, fictitious, and intended for young children. But the grandmother insists "either a story or nothing" (pp. 79, 82), and she tells a tale of the rat who wanted to laugh. Immediately afterward, when leaving her grandmother's apartment building, the granddaughter experiences something strange:

> My legs ran up the stairs. I don't know how to explain it, I don't know why myself, but I shut my eyes. I went up in the dark *and it was my own darkness*. I could taste it, chew it even. That darkness got stuck between my teeth, in my throat, in my stomach, between my legs…
>
> (p. 91)

What is happening here? What is this darkness that the granddaughter is describing?

This is not the last time that we encounter the darkness. Later in the story, ten years after the meeting between grandmother and granddaughter, an unidentified woman sends an email to a friend in which she describes what happened to her after discovering a website called "yalda&achbarosh.com" ("agirl&arat.com"). The site features a series of short and shocking poems, whose author and time of composition are unclear, that portray befuddled fragments depicting heroes in the form of a girl, father, mother, a rat, and a figure named Stefan. The woman describes what happened after she read the poems:

> I turned off the PC. I even unplugged it and *lay there in the dark*.[9] Suddenly it seemed as if the words were actually appearing on my body-like a luminescent tattoo. The nausea didn't stop until daybreak. [...] And I didn't even mean to... I mean, it isn't mine, and suddenly it is. Without meaning to, I saw my own world decompose into the most basic concepts, and I'm a little girl and a rat too.
>
> (p. 97)

The darkness appears yet again 100 years after the meeting between the old woman and her granddaughter. Y-mee Prana is a researcher at the anthropological institute who is drawn to study a popular myth about a girl and a rat that gave rise to varying forms of an entire culture – texts, comics, video games, performances, visual images, religious rituals, and others. Y-mee, like all of humankind in this futuristic era, does not operate and communicate in the physical world, but rather in a virtual realm, via a chip implanted in her brain. However, when she seeks to identify the origin of the myth about "a girl and a rat", she detaches herself from the virtual world. As Semel describes:

> "I turn off my 'implachip' and let my brain take over. *In the dark...* Tell someone that the little girl... I ...never had... A mother...Or a..." (pp. 147). She subsequently says that "From the deepest folds of the body... Rising...Outwards...*There in the dark*...Someone is laughing" (p. 161). and elsewhere "I hear a scream... Somewhere deep inside me... Not from any recognizable part of myself...The little-girl-who-once-was existed. The pit-that-once-was existed. *Darkness. Nothing more*".
>
> (p. 131)

Three women, three points in time, and a darkness that connects them to one young girl's traumatic story. These are three points on the old woman's journey of remembrance or, as Semel terms it, the relay race of remembrance, all without the lucid, factual, narrative traumatic story being told even once to one of those who remember it. Nevertheless, it is clear that these women have undergone an experience, some sort of memory that caused them to sense, even a sliver, of what the darkness was for that old woman, that caused them to connect with the source of the traumatic memory and feel something of it. As she writes: "Something that is not a chemical conductor, or an electrical one, or an electro-biological one...Carrying some secret information, with no name and no shape..." (p. 152).

Memory as an Uncanny Experience

Although not conveyed in verbal form, we can learn something about the force of the memory that passed to those bearing it from their uncanny (*Das Unheimliche*) border experience. According to Freud (1856–1939), the "uncanny" is not really something new or foreign, but rather is "something which is familiar and old-established in the mind and which become alienated from it only through the process of repression".[10] The presence of the silenced past in their present – those members of the second and third generations – creates a dualistic emotional stance of a desired horror: foreignness, fear, discomfort, and anxiety at the core of which flutter feelings of intimacy, familiarity, and hominess. Freud states that one of the characteristics of the "uncanny" experience is a mystifying repetition of similar experiences and that this impression is created both frequently and easily with the blurring of the border between reality and imagination.[11] Indeed, this is the way in which the repeated "darkness" experience of the different memory bearers is depicted. "I've never been so scared in my whole life" (p. 91), says the granddaughter of her feelings when the light in the stairwell goes out, although she adds that "it was *my own* darkness" (p. 92). "The nausea didn't stop until daybreak" (p. 97), says the person who revealed the poems of her sense of disgust while sitting in the darkness in front of the poems' words on the website she describes as "really weird, horrible, disgusting" (p. 95). At the same time, the intense physical sensation is accompanied by something familiar, even attractive "I mean, it isn't mine, and suddenly it is [...] and I'm a little girl and a rat too" (p. 97). "I was paralyzed with fear" (p. 147), the researcher Y-mee describes her first attempt to turn off the "implachip", in the darkness, but in its depths, she finds a connection to something within her: "I hear a scream... somewhere deep inside me" (p. 131). The feeling of familiarity and sense of home overpowers her to such an extent that she ponders whether the identification with the strange-familiar is absolute: "Maybe I am her" (p. 161). What then is that non-verbal memory that passed between its bearers and which generated the "uncanny" feeling? How did it pass through the tunnel of time?

Emotional Postmemory

Against the silent narrative memory, Semel posits the "emotional memory", a memory located beyond the events and the facts themselves. "She'd gotten used to not being able to remember the words", Semel writes of the old woman, "Darkness was what she could feel" (p. 72). The emotional memory preserves an emotional trace of the original trauma, passing under the threshold of the consciousness of the sender and recipients in whom it beats as a living heartbeat.

The transmitted emotional memory becomes "Postmemory": a transgenerational emotional-sensual sediment that contains and subconsciously transmits the core of the original trauma.

Semel marks the aesthetic-fictional realm as one that enables the transfer of the emotional memory and its conversion into postmemory. When the silent memory is processed into a fictional story, a poem, a myth, or other fictional work, it succeeds in making its presence felt as an emotional memory, in raising a voice.

> "Art", says Semel in one of her interviews, "is the arena of exactly the same things to which we cannot impart physicality, actuality, fear, horror, hunger. Hunger is a feeling. In the arena of art and an individual's destiny, even if conjured, I can allow him to undergo these experiences and, through them, to believe that a future reader... that it will happen to him. The memory will be generated within him".[12]

How does an aesthetic-fictional work enable the silent memory's transformation into an emotional memory?

The Transition of Emotional Memory through Art

As mentioned above, merely telling the story of a traumatic experience can itself become traumatic because it resurrects the feelings and suffering attached to the original experience.[13] The inability to process the trauma condemns the survivor to a life within it, a life in a past fossilized as if in an eternal present, as Semel writes of the old woman:

> When her time comes, the old woman will be lowered into the earth. Into the familiar darkness. She's not afraid. Unlike those who find refuge in the light, she has been there. She emerged from the darkness, and she has remained in the darkness.
>
> (p. 45)

This blurring of times erases the ability to create a distance between the individual and his experience and to disconnect between the "Self" and the feelings that accompany the experience.

The aesthetic experience, on the other hand, evolves solely on the base of the inhibitory action of distance and detachment, both emotional and physical. The theorist Edward Bullough (1880–1934) claims that the unique power of an artwork stems from what he terms "aesthetic distance" i.e., the artist's ability to strip the aesthetic experience of any personal impression, need, or end that lies within the context of "self", and his concrete experience (and the ability of the person perceiving the art to absorb an experience that lies outside his practical, actual self).[14]

As if in a mirror image of the pathological-psychological ordeal of the trauma described above, which nullifies any distance and detachment between a person and his experience, the aesthetic experience is based on the very ability to detach oneself and create a distance between the artist and his immediate perception. Giving the trauma an artistic form, such as rendering it into a poetic text, structures the distance necessary to prevent the trauma survivor from being swamped by his experience and enables him to give voice to his memories.

Bullough even points to the fact that many artists felt that the artistic formulation of their intense personal experience was "a kind of catharsis, a means of being rid of emotions and ideas, the acuteness of which they felt almost as a kind of obsession".[15] There is a marked similarity to the compulsive activity of the emotional mechanism experienced by the trauma survivor who over-obsessively experiences sights, smells, sounds, and emotions associated with the trauma. Artistic writing from an "aesthetic distance", as intimated by Bullough, not only enables the trauma story to emerge, but can also lead to a crystallization of the survivor's consciousness and his return to normality.

However, when faced with the aesthetic principle of distance that stresses the necessity of the detachment between the artistic object and the observing "self" or the artist, the question arises: how can any memory, such as emotional memory, be conveyed through a work of art as described by Semel?

Bullough stresses that the aesthetic distance is not the severing of the connection between the artistic object and the "self". Nor is it an impersonal, objective, purely scientific-intellectual connection, but rather a unique personal connection that has been cleansed of its practical and concrete nature. It can be therefore said that the aesthetic distance erases the factual-realistic dimension of the creative object but enhances its pure emotional dimension – that which is ultimately passed on through the work.

Although formal language can mediate the trauma's factual-realistic dimension, the shell of the events (the "slough of the story"), it cannot perceive and give form to the emotional dimension that transcends anything that can be said in words. This is the source of the survivors' familiar feeling according to which their personal experience is "unspeakable",[16] beyond indication, unnamable. In contrast, poetic language is created by means of the distance from the factual-realistic dimension, and yet is what succeeds to absorb and convey the emotional dimension of the experience.

To understand how poetic language facilitates the conveyance of emotional memory, we must ask: what exactly is the emotional dimension of the traumatic experience that eludes any formal-verbal representation? What is this "excess"[17] located at the heart of the traumatic experience that cannot be conceived via words, but is instead conveyed via works of art?

The Symbolic and the Semiotic Realms

In Semel's book, the pure affect attached to the traumatic experience is not purely a conscious entity. Emotion possesses a physical essence that is engraved into the body. It is branded into the flesh, sticks between the teeth, in the throat, stomach, and between the legs. It blazes visibly on the flesh like a tattoo, it pervades the blood, every cell, and neuron.[18] For those bearing a memory, it is accompanied by strong physical sensations such as nausea and vomiting. Even when the researcher Y-mee describes her quest in search of the memory, the emotion, it is connected to the body:

> If I write to you in my own handwriting, will you read it? A page with word on it, stained with the involuntary drippings of the body. Perspiration, saliva, urine, blood, tears...
>
> (p. 161)

The psychoanalyst and literary scholar, Julia Kristeva (1941–),[19] identifies the bodily sensory dimension as belonging to a pre-verbal semiotic realm in which the child experiences the bond with its mother via raw sensory impressions, bodily compulsions, sensual feelings, rhythms, and tones.[20] The semiotic physical-sensory realm is not identified by formal, organized, and symbolic language, is not subject to its rules, and cannot be expressed by it. This semiotic realm also encompasses the vivid physical-emotional impressions at the heart of a traumatic experience. Their existence in the pre-verbal semiotic realm precludes them from being coherently formulated via the organized grammatical and linguistic structures of symbolic language.

And what of poetic language? How does it enable the expression of a semiotic physical-emotional experience? Pre-verbal semiotic communication does not disappear when a baby begins to communicate via symbolic language. Instead, it takes a back seat to symbolic language, retreats to the unconscious. In order to reveal the presence of the semiotic behind the symbolic and to give voice to the physical-emotional impressions, we must use language in a way that will dismantle the organized, arranged, and disciplinary structure of the symbolic language, and return us to pre-verbal ways of thinking. Poetic language achieves this in several different ways which I will demonstrate via the lyric fragments in the third chapter of Semel's book.[21]

Exposing the Semiotic through Poetic Language in the Lyric Fragments in Semel's Book

The corpus of poems in this chapter contains violent and harsh texts that portray the same characters: a girl, father, mother, a rat, and Stefan. The poems do not form a coherent or evolving cycle of texts, but are isolated concise fragments, "words that have come undone" (p. 95) as the character in Semel's book supposes. The poems are flickers of a nightmarish consciousness that reveal a strange, terrifying, and threatening subjective world in which ideas from one semantic field are used to describe experiences and feelings from an entirely different one.

For example, in the poem **Cold-Warm**, the speaker uses markers familiar to us from the semantic field of "warmth" and "safety" – to wrap and cover oneself – in order to describe a terrifying experience: "I'll never be cold\For dirt is my blanket\I'll always be warm\ For I'll cover with blood" (p. 109). The expectation created by the use of familiar markers is shattered in the face of the unusual pairing with dirt and blood taken from the semantic fields of death and war. Similarly, in the poem **A Hug**, where the title indicates a gesture of love and affection, the marker is shattered later in the poem: "[…] The lice are free\To roam the place […] I lie there\And fell them tug\On my face\On my body\For me that's a hug" (p. 105). By disrupting the semantic fields and driving a wedge between markers and the indicated terms, the poetic language strains against the most fundamental infrastructure of symbolic language as a system of signals and allows urges from the semiotic world to rise to the surface.

Furthermore, using agreed upon delineated representations and words to describe terrifying sights and feelings detached from familiar daily reality creates a sense of hallucination, of a dream devoid of logic, or, more accurately, of a nightmare unfettered by the laws of reality and the bounds of discipline. The confusion between dream/nightmare and reality signals the existence of an internal physical-emotional reality that differs from our familiar natural and social reality which cannot be reduced to a symbolic language and allows a glimpse into that semiotic-primeval, individual, and uncommunicated world.

One of the most outstanding things when reading the poems is the dissonance between the shocking and sinister content replete with feelings of death, physical and sexual violence, and references to bodily secretions and repellent natural activities, and the childish, naïve, and innocent tone in which they described. See for example the opening poem of the cycle of poems **Ending**: "I so much want to be dead\ How can I get to be dead\\It isn't enough to want to be dead\ And it isn't enough to be dead\\Because even when I am dead\ It won't be over" (p. 99). The discordance is especially marked when reading the poems' titles and their childlike verse simply structured with a noun or adjective when contrasted with their content. For example, in the poem **Easy**: "It's easy\To get rid of a child who is small\With a rat\It's not so easy at all" (p. 104), or the poem **Colors**: "Green is what comes out of your mouth\ Red is what comes out of your legs\ Brown is what comes out from behind\Black is light" (p. 109).

The transgressive gap between the poems' linguistic register and their content does not allow the reader to accept them at face value. The words can no longer perform their role and convey meaning in a smooth and obvious manner. In effect, this dissonance exposes the symbolic language's means of representation, thereby removing the communicative-semantic veil, indicating the semiotic chasm over which it hovers.

Exposing the language's materialistic and formative aspects and the game in which it engages with them, also allows the semiotic to be exposed.[22] In the concise lyric text, Semel makes abundant use of various poetic elements that break up the structured and coherent part of the language, instilled with inconsistency and "disorder". Examples include the use of oxymorons and contrasts such as the sentence "Black is light" (in the poem **Colors**, p.109), or "At the tip of the root – the one close to the sky (**A Tree**, p. 113), and the use of metaphors and metonymies such as in the sentence "My body makes rain" (**Rain**, p. 113) or "A hole-child is running out of skin" (**Skin**, p. 106).

The texts feature numerous repetitions, such as in the poem **Why**: "Why potatoes?\Because. \Why lice?\Because. \Why darkness?\Because. \And why the Stefan?" (p. 101). The repetitiveness emphasizing the symbolic language's artificiality is also prominent through the use of anaphora and epistrophe such as in the poem **A Promise**: "I'll pee\I'll shit\I'll die\I'll give off a stench\That's all I can promise" (p. 115), or in the poem **A Name**: "A little girl without a name\ A place without a name\ people without a name" (p. 114). The compressed repetitiveness also sustains a rhythm and musicality which are some of the signs of the semiotic realm. For example, in the last poem of the chapter **Steps** that plots a real movement in the language: "Three steps\ Forward\Three steps\To the left\Three steps\Back\Three steps\To the right\\ That's how you cross yourself\That's how you're blessed\Maybe if I do it\The pain will be less" (p. 116).

The rhyming also creates rhythm, such as in the short sequential poems **Arithmetic** and **More Arithmetic**: "One two. That's that\One child\One rat" (p. 99), "Guess what it found\ One child in the ground" (p. 99).

On occasion, the poems' syntax is even incorrect, both a way to conform to the childish linguistic register and to wreak havoc with the symbolic order, like in the poem **Afraid**: "I don't know any more\if I'm afraid\Because if I stop being Afraid\I'll no longer be" (p. 115).

The process of breaking down the marking of the represented idea is also expressed in the poems' frenetic transition between subject (first person) and object (third person) – the narrator's leap from her viewpoint as being present (**Hide and Seek**): "Hide and seek\Just count to ten\No one will find me\ Ever again" (p. 107), to the concealed, external, and impersonal words (in **Addition-Subtraction**): "[...] Little girl [...] lives beneath the ground" (p. 100) undermines the language's ability to grasp the character and set in within agreed-upon markers.

Semel also uses different allusions to children's songs, stories, and games that she embeds in the poems in a way that flips their original meaning, presenting them in a threatening and disturbed light. In doing so, she undermines the ability of conventional language to convey a single clear and coherent narrative, instead highlighting the holes in the language through which its semiotic core can be recognized. For example, the poem **Food** begins with the innocent words that reverberate the mother's voice to her young child "Make sure you eat it all\To keep from being small". The somewhat rosy picture subsequently darkens however: "You'll swallow every crumb\For me you'll have your fill", eventually reaching its terrifying conclusion: "Eat straight out of my hand\And show me you can kill" (p. 107). The poem **Lullaby** also opens with words from a magical legend: "Once upon a time\ There was a little Jewish girl\And she had\Little Jewish hands…" but is quickly twisted into a nightmarish poem: "and a little Jewish body\ and a big hole…" (p. 110). The poems **Hide and Seek** and **Catch,** Seemingly Describes the familiar games, but their content reveals a horrific reality: "Hide and seek\just count to ten\No one will find me\Ever again" (p. 107), "If I run away\He gets even more wild\That's the game that we play\ The Stefan, The child" (p. 108).

Conclusion

Poetic language thus uses an entire poetic lexicon to resist the very words and sentences in which it is itself composed. The refusal to be written within the framework of the accepted marking conventions, and the act of revealing the accepted manners of representation, instill the poetic language with an element of subversion. It positions it as a liminal language that undermines and cracks the boundaries of symbolic language, thereby exposing the semiotic realm in which the trauma is seared in such a primal physical-sensory and pre-verbal manner.

"*Without meaning to, I saw my own world decompose into the most basic concepts…*" (p. 97), says the character who revealed the lyric fragments in Semel's book. Indeed, the poetic language succeeded in destroying the deceptive unified texture of the formal language, dissembling its fundamental concepts, and now, as "the innards pour out" (p. 95), the traumatic physical-emotional experience can raise its voice.

Semel sketches the contours of the emotional memory and its activity as part of the fictional-poetic world. This comes from an understanding that while symbolic language is *about* the body, poetic language is *of* the body,[23] and is the one in which the physically-emotionally engraved trauma can be told and moved on as a memory.

Notes

1 Semel, 2008, p. 110.
2 "[…] those who saw the Gorgon, have not returned to tell about it or have returned mute", Primo Levi, 1986, p. 83.
3 On the psychological crypt as a burial site for the lost "me" after a traumatic event see Schwab, 2006, p. 99.

4 Semel, 2008. All the English quotations from the book throughout this chapter are of Dr. Miriam Shlesinger.
5 Semel, 2008, pp. 6, 13. In her book The Parents Who Live Through Me (2005), Yolanda Gampel coins the idea of "Transgenerational Radioactive Transmission" to describe an unconscious penetration of violent and destructive aspects of events into the emotional mechanism of survivors and their descendants.
6 "The price of speaking" says the psychoanalyst Dori Laub, "is often reliving the past", Laub, 2008, p. 76 (Heb.).
7 Semel, 2008, pp. 6, 31, 39. Dudai (2009) stresses that the disappearance of the traumatic memory into the oblivion of the unconscious also stems from the unconscious desire to leave it "guarded and unchanged out of a total loyalty to the trauma, as the original copy of its memory" (Dudai, 2009, p. 215) (Hebrew). She raises the question there whether the adherence to the authentic memory hidden in forgetfulness is the most fitting ethical way to contend with such a phenomenon. Gampel also addresses the feeling of ethical prohibition among Holocaust survivors to transform the authentic incomprehensible trauma into a concrete representation (Gampel, 2005, p. 49) (Hebrew).
8 All references to a quote by page number alone relates to Nava Semel's book *And the Rat Laughed,* 2008.
9 All emphasized quotations from Semel's book are my own.
10 Freud, 1955, p.241.
11 Ibid. pp. 76, 80.
12 Semel, 2015.
13 On the reasons for the resurrection of the original traumatic feelings see Seligman and Nave, 2017, pp. 148-9 (Heb.).
14 Bullough, 1912.
15 Ibid. Aphorism 21.
16 Herman, 1992. P. 1
17 LaCapra, 2014.
18 There is a distinct similarity between the "physical memory" that Dudai finds (2005, p. 106) in Appelfeld writings – a memory experienced on a physical level that preserves the emotions and feelings of terror, anger, and pain related to the traumatic experience of loss in the clearest possible manner, and Semel's "emotional memory". "The war was secreted away in my body but not in my memory" says Appelfeld. "I do not invent, I draw from the inner depths of my body sensations and thoughts that I absorbed during my blindness" (Appelfeld, 1999, pp. 168–169) (Heb.).
19 Kristeva, 1984.
20 Kristeva calls this hypothetical realm "semiotic chora" after the Platonian concept "chóra" that appears in the Timaeus Dialogue and that means a nourishing maternal space through which the architect of the creation forms the world in his image.
21 The French thinker Jean-François Lyotard also claims that symbolic language is incapable of encompassing the memory of Auschwitz and that "idioms must be found" i.e., a new language must be created that can express what he terms "Le Diffe'rend" – that unstable state and instant of language "...wherein something which must be able to be put into phrases cannot yet be..." (Le Differ'end, p. 144) (Heb.). In his book "The Postmodern Condition", Lyotard claims further that art that engages in the sublime, being part of the sensory sphere, can give presence to the unspeakable experience while preserving the absolute otherness of this experience.
22 Feldhay, 1992, p. 77 (Heb.).
23 Friedman, 2007, p. 314 (Heb.).

Bibliography

Appelfeld, Aharon, 1999. *The Story of a Life*. Jerusalem: Keter (Hebrew).
Bullough, Edward, 1912. "'Psychic Distance' as a Factor in Art and as an Aesthetic Principle", in: *British Journal of Psychology*, vol. 5, pp. 87–117.
Dudai, Rina, 2005. "Poetic Language as a Means of Coping with the Trauma of the Holocaust in the Writings of Levi and Appelfeld", in: *Mikan - Journal for Hebrew and Israeli Literature and Culture Studies*, Vol. 5, pp. 101–110 (Hebrew).
Dudai, Rina, 2009. "Forgotten, Remembered and Re-forgotten: The Role of Forgetting in Working through the Holocaust Trauma within Literary Texts", in: *DAPIM: Studies on the Holocaust*, Vol. 23, pp. 109–132 (Hebrew).
Feldhay, Rivka, 1992. "Drash Nashi (A Feminine Interpretation)", in *Theory and Criticism*, Vol. 2, pp. 69–88 (Hebrew).
Freud, Sigmund, 1955. The Uncanny (*Das Unheimliche*), in: *The Standard Edition of the Complete Psychological Works of Sigmund Freud*, Eds. Strachey James. Vol. XVII, London: The Hogarth Press and the Institute of Psychoanalysis, pp. 219–253. (Original work published 1919).
Friedman, Liat, 2007. "Powers of Horror – Julia Kristeva and the Female Subject", in: *Ways to Feminist Thinking: An Introduction to Gender Studies*, Nitza Yanai, Yamar Elor, Orly Lubin, and Hana Naveh (eds.). Ra'anana: Open University, pp. 317–343 (Hebrew).
Gampel, Yolanda, 2010. *Parents that Live Through Me: Wars' Children*, Bet Shemesh: Keter (Hebrew).
Herman, Judith, Lewis, 1992. *Trauma and Recovery: The Aftermath of Violence- From Domestic Abuse to Political Terror*, New York: Basic Books.
Kristeva Julia, 1984. *Revolution in Poetic Language,* New York: Columbia University Press.
LaCapra, Dominick, 2014. *Writing History, Writing Trauma*. Baltimore: Johns Hopkins University Press.
Laub, Dory, 2008. "Bearing Witness, or the Vicissitudes of Listening", in: Shoshana Felman, and Dory D. Laub (eds.), *Testimony: Crises of Witnessing in Literature, Psychoanalysis and History*. Tel-Aviv: Resling, pp. 67–82 (Hebrew).
Levi, Primo, 1986. *The Drowned and the Saved*. Tel Aviv: Am Oved (Hebrew).
Libsker, Ari, 2005. "A Jew and a Girl: An interview with Nava Semel", in: *Globes* (Hebrew) https://www.globes.co.il/news/article.aspx?did=905773 retrieved on Nov. 25, 2021.
Lyotard, Jean, Francois, "Differ'end", in: *Theory and Criticism*, Vol. 8, pp. 139–150 (Hebrew). https://en.wikipedia.org/wiki/Jean-Fran%C3%A7ois_Lyotard1996
Nave, Orit, and Seligman, Tzvia, 2017. "Memory Processes after Childhood Trauma: The Special Case of Incest", in: *Mifgash: Journal of Social-Educational Work*, Vol. 25, No. 45/46, pp. 147–68 (Hebrew).
Sarig, Gissi, 2017. "The Past Moves Within the Present: Adler's Narrative Approach to Early Recollections", in: *Mifgash: Journal of Social-Educational Work, Special Edition on Early Childhood Memories*, Vol. 24, No. 45/46, pp. 49–76 (Hebrew).
Schwab, Gabriele, 2006. "Writing against Memory and Forgetting", in: *Literature and Medicine*, Vol. 25 (1), pp. 95–121.
Semel, Nava, 2001. *And the Rat Laughed*. Tel-Aviv: Yediot Aharonot, Hemed (Hebrew).

Semel Nava, 2008. *And the Rat Laughed* (M. Shlesinger, Trans.). Melbourne: Hybrid Publishers.

Semel, Nava, 2015. "The Paths to Memory", in: A Panel Discussion at the Conference: *on Challenges in Designing the Memory of the Holocaust*, Center of Organizations of Holocaust Survivors in Israel and Yad Vashem (Hebrew): http://www.holocaust-s.org/%D7%9B%D7%AA%D7%91%D7%95%D7%AA/%D7%90%D7%AA%D7%92%D7%A8%D7%99-%D7%A2%D7%99%D7%A6%D7%95%D7%91-%D7%96%D7%99%D7%9B%D7%A8%D7%95%D7%9F-%D7%94%D7%A-9%D7%95%D7%90%D7%94-%D7%9B%D7%A0%D7%A1-31-12-2015/ retrieved on Nov. 25, 2021.

Chapter 10

The Presence of Absence; Postmemory in My Life

Naomi Shmuel

I Was Not There

> The morning they set out from home
> I was not there to comfort them
> The dawn was innocent with snow
> In mockery – it is not true
> The dawn was neutral was immune
> Their shadows threaded it too soon
> They were relieved that it had come
> I was not there to comfort them.[1]

I was never there. It all happened before I was born, yet these events have a presence in my life so strong that I could say they have defined me. The memory was embedded in me as part of my childhood, unfathomable, perhaps dormant, until I dared to examine it. It is a memory forged by absence, sealed by mass murder, symbolized by the faces of my grandparents, defining me as a continuation long before I was even aware of my own existence. It contains an obligation to justify that existence, to fill it with meaning, to tilt the balance of good in a world full of evil – a daunting task for a child to carry into the world as her birthmark.

Background

The poet and writer Karen Gershon (1923–1993) came to England at the age of 15 as Kaethe Loewenthal, on one of the first *Kindertransports* from Germany just before the Second World War. Her two sisters, Anne (17) and Lise (16), also arrived in England, but they were separated soon after the arrival: Lise traveled on the last legal ship from England to British Mandate Palestine, and Anne was to die of a rare blood disease soon after joining the British women's army.[2] Their parents and extended family were killed in the Holocaust.

They Came as Children

Perhaps Gershon's most well-known work is the book "We Came as Children" (1966),[3] the collective story of child refugees who came to England on the *Kindertransports*. There were 10,000 such children in total, ranging in age between 3 and 17. Like the Loewenthal sisters, many of the children never saw their parents again.[4] Two hundred and thirty-four child refugees contributed to the book, for which she received the Jewish Chronicle Book of the Year Award in 1967. The book praised as "overwhelming" received a lot of publicity at the time, when the existence of the child refugees and the plight of their families was not common knowledge in England.[5] This publicity included an interview on national television, which made it suddenly clear to us, her children, that we were Jewish.

We are all born as part of someone else's story – our parents' narrative – struggling to claim possession of our own being through self-assertion, under the illusion that with will power alone we can take charge of our lives. At some point, it became apparent to me that all the decisions I felt to be my own, all the paths taken through my independence, were also forged out of the greatest catastrophe mankind has ever created against mankind. My choices, my being, my very existence, have always been singed by the heat of those furnaces. My name, my facial features, my temperament, even my dreams, carry images of others – the dead who inhabited our family home alongside us, never spoken of, always present. The family my mother created to replace the one she lost was always lacking – a carbon copy of a faded memory, disconnected, homeless, speechless.

The poem "I was not there" has become my mother's most famous poem. Once, when I was a teenager, a teacher read it out loud in class. My mother's poems, autobiographies, and novels became the voice of a whole generation. During her lifetime she published six volumes of poetry, eight books (three non-fiction and five fiction), and in 1989 British Television's Channel 4 produced the film "Stranger in a Strange Land" about her life.[6] The Times obituary (1993) described Karen as "a lone voice in the Holocaust poetry of the 1960s."

It was a monumental task to find the words to express the unthinkable that had happened, a task she took upon herself with a passion. Having been a writer since her youth when her poems were published by the *Judische Rundschau*,[7] she had a talent for words which would have made her the equivalent of another Rilke or Heine. Instead, she was cast out not only from her family and home but also from her language. The soundtrack of my childhood is narrated by her voice, English spoken with a thick German accent. To this day, I cannot hear such voices without a strong emotional reaction.

Postmemory

I am not sure that postmemory can be disentangled from other influences, specifically being the daughter of a Holocaust survivor: how can I differentiate what was absorbed in childhood from the pattern embedded in my existence by the events that preceded my birth? I think these are intertwined, an intense web of meaning which contains my story as a direct continuation to hers, as a testament to the historical fallout of the Holocaust.

During the past year I have been working on the daunting task of writing her full biography based on her archive, which aside from her published books contains many unpublished manuscripts, and hundreds of letters in German to her sister Lise who lived in Italy. The task is daunting not only because of the magnitude of the materials (and the fact that I do not know German), but also because it is the story of my family of origin, in all its bare complexity. And while working on this, the parallels between her story and mine have become so blatantly apparent that they sent me to seek therapy, as the realization that forces beyond my understanding have forged my own reality without my awareness, was simply mindboggling. The result, aside from the evolving book, has been deep introspection, and a critical reappraisal of my own life, including some very drastic personal changes.

Writing and Therapy

The fact that there is a deep connection between writing and therapy is something I have always been aware of. I intuitively understood that to my mother (who never participated in any form of therapy) writing was an invaluable lifeline to mental health. In fact, she often said she could not live without it. I will elaborate more on this soon in discussing her transition from German to English, but the process that I was going through was different. It involved an interplay between reading her literary texts and private letters, and my own writing, forming an eerie timeless meeting place of past and present, the dead and the living, with uncanny extensions to previous and future generations.

"To grow up with overwhelming inherited memories, to be dominated by narratives that preceded one's birth or one's consciousness, is to risk having one's own life stories displaced, even evacuated, by our ancestors. It is to be shaped, however indirectly, by traumatic fragments of events that still defy narrative reconstruction and exceed comprehension. These events happened in the past, but their effects continue to the present."[8]

When I write, the material often comes from somewhere way beyond conscious thought. It is a mental process of freeing the mind from distractions to enable the words to flow of their own accord, unhindered by an attempt to mold them. Thus, an unconscious process precedes the final product, which explains the resulting sense of surprise, or feeling influenced by forces beyond my control. The next stage, "polishing" the text, is a conscious mental process that can involve further drafts until the final completed version.

"Mental experience is shaped and developed through a series of thoughts which are had by writer and (subsequently) by reader. Looked at it this way, we could say that writing is shared thinking."[9] In my case, it became a powerful reflection of something shared across generations. So, while the process of writing could provide the insights, therapy was to me a logical means to understand these in the current context, and to reach the necessary conclusions for myself. In contrast, Gershon's writing was a form of self-therapy which often took her away from us, her children. In fact, her obsessive-compulsive writing created a form of absence. In one of her letters (from 1956) she states: "I am so engrossed in my books that life in the real world takes place behind my back."

Transmission and Translation of Memories

Perhaps an understanding of the process of transmission and translation of memories[10] across the generations can be better understood through looking at specific examples, in my case the most prominent are the issues of language (and writing!), concepts of home, family, and belonging, and the lifelong struggle against prejudice and discrimination. These themes are interwoven into my mothers' life and work as they are in mine, and yet not as inherited or taught, but as intrinsic to my sense of self. They are patterns on our family tree formed by the interaction of time and space, tragedy and renewal, and devastation and re-birth.

Language and Creative Expression

Having lost everything when she came to England as a teenager, Gershon herself disowned her initial poems about her experiences for being written in the language of those who had exiled her.

"Those who arrived in England on the Kinder-transport had become strangers to themselves. The feeling of being a stranger to oneself prompts the traumatized survivor to translate his\her experiences. Revisiting the traumatized experiences is in many ways an act of translation. [.....] translation allows for language to engage again, for the writing process to resume, to represent or support a healing process coping with trauma."[11]

Gifted children who arrived in England as German Jewish refugees before the Second World War were sponsored to develop their talents as musicians or artists, but it was assumed by all that poetry must be written in one's mother tongue. Gershon learnt to hide her passion, and with great determination taught herself how to master the English language by reading avidly. She did this as she struggled to support herself at an age when her English peers still lived at home. Her accomplishments are a testament to her success, against all odds, and with little encouragement from her surroundings. Her writing was a lifeline to salvage what was left of her sense of self. It was her means of reaffirming agency in a situation of helplessness, being at the mercy of strangers.

"Writing decisions are clearly connected to meaning-making. We can choose the moral of the story; we choose what we record and explore. Writing, therefore, celebrates and records the writer's agency."[12]

Gershon's words gave meaning to her experiences, the acceptance and publication of her work gave her feelings legitimacy, and her public readings gave her a sense of worth. Often rejected by the British as a person because of her identity as a German Jewish refugee, her writing earned her a place of belonging of sorts, anchored in the English language she had adopted. When I attended her reading at the Author's House in Tel Aviv during her last visit to Israel in 1991, several people from the audience thanked her for being the voice of a whole generation. Her writing remains a testament to the paradox lived by all children of the *Kindertransport*: the need to celebrate life mixed with the guilt of survival.

Although Gershon lived in Israel for six years, she never managed to write in Hebrew, and her work did not receive the recognition it deserved.[13] Correlating the dates of her major works with the reality of her life during those years, reveals the journey she made in coping with the tragedy of her losses and the enormity of the Holocaust. Her writing also reflects her gradual return to her Jewish roots, rejected after learning of her parents' fate as a curse with which she did not wish to burden the family she was about to create. Many years later, in some sense, Hebrew texts and stories familiar to her from her childhood became a safe haven, an alternative home when there was no longer a physical home.[14] The deep sense of belonging she experienced in Israel, and her creative home in the English language always remained a paradox for her.

I have managed to reconcile my creative identity with my sense of belonging through living in Israel and writing in Hebrew. It is only here that I have a sense of home, that I feel I can give meaning to my life. I never knew my grandparents – I was never there – and yet I have always had a sense of their presence in my life, a knowledge about them that goes beyond the fragmented memories my mother talked or wrote about. Is this postmemory? It is a presence beyond words, a knowledge beyond facts, an influence through absence, a sense of connection beyond thought. When I wrote about my mothers' childhood they entered my dreams, they were real people present in my life as never before.

Concepts of Home, Family, and Belonging

Separation, longing, and loss are the imprint on our family tree – they have shaped relationships across the generations, and they have demolished and rebuilt the meaning of "home."

> What becomes clear throughout Gershon's oeuvre is that her sense of home is always provisional. As she writes in the poem 'Married Love' (1975) 'I sought a home it would not hurt to lose, which would outweigh for me the one I lost.'[15]

The words "family" and "home" are loaded with personal, cultural, and historical perceptions and interpretations.[16] We are each pieces of our families, whose existence within us shapes our very being, we create similar or alternative versions to our families of origin – always forged in relation to them. Families inherently contain continuity alongside change.[17] As such "[…] development is not conceived of as lying in either the individual or the social group, but as evolving from the dialectical interaction between the two."[18]

The relationships in our lives are modeled on concepts of interaction, reciprocity, and connection which we learned during our childhood. Through postmemory they contain invisible ingredients – splinters from a past destroyed before our birth, scattered across time to keep us vigilant and appreciative of the small mercies in our lives. The next generation is resilient and strong, in Israel they have to be – there is no choice – they bear the burden of their birthright together with the obligation to take responsibility for it all from now on. An invisible torch is passed between the generations – it is the light burning from all time, giving hope where there is devastation and destruction. It is a light from the past showing the way forward, as my mother wrote:

> The eternal light which laid
> Its mercy on my childhood days
> And commanded me to be
> Servant of its mystery
> Lodged a splinter of its grace
> In my consciousness and throws
> On the reality I face
> A radiance it cannot lose.[19]

The Lifelong Struggle Against Prejudice and Discrimination

Prejudice and discrimination combined with moral corruption are the pillars which held up the Nazi regime. They are powerful undercurrents that continued to effect the life and work of Karen Gershon long after she left Nazi Germany:

> Both writing and an imagined homeland (Jerusalem) offer young Gershon escape from the alienation of her refugee experience. Such alienation relates to gender as well as Jewishness, sexism as well as antisemitism. [….] In England […] there is hostility towards Gershon as a Jew, a German, a refugee, and a woman.[20]

What was affecting my mother was her intersectionality: this is a conceptual framework for understanding the ways in which aspects of human identity (such as gender, race, and socioeconomic status) simultaneously interact and intersect to shape lived experiences and life chances through interlocking systems of bias and inequality that exist at the macro social-structural level (i.e. sexism, racism, and classism).[21] At the micro-individual level, categories of difference such as gender, age, sexual orientation, or socioeconomic status are understood not as independent dimensions of human diversity, but rather as interconnected and in interaction with each other.[22]

In other words, the negative forces that carved out the Holocaust from the multitude of human ventures over all the generations continue to play a role in society long after. I have always felt that it is our duty, as the descendants of the victims, to devote our energies to prevent or minimize the effects of bias, prejudice, racism, and discrimination of all kinds. I have devoted my life to this in my books and my academic and professional work in training professionals to work with diversity. I see a direct correlation between this and my own past, this is a duty not a choice.

A Summary in Context

As an anthropologist with an interdisciplinary background, I have come to value the perception of complexity as integral to understanding human reality. Part and parcel of this perspective is understanding context: social and historical context is created by people, and people are formed by their social and historical contexts. A person never exists in a void, but always in a context. Contexts are complex because they change constantly over time, as do human beings. Context means a set of circumstances or facts that surround and contribute to the full meaning of an event or situation.[23] Every child is born into a certain context that was created long before they were born, but it will shape their whole existence. This is true both for the descendants of the Nazis and for the Jewish victims. It is also true for all the people in the world, especially those born as refugees, or in regions of conflict or bearing the aftereffects of prejudice or racism. There is no competition on human suffering, it is not about identities or justice. In the long run, all that we have is our capacity for empathy and our common humanity. Thus, I will end with another powerful quote by my mother:

> Who wants the future must
> Come to terms with the past
> That people rise and fall
> Makes equals of us all
> Let none claim precedence
> For his inheritance
> And there shall be no cause
> By which men die by force.[24]

Notes

1 Gershon 1990:7.
2 After being released from internment as an "enemy alien."
3 Republished by Macmillan in 1989.
4 "One surprising outcome of the survey has been the realisation that maybe more children than previously thought were reunited with one or both of their parents. It had previously been assumed that over 90% of Kindertransport children had suffered the loss of both their parents. According to the survey 54% of the children's parents were believed to have been murdered and 41% of the respondents never saw both their parents again. The authors of the survey now believe that 60% of all Kindertransport refugees lost both their parents." http://www.ajr.org.uk/kindersurvey
5 Raymond Mortinmer, "We came as children", *Sunday Times*, London 15.5.1966; Lena Jeger "Body, Soul and Passport", *Guardian London* 13/5/1966, Julia Neuberger, "A Growing Disquiet", *Observer*, London, 11.3.1990.
6 After her death another autobiographical book (Gershon 2009) and a volume of poetry (Gershon 2002) were published.
7 The *Jüdische Rundschau*, published in Berlin from 1902 to 1938, was the largest and most important Zionist weekly newspaper in Germany.
8 Hofmann, B. & Reuter, U. 2020:7
9 Sampson, F. 2007:315.
10 Discussed in Houswitschka 2020.
11 Houswitschka 2020: 185.
12 Sampson 2007:317.
13 The only Hebrew version of Gershon's writing is a small volume of poetry translated by Rachel Halfi: Gershon 1970.
14 Discussed in Lawson 2006:139–164.
15 Lassner & Lawson 2009:xxi–xxii.
16 Examples of cross-cultural comparisons can be found in: Rubin 2006; LeVine 2008:55–65. Lancy & Bock & Gaskins 2010:65–84.
17 Keith & Whitaker 1988:431–448.
18 Falicov 1988:39.
19 Gershon 1990:8.
20 Lassner & Lawson 2009:xxiii–xxiv. Also relevant: Sicher 2012.
21 Crenshaw 2017:139–167.
22 McCall 2005.
23 On the context informed perspective see: Askeland & Døhlie 2015; Roer-Strier & Nadan 2020.
24 Gershon 1990:14.

Bibliography of works cited

Askeland, G. A., & Døhlie, E. (2015). "Contextualizing international social work: Religion as a relevant factor", *International Social Work,* Vol. 58, No. 2, pp. 261–269.

Crenshaw, K.W. 2017. *On Intersectionality: Essential Writings.* The New Press.

Falicov, C. 1988. "Family sociology and family therapy contributions to the family development framework: A comparative analysis and thoughts on future trends", in: C. Falicov (ed.), *Family Transitions: Continuity & Change Over the Life Cycle,* New York: Guildford Press, pp. 3–54.

Gershon, K. 2009. *A Tempered Wind*, USA: Northwestern University Press.
Gershon, K. 2002. *Grace Notes*, UK: Happy Dragons Press.
Gershon, K. 1990. *Collected Poems,* UK: Macmillan, Papermac.
Gershon, K. 1970. *The Pulse in the Stone: Jerusalem Poems,* Tel Aviv: Aked.
Gershon, K. 1966. *We Came as Children*, London: Gollancz. (Republished by Macmillan in 1989).
Hofmann, B. & Reuter, U. 2020. "Introduction", in: B. Hofmann & U. Reuter (eds.), *Translated Memories: Transgenerational Perspectives on the Holocaust,* UK: The Rowman and Littlefield Publishing group, pp. 1–18.
Houswitschka, C. 2020. "Vicarious witnesses and translation in Kindertransport poetry", in: B. Hofmann & U. Reuter (eds.), *Translated Memories: Transgenerational Perspectives on the Holocaust*, UK: The Rowman and Littlefield Publishing Group, pp. 183–198.
Keith, D. & Whitaker, C. 1988. "The presence of the past: Continuity and change in the symbolic structures of families", in: C. Falicov (ed.), *Family Transitions: Continuity & Change Over the Life Cycle,* Guildford Press, New York, pp. 431–448.
Lancy, D. & Bock, J. & Gaskins, S. (eds.), *The Anthropology of Learning in Childhood*, UK: Alta Mira Press.
Lassner, P. & Lawson, P. 2009. "Introduction", in: K. Gershon (ed.), *A Tempered Wind,* USA: Northwestern University Press, pp. ix–xxvii.
Lawson, P. 2006. "Karen Gershon exile and diaspora", in: P. Lawson (ed.), *Anglo-Jewish Poetry from Isaac Rosenberg to Elaine Feinstein*, London: Vallentine Mitchell, pp. 1–18.
LeVine, R. & New, R. (eds.), *Anthropology and Child Development: A Cross-Cultural Reader*, Oxford, UK: Blackwell Publishing.
McCall, L. 2005. "The complexity of intersectionality", *Signs,* Vol. 30, pp. 1771–1180.
Roer-Strier, D. & Nadan, Y. 2020. "Introduction: The Israeli stage for context-informed perspective on child risk and protection", in: D. Roer-Strier, & Y. Nadan (eds.), *Context-Informed Perspectives of Child Risk and Protection in Israel*, USA: Springer's Child Maltreatment Series.
Rubin, K. & Boon Chung, O. 2006. *Parenting Beliefs, Behaviors, and Parent-Child Relations: A Cross Cultural Perspective*, New York: Psychology Press.
Sampson, F. 2007. "Writing as therapy", in: S. Earnshaw (ed.), *The handbook of creative writing*, UK: Edinburgh University Press, pp. 312–319.
Stratton, P. 2003. "Contemporary families as contexts for development", in: J. Valsiner and K. Connolly (eds.), *Handbook of Developmental Psychology*, New York: Sage, pp. 333–357.

Chapter 11

I Was a Child of Holocaust Survivors

Second Generation Postmemory in Animated Documentary

Liat Steir-Livny

Since the 1980s, numerous representations in the Western world have introduced second-generation Holocaust survivors as protagonists and describe growing up in the shadow of the parents' trauma. They include literature, poetry, popular music, autobiographies, art, graphic novels, various cinematic genres (experimental, fiction, documentary), TV, social media, and others. These representations describe various forms of what Marianne Hirsch called postmemory: the experience of those controlled by events that happened before they were born, and who apply their imagination to places where they cannot remember.[1]

I was a Child of Holocaust Survivors (15 minutes, Ann Marie Fleming, 2010) is the first animated documentary dealing entirely with postmemory of a second-generation Holocaust survivor. The film is based on the graphic novel of the same name by Bernice Eisenstein (2006) in which she describes in the first person growing up in the 1950s in Toronto's Kensington Market neighborhood. Eisenstein took an active part in the production of the film and her voice narrates the animated documentary.

The article analyzes how through the particularities of the animation's textures, the film opens up new ways of visualizing themes that previously eluded live action films: Holocaust-related fantasies, dreams, and hallucinations. These textures enable to deepen the understanding of what Rony Alfandary refers to as "postmemorial work" – the realization that one is affected by events he/she did not experience and haunted by patterns of behavior, forms of relationships and emotions which cannot be explained solely by his/her own individual history".[2] The article shows how director Fleming, who is not a second generation, and Eisenstein, who is completely conscious about the Holocaust's effect on her life, use this medium to manifest what postmemorial work is, by representing a thorough, in-depth, creative investigation that uncovers the roots of the repetition Eisenstein is engaged in.

The Production of *I Was a Child of Holocaust Survivors:* Why Animated Documentary?

I was a Child of Holocaust Survivors is the first and as of now, only animated documentary devoted solely to the way a second generation experienced growing up in the shadow of the Holocaust. It reflects what Charles Figley referred to as secondary traumatic stress disorder; namely, indirect exposure to the trauma that affects those who were not themselves involved in the traumatic events. Secondary traumatic stress can manifest in friends and relatives of the traumatized persons, as well as in wider circles.[3]

Animated documentary researcher Annabelle Honess Roe[4] defined the specific epistemological potential of the animated documentary and suggested that animation can achieve certain ends that live-action cannot. She suggested three functions (that can overlap): mimetic substitution (the animation visualizes what was not captured on camera and reenacts historical events), non-mimetic substitution (where there is no visual link with reality in that the animation uses metaphors to overcome the absence of filmed material), and evocation (the animation points inward, represents internal worlds, and visualizes invisible aspects of life). These functions underscore how animation can broaden and deepen the range of what can be learned from live-action documentaries by opening them up to subject matter that previously eluded live-action films, such as un-filmable events, and the inner worlds of the protagonists which invite the viewers to imagine and bridge between non-realistic images and reality. The sections below analyze the way *I was a Child of Holocaust Survivors* enriches our knowledge and understanding of the Holocaust by making use of these key functions.

Subjective Memories of Un-filmed Events

According to Honess Roe, one way that animation functions in animated documentaries is by substitution. In these instances, the animation illustrates something that was not filmed and replaces live-action footage. *I was a Child of Holocaust Survivors* returns to the past to visualize what was not filmed – growing up in a family of Holocaust survivors. This is a visualization of subjective recollections of the child from her past.

The movie alternates between the mimetic and the non-mimetic without signaling these transitions. Although the images are human, the colors (black and white dominate the film, with touches of yellow, blue, and red in some scenes), the often deliberately unrealistic camera movements, and the constant blurring of real events, dreams, fantasies, thoughts, and hallucinations, strengthen this non-mimetic quality. This produces a type of aesthetic that does not achieve ever-increasing levels of verisimilitude, but calls on the audience to consider a new way of dealing with reality and truth. This aesthetic echo animator Orly Yadin's claim that animated documentary is the most honest form of documentation because there is no pretense of its reflecting reality. Rather, it affirms itself as a representation of a subjective memory, thus making its intentions crystal clear.[5]

This shield enables to openly represent the intimate world of Eisenstein's parents, their relatives and herself, in which the trauma is interwoven in the survivors' life, penetrates the next generation, and prevents both generations from experiencing complete happiness. In the scenes depicting parties with friends and family, the guests greet each other with the familiar phrase in Yiddish *"auf Simches"*, which is used both on celebratory occasions and when offering consolation. This impossible yet very vivid combination is strengthened by the image as the party scene turns into a scene of a concentration camp inmate standing on a small stage behind barbed wire saying *"auf Simches"*. As the animation morphs from a swastika to the entrance to Auschwitz to the image of two frightened inmates in striped uniforms, Eisenstein's voice-over explains what the phrase means. Its dual meaning is symbolic of the author's life in which even the happy occasions are marked with constant grief through the presence of trauma.

The acting out of the trauma is visualized in other party scenes, in which the camera moves between family members, and the protagonists briefly summarize their past ("Norman had a wife and a young child before the war, but they died in a concentration camp. [...] Rose saved my mother's life when they were both in Auschwitz [...]"). A close-up of another family friend has a background soundtrack of train noises ("On a transport [...] Carola was able to jump out of the moving train"). The present is always mixed with the past.

According to the film, Eisenstein the child feels like an outsider but is not entirely an outsider, since the trauma she did not experience dominates her life as well. Even her seventh birthday party is described through the lens of trauma. A cake with seven candles appears, bringing a touch of yellow light to the black and white animation. Eisenstein, however, does not only talk about the party but deals with the past. As the camera focuses on the face of an old man, her voice is heard:

> My mother's father had been taken from his home in Benjen, Poland, to a labor camp. My grandmother found him after the war in Sweden. She and the rest of the family had been taken to Auschwitz. Their son Lemel didn't survive.

I was a Child of Holocaust Survivors uses black humor to sensitively present the way Eisenstein learned to use her parent's past as leverage. Three scenes provide examples. When a classmate pulls her hair, she yells at him to stop because "my parents were in Auschwitz"; sitting around a bonfire with friends, no one can top her story ("my parents were in Auschwitz"), and as an adult visiting a therapist, she uses the same phrase to explain her problems.

Evocation: Representing Thoughts, Dreams, and Hallucinations

According to Honess Roe,[6] evocation is the third function in animated documentaries. It means depicting stream of consciousness, unconscious elements, dreams, imagination, etc. Instead of pointing outwards, this type of animated documentary turns inwards. These scenes aim to evoke rather than represent the experiences. By visualizing the invisible aspects of life, often in an abstract or symbolic style, animation enables viewers to imagine the world from someone else's perspective.

In *I was a Child of Holocaust Survivors* the representation of the inner world takes on a prominent role. Although the film is based on an autobiography, the title refers to a collective story. There is no specific label given, but rather an affirmation that the children of Holocaust survivors are different from other groups of children. The teaser starts with melancholic music. An animated image appears of a child sitting naked on a rock on which the names of Jewish communities in Europe have been carved. In a zoom out, the scene shows that the rock is positioned on top of a globe. This scene gives the feeling that the child was born out of this rock, and from the memory of the Jewish communities that were destroyed in the Holocaust. Since the film is from Eisenstein's perspective, this signifies that in her view, the entire world was created from Jewish ashes. The rock that commemorates the Jews who perished in the Holocaust is the center of the world in this child's eyes and represents the world she knows. In the next scene, as the Earth turns, Eisenstein's voice is heard as she reflects on her life. The first thing she says is "I'm lost in memory". Since this is the voice of a woman, and not a child, this double perspective clarifies that she is telling a story in which awareness of the Holocaust was the center of her world from her childhood and remains so in her adult life.

The child, who is depicted in different stages of development, appears adult-like, with the sad, serious face of a grown-up in the body of a child, as though the secondary trauma had deprived her of childhood. From the moment of birth, an adult emerged from the ashes of suffering. This is apparent when she explains that *Shloshim* is a "time of transition for the mourner" as her own image changes from child, to teenager, to wrinkled old woman. As the eternal mourner, she cannot be a normal teenager; hence, her face and neck appear wrinkled. The memories of her parents' past that she inherited do not let her be young and free. She is forever suspended in this child-adult limbo.

The reason for the constant sadness is explained as the opening titles appear. The music changes from melancholic to frightening, as if taken from a horror movie. The visuals include a frightened child hugging a doll, taken from a high angle that minimizes her even more, as a shadow takes over the frame threatening to swallow her up. The film's title which then appears, mimics B movies of the horror genre from the 1950s. This tribute to B horror movies appears again later in the film, as a constant reminder of how the shadow of the Holocaust is always there, threatening and creating constant anxiety.

Animation and Postmemory

According to Fleming, "It's really about a state of mind almost, and how you deal with this in a family: how you deal with horrific events that have shaped a generation's lives".[7] The combination of mimetic and non-mimetic forms is used to represent not only Eisenstein's familial past but also her postmemory.[8] Animation is used to visualize parts of her parents' Holocaust stories and how she imagines them. For example, she tells the story of the ring in a sequence of black and white scenes of her mother in which the ring is singled out in yellow. The camera zooms in on it to highlight its importance. She tells her mother's story in the voiceover as the animation visualizes her postmemory – what she imagines it looked like – an image of Auschwitz-Birkenau which shifts to inmates entering "Canada" (where gas chamber victims' clothing and belongings were sorted by inmates and sent to Germany). Then her mother is shown sorting the belongings and finding a coat. Eisenstein recounts her mother telling her that one day she was so cold she asked the guard if she could wear one of the coats. Her mother's head is not seen in the scenes as though she has no image: the Nazis had taken it from her. Her daughter cannot imagine what she looked like in the camp, and hence her head cannot be animated. When her mother puts on the coat, the scene is depicted in color, since this is the coat brought her not only warmth but also good luck. Without a temporal transition, the scene shifts to one where her mother and father are shown together, happy, hugging after the war, as Eisenstein says that her mother gave the ring she found in the coat to her father when they were married. The scene ends emblematically as in silent films by turning into a small circle that closes in on the figures until the screen goes black, as Eisenstein says that this was the only thing she had to give him, and he wore it forever. This is how Eisensteim and Fleming chose to imagine this Holocaust story as one with a happy end.

In other scenes, animation is used to portray Eisenstein's postmemory of her father's Holocaust experiences. Eisenstein remembers that as a child, after her father ate dinner, he used to lie in bed and watch TV. She segues from the horses shown on TV to tell his history:

> When war began, my father was drafted into the Polish cavalry. After his horse was wounded, he went back to his family in Michałów, only to be taken to a labor camp with his brother. Eventually they were separated, and my father was sent to Auschwitz.

The animation morphs from a horse to a hand patting a horse, to silhouettes of men with their heads lowered who climb a mountain to the entrance of Auschwitz. The scene mixes black and white with yellow. "His mother, father, and two sisters didn't survive. He was not able to save them" she concludes as the gates of Auschwitz turn into a moon and stars, like a metaphorical night encompassing the family, which then morphs into an eye, possibly her eye, as she "sees" the past in her memory.

Wishful Postmemory

The film shows how by using animation one can expand Hirsch's postmemory and represent what I refer to as "wishful postmemory" – what Eisenstein wishes would have happened. For example, after representing the postmemory of her father's Holocaust, in the subsequent Holocaust scenes the horse comes back, this time in a different form. Her father, who became a fan of Westerns after he immigrated to Canada, rides the horse, this time as the town's sheriff, and the yellow badge the Nazis forced Jews to wear now becomes the badge of a sheriff who throws open the gates of Auschwitz in a dramatic gesture. Through his cosmic powers, he opens a vast pit in the ground, an inferno that swallows up all the Nazi soldiers. He lifts the barbed wire, allowing the inmates to escape and at the end winks at the "viewers", tipping his hat in a gesture reminiscent of Westerns, as he rides off into the sunset with the woman he has saved (who is dressed in a striped uniform) while cowboy music plays in the background. These scenes, dominated by blue and yellow, bring smidgens of color into their black and white trauma-filled lives. As the scene ends, the cowboy asks: "how do I look?" a question that surfaced before during her description of their life in Canada. She answers, as before, "you look great, Dad". Thus, animation is not only used to reenact the un-filmed past or imagine the unknown portions of the past (postmemory) but is also used to visualize what Eisenstein *wished* had been (wishful postmemory) with this visualization of the protagonist's inner world enriching the viewers understanding of secondary trauma.

Visualizing Holocaust Obsession and the Effects of Secondary Trauma

Dominic La Capra[9] suggested that second-generation survivors may experience the feeling of a missing link, which creates a lacuna in their identity and existence as a result of the total destruction and obliteration of places, people, communities, and memorabilia. This "ontological absence" can create an obsession with the past, and with the Holocaust that is aimed at giving this eradicated past a representation, language, and story. According to second-generation literature researcher Iris Milner,[10] an imposed disconnect with the past can lead to a compulsive obsession with forbidden knowledge, and a longing and desire for it. The feeling of a past which was torn asunder is accompanied by feelings of isolation and loneliness, and thus creates a "memory obsession", a desire to know the "causative trauma", the "formative trauma", with its unceasing influence on the present. This epistemophilia (love of knowledge), this unending quest for the missing link, is a search that affects the very foundations of identity.

The animation breathes life into this longing and enables the viewer to plunge into Eisenstein's consciousness by visualizing her growing obsession with the past. She states that the Eichmann trial was the catalyst for her Holocaust obsession. "Knowing that the Holocaust happened wasn't enough. I needed to know what it had done to my parents", she says. From that point on, she became addicted. "Suddenly I'm injected with the white hit rush of a new reality: The Holocaust is a drug, and I've entered an opium den".

The change brought about by the Eichmann trial (1961)[11] and her sudden addiction is illustrated as a dark vortex pulling her in, as the child falls deeper and deeper into it with a look of terror. This scene appears between two sequences depicting the family watching the trial, thus enabling the viewers to understand the trial's deep emotional effect. "I've been given my first taste [of the drug] for free from everyone here", she says in a voice-over as the animation zooms out of the drawings of the adult family members, dissolving to her parents and relatives pulling up their long sleeves, showing her and the audience the number tattooed on their arms. The numbers turn into a rope that is tightened, which turns into barbed wire, behind which the blurred images of concentration camp prisoners can be seen. "This is when my addiction takes hold. [...] There is no end to the dealers I can find for just one more hit". She defines her obsession as "one more hallucinatory entry into the world of ghosts"; a world that is both intimidating and intoxicating at the same time.

Scene after scene visualizes her "addiction". According to her, "H" (the Holocaust, but also heroin) gives a "high". This metaphor takes on mythical power as the child is shown pleading with an old man who stands, like the biblical Moses, on top of a mountain holding the letter "H" instead of the tablets of the covenant. Everything around him is black, and only the letter "H" stands out in white, surrounded by a halo. This image turns the Holocaust not only into the most important part of her Jewish identity, but the constitutive event for the entire Jewish people. The child jumps over the dark pit that is the Holocaust and lands in a movie theater as Holocaust books appear on screen, while in the background, her emotionless voice describes how this desire to know sends her "out of my home, alone, to the cinema, to the library, where I can see any movie and read any book". Suddenly, the little girl from the first scene reappears, but this time, instead of sitting on top of the world, she is perched on top of a pile of books. Some of them are written by survivors and others by members of the second generation; for example, *Night* by Elie Wiesel (1960) alongside *Nothing Makes*

You Free edited by Melvin Jules Bukiet (2003), which introduces writings by descendants of Jewish Holocaust survivors. She is still naked, as though she was born from these books.

Like any other addict, the obsession is visualized as mixed with a desire to get clean. In later scenes, a little girl appears pushing a big rock up a hill. The rock falls, crushes her, turns into the sun, and then becomes a ball that she rolls in her hands. "Here I am, some Jewish Sisyphus, pushing history and memory up the hill, wanting to stand in front of my parents and say "here, take it, I don't want it. It yours". However, her father sits with his hands in his lap, as if unwilling to take it. The little girl is therefore "stuck" with the transgenerational transfer of the trauma and the perception that the Holocaust is the center of the world, like the sun. In her world, it is no wonder that she refers to Eli Weisel and Primo Levi as the "forefathers of memory". They take her hand and guide her gently through the dark door of memory.

The circle is a leitmotif that repeats in the film. The circle is Eisenstein's father's wedding ring, the hole in her soul, and the pretzel she eats as she talks about her Holocaust addiction and Holocaust craving. The Shtetl, Holocaust survivors, and the trauma cannot be organized into a linear narrative in a world where the imagined past constantly bursts into the present. "There is no center to be found in memory" she says in a scene in which she is portrayed as a child throwing pebbles into the water. The pebbles create ripples in the water which grow larger and take over the frame.

The circle appears also in the final scenes, which highlights the fact that Fleming did not give in "to the temptation of closure".[12] These scenes represent Eisenstein's son's circumcision ceremony, which takes place after Eisenstein's father died. Her husband is seen holding the baby, flanked by his brothers, who are soon encircled by a ring drawn by an invisible pen, which morphs into the wedding ring, this time topped by her father as an angel watching from above. The men are soon replaced by an image of the crying baby, which turns into the naked child sitting on the globe; the same image is shown at the beginning of the film. The globe rotates as Jewish music is heard in the background and the film fades out. This is the circle of life, which captures the second generation and the next, the third generation, in an endless traumatic memory which clutches onto the children and grandchildren, locking them within. Even though time marches on and the children grow up and the elderly die, the circle lives on in parallel to linear developments.

Conclusions

Based on Annabelle Honess Roe's three functions of animated documentary, this article discussed how *I was a Child of Holocaust Survivors,* which combines all three, expands the range of what and how we can learn about transgenerational transfer of trauma and postmemory – in this case study – a second generation Holocaust survivor.

Through mimetic substitution, non-mimetic substitution and evocation, animation straddles the boundaries between past and present, dreams and reality, recollection and hallucination and offers a deep understanding of the profundity of transgenerational transfer among the post-Holocaust generations.

Scholars have suggested that animated documentary is less exploitative of its subjects than live action documentaries because it conceals the identity of its protagonists.[13] The animated documentary consists of a "multiplication of what was originally there" masks its protagonists and can "conceal and expose" at the same time.[14] It can address shocking, traumatic or painful personal themes while protecting the documented subjects, preserving their anonymity and thus resolving the ethical dilemma of disclosing them to the viewers, because in animated documentary, the real person is represented through a completely fabricated construction.[15]

I was a Child of Holocaust Survivors takes a mimetic and non-mimetic aesthetic position from the outset which communicates that this is a subjective perspective, a profound look into a family and a community's traumatic experiences but without being voyeuristic, because it shields characters through animation. In so doing, Eisenstein and Fleming "defend" not only Eisenstein, but also her parents and relatives whom they represent. They are there, their stories are visualized, but they are unrecognizable. This is not only an aesthetic choice but an ethical stance as well.

Are these mimetic and non-mimetic visualizations of the familial past an accurate description? No film is an accurate description. It is always the subjective outlook of its creators. In addition, According to Skoller,[16] animated documentary allows for speculative and subjective imaging in situations for which there are no images to otherwise express experience or states of mind. Animated documentary is a tool that enables reflexive perception and is able to generate a deeper affective insight into the situation explored.

Animation also enables the representation of the inner world, which takes on a prominent role in the film. The combination of mimetic and non-mimetic forms is used to represent not only the familial past she experienced but also the protagonists' postmemory – the way she imagines her parents' whereabouts during the Holocaust, and the effect of postmemory on her hallucinations. In addition, animated documentary enables what I termed "wishful postmemory", as the animation shows an imagined narrative of alternative history in which Eisenstein's father, the lone ranger, rescues all the inmates of Auschwitz-Birkenau. Entering her mind clarifies how the Holocaust became an obsession, a drug which takes over the second generation's soul.

The combination of these three functions of animated documentary makes it possible to visualize the unfilmed past and provides new perspectives by visualizing the inner world, bringing to life secondary traumatic stress, postmemory, wishful postmemory, and the acting out of the past by those who did not experience a trauma.

Notes

1 Hirsch, 1996.
2 Alfandary, 2021, p. 12.
3 Figley, 1995.
4 Honess Roe, 2013.
5 Yadin, 2005.
6 Honess Roe, 2013.
7 Dallian, 2010.
8 Hirsch, 1996.
9 La Capra, 2000, 47.
10 Milner, 2004, pp. 19–35.
11 Adolf Eichmann was one of the high-ranking Nazi officers. He oversaw the logistic of mass deportation of European Jews to the concentration and death camps in Poland. After WWII he managed to escape to Argentina. He was captured by the Israeli Mossad in 1960, tried in Israel in 1961 and hung in 1962.
12 Friedlander, 1992, p. 52.
13 Landesman and Bendor, 2011, p. 359.
14 Ehrlich, 2015.
15 Ehrlich, 2010.
16 Skoller, 2011.

References

Alfandary, Rony. 2021. *Postmemory, Psychoanalysis and Holocaust Ghosts: The Salonica Cohen Family and Trauma Across Generations*, London: Routledge.
Dallian, Wendy, 2010. "I Was a Child of Holocaust Survivors", in: *Vancouver Observer*, September 17, 2010.
Figley, Charles R, 1995. "Compassion Fatigue as Secondary Traumatic Stress Disorder: An overview," in: Charled R. Figley (ed.), *Compassion Fatigue: Coping with Secondary Traumatic Stress Disorder in Those Who Treat the Traumatized*, New York: Brunner-Routledge, pp. 1–20.
Friedlander, Saul, 1992. "Trauma, Transference and 'Working Through' in Writing the History of the Shoah", in: *History and Memory*, Vol. 4, No. 1, Spring–Summer, pp. 39–59. https://bit.ly/3C7bvfY
Ehrlich Nea, 2011. "Animated Documentaries as Masking," in: *Animation Studies Online Journal*, Vol. 6. Retrieved January 6, 2015 https://bit.ly/3Cba8MZ
Eisenstein, Bernice. 2006. *I was a Child of Holocaust Survivors*. New York: Riverhead Books.
Fleming, Ann Marie. 2010. *I was a Child of Holocaust Survivors*, 15 min.
Hirsch, Marianne, 1996. "Past Lives, First Memories in Exile," in: *Poetics Today, Winter 17*, pp. 659–667.
Honess Roe, Annabelle, 2013. *Animated Documentary*, London: Palgrave Macmillan.

La Capra, Dominic, 2000. *Writing History, Writing Trauma,* Baltimore, MD: Johns Hopkins University Press.

Landesman, Ohad and Bendor, Roy, 2011. "Animated Recollections and Spectatorial Experience in Waltz with Bashir," in: *Animation: An Interdisciplinary Journal,* Vol. 6, No. 3, pp. 353–370.

Milner, Iris, 2004. *A Torn Past.* Tel Aviv: Chaim Weizmann Institute for the Study of Zionism and Israel, Tel Aviv University/Am Oved [Hebrew].

Skoller, Jeffrey, 2011. "Introduction to the Special Issue Making It (Un)real: Contemporary Theories and Practices in Documentary Animation," in: *Animation: An Interdisciplinary Journal,* Vol. 6, No. 3, pp. 207–214.

Ward, Paul, 2008. "Animated Realities: The Animated Movie, Documentary, Realism," in: *Reconstruction: Studies in Contemporary Culture,* Vol. 8, No. 2. Retrieved June 1, 2010 https://bit.ly/3z0yPK0

Yadin, Orly, 2005. "But Is It Documentary", in: Toby Haggith and Joanna Newman (eds.), *Holocaust and the Moving Image: Representations in Film and Television since 1933,* New York: Wallflower Press, pp. 168–172.

Chapter 12

"If It's ME Reading the Signs"
Carl Jung's Synchronicity and the A-Causal in Holocaust Postmemory at the Movies

Michelle Lisses-Topaz

Introduction

I am blessed with two distinct early memories. They are ostensibly separate, but truly very much intertwined. They both involve my maternal grandfather; one more directly, one inadvertently. Both memories have haunted me for years. Only recently have I made sense of why they are so persistent, so vivid.

In the first memory, I am about three years old. I am standing with my little feet in socks on Grandpa Salvator's big feet, and he's wearing shoes. He hums a tune of his own making; "tee-neigh, tee-neigh, tee-nee-nee" over and over again while he holds my little hands in his big, soft, but strong ones. We sway back and forth, dancing in the doorway of a hall between the two sections of his and my Grandma Sarah's Los Angeles home. The floorboards beneath our interconnected feet creak as we sway, giving the dance a slightly precarious feeling to a three-year-old, while simultaneously feeling safe and protected, enveloped by love. The sensation is palpable; a feeling of being cherished as he gazed down on his eldest grandchild's fine brown hair and big eyes which met his sparkling, kind blue ones.

The second memory is from when I was five years old. My mother, Salvator and Sarah's eldest, also a Salonican native, born after they survived the War, who came to America when she was three years old, comes to pick me up unexpectedly from kindergarten. With not many words, she drives me in the 1970s Pontiac to "a surprise", she says. We reach a building; she buys some tickets from a lady in a booth with a window that has a hole in it. The woman takes my mom's money and slides two strips of paper out toward her. We walk little hand in big hand into a cool, dimly lit room with many velvet-lined seats and sit down, side by side in two of them, just left of center. My little feet dangle off the chair. It's fun, if not a bit precarious. The already dim lights get dimmer, eventually going pitch black as a big white light which turns different colors and shows shapes and pictures is projected onto a wide, rectangular screen in front of us. As the music rises, I feel a shiver, the good kind, envelope my entire body. She has taken me to see my first movie in a movie theater, Walt Disney's "Dumbo".[1]

From that moment forward, every time I enter a movie theater, even now as an adult, I get that same little shiver, and a thought crosses my mind: "All of us here in this room are going together on a journey...who knows where it will lead. Sit back and trust it, let it unfold".

Early Foundations

Today, as a psychologist, I reflect on these two memories with a professional eye. It is obvious to me when examining the content and sensations I retain regarding both experiences, that Jean Piaget (1896–1980) was on to something. He posited that young children learn from (and often remember) their earliest experiences with a very distinct quality. He observed that infants and young children tend to take in the world with the force of all of their senses, and explore with the full extent of their motor volition.

Piaget, who changed the face of thought regarding the field of Child Development, termed his first stage, which extends from birth to approximately two years of age, "The Sensorimotor Period". During this first stage, he links "the construction of temporal succession and elementary sensory-motor causality". These intertwined feelings of "what I felt happen" (the sensory motor aspect) and "when I felt it happen" (the temporal aspect) are in his words "indispensable for the structures of later representational thought".[2] Although children above the age of two progress to other modes of thinking, learning, and exploration, their memories, especially the ones from early life, may take on a very "body-mind" quality, even when accessed later on. Since for me, the experiences mentioned above occurred on the cusp of language development, symbolic thought, and representation, they retain both a time and place feeling, but also physical sensations.

In other words, it is apparent when examining both of my memories that they have crystallized in my mind and incorporated many visual, tactile, and auditory components, well preserved with those sensations intact. However, because I was slightly older in the second incident, that memory is also accompanied by a clearer verbal thought which has come to develop personal meaning and significance.

It is important to note that development and gathering of knowledge generally continue from this point forward into late childhood, adolescence, and adulthood to have a very linear, "logical" quality. This is especially true in Western society, with its high regard for and reliance on the scientific method.

In retrospect, these memories lay the groundwork, or set the stage. As time goes on, additional meanings become attached to the cognitions. For instance, when I was five years old, I did not know that Grandpa Salvator had been a projectionist in a movie theater in Salonica; that knowledge came later, at about eight or nine years old.

It came from my mother who used to talk about how much she and her sister loved movies when they were children. As the eldest children of new immigrants to the United States who had to make a living, they would do the household chores while watching a movie on the small black and white television in the living room, at the front of that same creaky house where I danced in with Grandpa decades later. Doubtless, they viewed some of the same black and white films he had projected decades prior and miles away, in another world, in another lifetime. Alternatively, my grandparents would drop them off at the movie theater on a Saturday or a Sunday morning, armed with food and beverages, and would return to pick them up only in the afternoon hours. My mother, Rachel and her sister, Flora, would watch the feature twice, with the cartoon and newsreel in the middle. No one would shoo them out of the theater. It was the 1950s! My mother said that my grandparents would use the time to sell flowers or work in the small grocery store they eventually purchased and ran, just like my grandmother's family did in Greece.

As a child of the 1970s, that last bit of information both enchanted and scared me a bit. How could my grandparents do such a thing? In so many other ways, they were so protective of their four children, my mother, my aunt and my two uncles, all namesakes of their parents who either perished in the concentration camps or died in Greece, with the exception of one who immigrated to Israel after they moved to Los Angeles in 1951. It made me think and ponder.

The questions were endless. I knew Grandma Sarah had some relatives, a brother and her mother who survived with her in the hills of Northern Greece, but they made *aliyah* (emigrated to Israel). Why did they live abroad? Why didn't I have great aunts and uncles, cousins of cousins, not even overseas? Explanations were given, some vague, some slightly more explicit, but many of my questions were not voiced. They percolated alone in the recesses of my mind.

But his family? Why did Grandpa Salvator have no one? No one. Not even overseas. Why didn't he talk about it? What happened?

Only once in a while, generally after a Passover Seder in Ladino and the traditional four cups of wine, surrounded by his four namesake children and three or four precious grandchildren at the time, he would he break down and say in a blend of languages, "There were so many. So many. It's all gone. Where did they go? Why…". My uncles, Jack (Jacob) and Lee would try to comfort him, as he choked back his tears, "We're here Daddy. We are here Papu". It makes an indelible impression on a small, wide-eyed child.

Where *did* they go? Who were they?

(In good movie genre style, prepare yourself for the flashback).[3]

He Who Surely Will Be Saved

Salvator Yehoshua Segura was born in 1914 in Salonica, Greece. He was the youngest of seven children, four boys and three girls. His father, Yaakov Haim, was a shoemaker. His mother, Rahel, apparently was a very good cook. They loved each other. They cared for their children and like good Sephardic families, they honored traditions. Children got married in chronological order. You didn't jump the queue; it just wasn't done.[4] Children, especially the youngest, stayed near their parents and did not leave the family, even when they came of age. The family was valued, and it was above all.

Salvator's earliest memory was of the smell of smoke in his nostrils from the 1917 conflagration that devastated much of the city of Salonica. When he mentioned that fire when I was a child (one of the few memories I heard from him directly), I thought he was exaggerating. Only later, when I read about the extent of its ruin, did I understand. And then I asked myself: when he looked down at me with loving eyes when I was three, did he think to himself, "God willing, she will never know this or any other hardship like I did". Was that his unspoken wish for me?

He was a smart and ambitious child, a good student, a lover of languages and history. His talents caught the eye of a teacher at the Alliance Israélite Universelle. When he was 15 years old, he was given the opportunity to take exams to determine if he was capable of being sent to Paris to learn to become a scholar himself, a teacher. His parents allowed him to take the exam and he was accepted. As he tells it in his testimony, his bags were packed and all the necessary arrangements were made, when his mother intervened and forbade it, citing the fact that he was her youngest. Needless to say, he stayed in Salonica.

He tried again, about five years later in 1935, when he was approximately 20 years old, to immigrate to what was then called Palestine, the Land of Israel. He got all his papers together, went to the British Consulate, and was successful in receiving a visa. Again, arrangements were made, bags were packed, and his mother once again blocked him at the last minute.

I assume this makes a young man despondent; to have his ambitions and dreams dashed time and time again. But he was a dutiful son; he was expected to work with his father as a shoemaker. He did for a while, but it didn't feed his soul. Somewhere along the line, he found himself a projectionist in a movie theater. That's what we knew anyway…

On tape, he omits the information of his former profession completely. However, he relays in startling detail all that surrounds the Nazi invasion of Salonica and the events pursuant, and not only because he is asked about it explicitly. His voice is clear and confident. He is speaking for posterity, and he is fully aware of the verbal will he is conveying.

He recalls in chilling detail the sight of a motorcade rolling into the streets of his beloved city. He notes that the Nazi soldiers rode in on motorcycles and that you could only see two slits for their eyes and one for a mouth under the dirt and dust that was caked on to their faces from the filth of the road and the length of the journey. Later, when he saw them standing on the streets in their grey coats, he wondered to himself were they really that large, that towering, like giants, or was it just his fear that made them seem larger than life?

He relates in detail the occurrences in the early days of the occupation, explaining the actions of the Jewish community, the attempts to process it all and determine what it meant. He speaks of his change of residence in February 1943, when he found himself living with two of his brothers, one of them married, in a house that was already within the confines of the newly established boundaries of one of two Salonican neighborhoods that were now considered the Ghetto.

On the morning of 25 March 1943, the household was awakened by the Jewish Police who were doing the bidding of the S.S. command. Salvator and his two brothers were told that they were to bring only a blanket and that they would be taken for one day of work. He describes the humiliation of being marched through the streets, some onlookers crying, others cursing and laughing at the lines of Jewish men being paraded by them. He recalls that more than 800 men were taken that day.[5]

He mentions the shred of hope he held on to when he was put on a train some weeks later with his brothers and many of the same young men who had been held together in the Baron Hirsch compound. He maintained some hope because out of the window of the slow-moving train, Salvator noticed that instead of heading out of Greece toward Albania in the direction of Europe, it traveled to the South of Greece, eventually to a forced labor camp near the ancient city of Thebes.

In the camp, the young men were put to work, mainly building a railroad track. He describes hard labor and bad conditions, including rancid and sparse amounts of food. As the youngest of his brothers in the camp, not yet married and without children, he constantly prodded and pushed them to try to escape with him. They were older, and either more naïve or settled and set in their minds that this would soon pass, and they could get back to their lives and families. And so, Salvator swallowed his better judgment and stayed with his brothers, until an incident that changed his perspective and made him see the gravity of the situation with clear eyes.

One day the men were led to a warehouse of sorts. Inside were hundreds of sewing machines, Singer sewing machines, he notes. Pillaged, stolen bounty, remnants of the dowries of Jewish girls. Each symbolized a hope, a future, and a family. I can only imagine that to the son of a shoemaker, they also symbolized a livelihood, a way of life, and his father. The Nazis gave each man an implement – a sledgehammer, a stone, whatever was available and commanded them to destroy those machines, to pound them into oblivion. The senseless destruction finally drove the point home for Salvator, and all illusion was lifted. He heard a voice in his head saying, "If they can do this to machines, imagine what they can do to people".

He resolved that he would no longer stay. Despite the natural order of things and the expectation to stay with the family come what may, to honor your elder siblings and their wishes, he was resolved that he would take his next opportunity and flee.

When one looks for opportunity, it often presents itself. This kind of awareness sharpens the senses. It did not tarry.

One morning the men were lined up and told that there would be a need for workers outside of the confines of the camp. Salvator immediately made one last attempt to enlist his brothers in his plan. This is one of the advantages that Salonican Greek Sephardic Jews had: languages that the Germans could not comprehend, such as Ladino.

"Let's go. This is our chance.", he implored them. "No, this will all be over soon. Who knows what kind of work they will make us do...", they replied.

Salvator jumped on the back of the truck without much more thought than that, and at the last moment he plucked up his jacket with the yellow star from the branch of a nearby tree that was adjacent to the truck. In retrospect, he says he did this without much thought either.

It was just him and the guard. He did some work, moving this pile of rocks over here, that pile of rocks over there, digging and filling sandbags for the construction of a platform for one of the train stations. The details are no longer of consequence, because at some point, a woman approached him, she spoke to him in Greek, under the linguistic radar once again. She told him she knew he was from the camp, that he was Jewish. The words she uttered then are seared into his memory. In the moment, he couldn't believe his ears. "Young man, I will give you a chance. Take it".

She proceeded to distract the guard, in a way only certain women can, eventually getting into the truck and convincing the Nazi guard to drive a bit down the road for some privacy.

Salvator was alone at a crossroads. His heart pounded. He found himself suddenly in a flashback in his mind, recalling a moment from before he was arrested with the other Jewish young men. He was sitting in a café in Salonica with his fiancée. A woman approached him and said she could read his palm. He didn't want to look stingy in front of his intended, so he paid her a few coins. Besides, he was intrigued. What she said rushed back to him at this moment. "I do not see transfer in your future. I see you at a crossroads".

He blinked, was this what she had meant? Was this his moment? A split second later, he took off running, ripping the yellow star from the jacket he had prudently, even though mindlessly, snatched up earlier that day. Where he was running, he did not know. He just ran. The date was August 4th, 1943.

He eventually found himself in the hills near the village of Moustafades, made his way to the Greek partisans of ELAS. He convinced them to help him make a safe passage to Athens, where he knew the Italians administered the city and the conditions were somewhat better. He wanted to make his way to his cousin Eli's house.

He knocked on the door. Eli's wife Zafira, who had never met Salvator, opened the little window of the front door, and the resemblance between the cousins was so striking that she immediately called out to her husband, "Elias, your cousin is here!". They took him in, and he lived with the couple and their young daughter, Kelly. He remained in Athens until the end of the occupation under an assumed Greek alias.

There are many more stories. But this is how he survived. When he returned to Salonica after the war, he waited, even working for UNRRA to take down the details of the survivors as they slowly returned from the ashes and the horrors. He hoped to find his brothers, his sisters, his parents. No one returned.

Continuing Connections

I reflect on these facts and stories, which he relays in his testimony as recorded in 1987. Suddenly, this man, who rarely to never spoke of his past and the hardships he endured, talked on tape for more than an hour continuously, with a sharp, stunning recollection of exact names, dates, and places. I was almost 18 when I saw it for the first time, and I was riveted. However, I noted that with all the richness of narrative he imparted, he did not mention being a projectionist. Perhaps this memory was too painful? Perhaps screening those movies in a dark hall allowed him to hold on to his dreams in some manner, see the world, and live vicariously? Perhaps the people he lost are involved with this portion of his life?

When I viewed his testimony again with my own almost 18-year-old daughter before she was to depart on a journey to Poland and Auschwitz with her high school graduating class, I was struck with things I had missed as a teen. This man is articulate and highly intelligent. Moreover, he is incredibly cognizant of *all* the details of his narrative – those related to his personal story no less than those related to its historical context. It's the Greek history lesson that he as a young, ambitious man never had the chance to impart to a class of students, and he is a first-hand, reliable source.

The thing that stands out the most for me during this viewing is that he keeps repeating a phrase, again and again. "It's unbelievable, you cannot believe this [what happened to me/us]. Somebody needs to write this down".

Sitting with my daughter, Salvator and Sarah's first great-grandchild, in our home in Israel, tears stinging my eyes, I suddenly realize, "somebody" is me. I'm the one who is supposed to write this down. It is as if he is giving me an imperative from the great beyond. Maybe he is?

A third memory rushes back to my mind, strong and brilliant, as if I'm reliving it.

We are walking down the street outside my parents' house in the mid-1970s. It's a day or two before Yom Kippur and I am about seven years old. The sun is slowly setting as Grandpa looks up at the sky, his hand in mine. He tells me that the sunset after the day of fasting and prayer is the most important one. If I look up at the sky at just the right time, I will see the gates of heaven slowly closing. That is the time to make the most solemn prayer deep in my heart. As long as the gates are still open, my prayer will be heard. I am enchanted by his words, and wonder if I'll see the gates he tells me about, and if I'll look up at just the right time.

And then he sighs.

"Ija",[6] he says, "you know, nobody really dies". I nod, filled with both interest and fear. He continues, his voice in a dream like state, miles away from my hometown. "As long as we remember them, nobody ever really dies".

I am the recipient of a postmemory imperative, and a clear directive.

Carl Jung and the A-Causal

Where does Carl Jung (1875–1961) and his theory of synchronicity and the a-causal fit into all this? For that we must focus our sights on March 2018. First, let us understand a bit about Jung's theory.

In the field of psychology, Carl Jung and his theory are often regarded as a bit of an outlier. At times, he has been discounted as the father of a theory that is more spiritual than scientific. One of his more well-known and popularized concepts is that of "synchronicity" which he bravely began to write about in the 1950s and 1960s with a fair amount of trepidation, knowing that it could be misconstrued and even dismissed by linear, logical, causal, Western culture.

In the simplest of terms, synchronicity is "a meaningful coincidence".[7] In his concise article, focusing on some of Jung's personal experiences that led him to coin his terminology and summon the courage to publish his ideas,[8] Forrer states that an encounter with synchronicity is a "puzzling experience".[9] Jung links the term synchronicity to an "acausal law" or principle which is "composed of the triad of space, time and causality"; and he asserts a fourth dimension of synchronicity and therefore terms it a "quarternio".[10]

Instead of the typical laws of causality to which we have become accustomed in most western societies, Jung goes out on a proverbial limb. He presents us with an alternative thought that calls into question the typical "x leads to y" thinking, and allows for a more circular and intuitive way of understanding causality and other psychological phenomenon such as thoughts and ideas. These concepts are useful when thinking about dreams and dream-thought processes, and in that way, Jung stayed in Freud's good graces. Where he departs from Freud and shakes up the concept of logical and linear causality is when he advocates that *even in a waking state* one may have a type of insight, or foreknowledge.

It is in this manner that we may begin to connect the concepts of Jung and Piaget.

If a young child has a predisposition to learn about the world in a visceral, sensory manner, and at least some experiences become attached to personal meaning and therefore are well preserved and carry through into adulthood, then he or she may experience a unique level of awareness when he/she encounters a similar sensation or piece of information in later life. Some people consider this kind of awareness supernatural; others will think of higher awareness attributed to certain cultures, or those who take part in spiritual/religious endeavors. In this day and postmodern age, perhaps we can liken it to a kind of mindfulness, which incorporates the practice of some aspects of meditation, Eastern practices, and awareness training.

Whatever the case may be, the feeling one gets when experiencing synchronicity and the a-causal, is like no other. If one is open to it, it is thrilling and undeniable. It feels other-worldly, even when you belong to a profession that encourages awareness of psychological phenomenon and one's own thoughts.

Thus, we return to the unusual events that transpired.

Synchronicity Sparks the Desire to Discover

On 18 March 2018, I awoke to find that my cousin Josh (Salvator's namesake) had sent me a rare email. No title, no note, just a link. I must say I suspected it was a virus, or at the very least spam and nearly erased it without opening it. But something tickled my curiosity. Josh is a busy, young father who doesn't send emails every day.

The link I clicked on was a human-interest story from an Israeli journalistic website that commemorated the approaching septennial Israeli Independence Day. It detailed the story of a 90-plus-year-old couple who wed by chance on 29 November 1947, the day of the United Nations approved the partition plan of British Mandatory Palestine, essentially allowing the terms of the right to the State of Israel to exist. The names of the couple: Moshe and Toni Segura. My heart skipped a beat.

As I read down the article, and a website I found simultaneously, it detailed that Moshe was the son of a Salonican movie theater owner. I felt a familiar shiver in my spine.

As I scrolled down, I found a video clip of the couple telling their love story and how it intersected with the birth of the State of Israel. Toni did most of the talking at the beginning of the clip, but when Moshe appeared on screen, I froze as I saw before me the spitting image of my grandfather who had been deceased by then almost 25 years.

I immediately began to sob uncontrollably, shaking. "We found him, we found him", I cried aloud, without fully knowing the extent of treasure we had stumbled upon and who we had found. All I knew is that instantaneously I was back at the Passover Seder table. And I knew in my bones that this is what we had been looking for (Figures 25 and 26).

With concentrated efforts and intercontinental familial consultation among Salvator and Moshe's proud descendants, we were able to determine that they were second cousins (see family tree in the Appendix at the end of this chapter). Moshe's grandfather, also named Moshe, was one of Yaakov

166 Michelle Lisses-Topaz

Figure 25 Left, Moshe Segura. Right, Salvator Segura.

Figure 26 On the left Salvator Segura in 1987, at the age of 73. On the right Moshe Segura in 2018, at the age of 93.

Haim's brothers, the family originating in Izmir (or Smyrna), Turkey. Of course, the family roots, generations beforehand, originate in Spain. But that is a different film, for another time and place.

More earthshaking was the newfound knowledge that Moshe's father Peppo (Yossef) had been in the movie theater business in Salonica in the 1930s until the Holocaust with his brothers, namely, Leon and Benico Segura, also joining forces with their brother Eli who was born in 1910.

Yes! The same Eli whose door Salvator had knocked on in 1943 after escaping the Nazi forced labor camp in Thebes. This was confirmed when we were reunited with his daughter, Kelly. She remembered Salvator and was full of information regarding the family business and her uncles.

As early as the 1920s, the older brothers entered the movie theater business. Purportedly, they even initiated a venture for a venue with many kinds of entertainment besides cinema in the well-known Salonican landmark, The White Tower. Over time they ran and owned (and partnered with others including Greek Christians) no less than five movie theaters! A Greek "Cinema Paradiso"![11]

It seems that Leon was the visionary, the risk taker. Peppo had a head for the business side, and Benico had a foothold in advertising.[12] A younger brother, Yitzchak, had connections with someone who eventually became a well-known cinematographer, screenwriter, and entertainment mogul in Greece, Nikos Bililis. Together they created and marketed a small, affordable projector to show movies even after the Nazi invasion, and surreptitiously filmed the Nazis and their atrocities in the city of Salonica.[13] Apparently, Eli was very good with languages. He viewed several movies in a day in different languages to determine which of the family theaters was appropriate for the initial screening, basing his decision on the local demographic in the area where the theater was located, and the viewers who tended to frequent the establishment. Sometimes they would stagger the screenings and another brother, Adolfo, would run a reel by bicycle from one theater to the other at intermission, regaling the crowd with magic tricks and playing music while it was being set up by the projectionist.[14]

One of the theaters was called "Alkazar"[15] and was housed in the structure of the Hamza Bey mosque, that was no longer in use following the change in population after the fall of the Ottoman Empire and the establishment of Greece as a nation state. Alkazar served both as an indoor movie theater for winter showings and an outside courtyard to project films in the summer, as is traditional in the warm Mediterranean city of Salonica. Apparently, the complex was large enough that, over time, shops were added in the nearby halls and rooms of the *mosque*, thus completing the modern entertainment and leisure experience.

This newfound knowledge sparked a memory in my Uncle Jack's mind (namesake of the patriarch, Yaakov Haim). As Salvator's eldest son, he told me a story that his father would tell his four children from the days when he was a projectionist before the Holocaust. In his words, as he wrote them to me:

Dearest Michelle,

...As you know, one of several movie theaters which was owned and operated by the Segura Family was the "Alkazar". Papu told me he was the projectionist in this theater. One particularly interesting incident Papu related to me was the time he was screening the famous 1939 American film "Gunga Din" for an audience that included many British troops who were members of Britain's Nepalese "Gurkha" division, after the start of the war, but before the German occupation of Salonica. These Gurkha soldiers were all in uniform and well-armed as they watched the movie.

As you may know, "Gunga Din" exalts and glamorizes the might and glory of the British colonial "Raj" on the Indian subcontinent. The plot focuses upon the loyalty of one particular Indian water carrier who sacrificed his life by blowing a bugle to warn the unsuspecting British troops of an impending attack by "anti-colonial" fighters of the Indian "Thuggee" cult...

It seems, however, that the Ghurka soldiers harbored some resentment against their British overlords because when the movie's forewarned British soldiers started knocking off the Indian fighters, the Ghurkas stood up, got out their Tommy guns and started blasting away at the movie screen, tearing it to shreds, as Papu witnessed everything from his perch in projection booth at back of the theater.

A wonderful puzzle piece slid perfectly into place, making the whole picture that much richer and alive. From this moment, a new desire began to bloom in me. What else could I find out about the family business? Could I find evidence of this particular incident? My heart pounded and the familiar shiver went down my spine. But how? Where to start?

Fast forward to 2020. As the pandemic hit, time began to stand still, fear began to rise, and Grandpa Salvator "visited" me almost daily in my dreams and waking thoughts. I was enveloped by a sense of urgency; I must discover, I must uncover, before heaven only knows what happens.

The signs began in strange ways. Lines from movies began to flood my thoughts. Although this is not an uncommon occurrence for me (as a child, my sister and I would play "Guess what movie this line is from?" on long car journeys and in dark bedrooms, staring up at the ceiling and avoiding sleep together), this time it was different. The lines felt not like a game, but like messages, often insistent and nudging.

Initially, some were comforting. At the height of lockdown and stay at home orders came the voice of Judy Garland, reverberating in my mind, "There's no place like home. There's no place like home".[16]

Others were more ominous. "Get busy living or get busy dying",[17] I heard Morgan Freeman's baritone voice prodding me. Finally, there was one I could not ignore and flooded me with emotion. It whispered and it did not relent; haunted me as it had Kevin Costner. "If you build it, he will come".[18] I did not know what to do about that last one. What was I to build?

Intuitively, I began to schedule video conferences with descendants of former Salonican citizens. None of them were survivors themselves, they are so few these days, and I had to rely on technology because of the virus raging outside. I interviewed and listened to their stories, asked them my questions, searching for details. I did not know where it would lead but had a feeling that it was right; this was my path, and I should follow it. The time at home, lockdown, became a blessing and not a curse. Eventually, these interviewees helped me find my way to The Salti Institute for Ladino Studies at Bar-Ilan University. As many institutions had during the pandemic, they had transferred all of the coursework and gatherings online.

Through my newfound connections, I encountered a doctoral candidate[19] who is researching in the Ladino press, looking through various newspapers that still exist in different archives in Israel. She was receptive to watching Salvator's testimony and agreed to keep her eyes open for movie advertisements or articles involving the movie theater business. I told her the names of the theaters that I knew were part of the family's livelihood and waited with bated breath.

On June 1, 2021, she sent me a message: "I found a movie advertisement from the Alkazar theater".

Before I opened the message, I knew. I just knew. Although I had not told her Uncle Jack's story, although it was inconceivable, I knew (Figure 27).

Figure 27 Advertisement for the film "Gunga Din".

The movie advertisement is from Christmas eve 24/12/1939. It is for the film "Gunga Din" to be shown the next day at the Alkazar theater in Salonica, Greece.

It is written, as the majority of advertisements and articles were in the Ladino press, in the language of Ladino, which is a language that combines a medieval Castilian Spanish dialect with words from many languages including Hebrew, Arabic, Turkish, French, Italian and Greek. It was the vernacular of Sephardic Jews in many places throughout the Balkans prior to the Holocaust. In its written form, and in the Ladino press, it is presented in Rashi Script, which looks like Hebrew in many ways, but the words are in the language of Ladino.

This advertisement was found in the archives of the Salti Institute in the Mesajaro newspaper, no. 1320, page 2.

At a later date, another advertisement surfaced. This one helped me consider how my grandparents allowed my mother and her sister stay for hours alone at the movie theater in Los Angeles when they were children. I needed more explanation than the drive to make a living in a new country. How could they leave their precious children alone for so many hours? (Figure 28)

Figure 28 Advertisement for children's Chanukah program at the movie theater.

This detailed advertisement is from the Aksion newspaper and features a rich program that was put together at the Alkazar theater specifically, as it is worded "for Jewish schoolchildren" during the holiday of Chanukah. It was advertised in the Ladino newspaper (no. 1900, page 3) on December 13th, 1935 and was found in the archives of the Ben Zvi Institute in Jerusalem.

The program entails five activities at the theater for children at reduced rates and says that parents may accompany their youngsters at a special price.

The activities planned are:

1. A play presented by a Hungarian artist named Francesca Gaal entitled "The Smallest Demon Driver".
2. A Fox-Movietone Newsreel translated into Greek.
3. A Mickey Mouse Film.
4. An acrobatic show.
5. A film presenting a ceremony that took place in Athens involving the Greek armed forces who pledge allegiance to his majesty, King George.

This information settles my mind and allows me to understand better my grandfather's mindset. A movie theater is a safe place for children. It is a place to be entertained and learn about the world at the same time. But more importantly, a movie theater is home. And "there's no place like home".

I picture him and his cousins planning out the coming attractions, arguing like the brothers in the movie "Avalon",[20] all the while knowing that they had each other, and so they were rich. They had it all.

Since then, we have uncovered many more advertisements for movies shown in Salonica before the Nazi invasion, as well as articles regarding the movies and their owners, and this vein of Salonican Ladino culture prior to the war. We now know things about the business and the way the people spent their leisure time, occupied their minds, and enriched themselves in ways that have yet to be documented in the history books regarding this particular society.

Preserving a Continuing Legacy

There is now an entirely new chapter of the story to tell; and yes, it needs to be told. As Grandpa Salvator said, "It's unbelievable. Someone needs to write this down". The details that are uncovered help me to sketch a clearer picture. With each detail, we get closer to knowing a bit more about the people that he missed around the Seder table, and the experiences he had as a young man before the destruction. Who he, and we all, lost. Forever.

The least we can do is not let them die in our memories, and honor them in the sense that Grandpa Salvator imparted to me so many years ago on Yom Kippur, by remembering them.

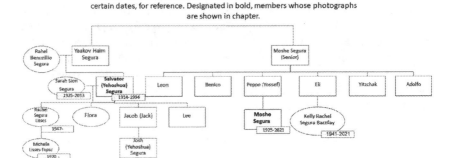

Figure 29 Selected members of the Segura Family, as mentioned in the chapter with certain dates, for reference. In bold, members whose photographs are shown in the chapter.

As illustrated in the work of the great narrative therapists Michael White and David Epston,[21] remembering is in a sense, bringing back to life. We, as witnesses, become "members" of their stories.[22] We also labor to give them new life by piecing them together once again. I espouse that a member may also be likened to a "membrane", a living organ, and as we re-piece the hearts and the souls together, we recreate their image. We, literally, re-member.

As for me, and the strange, eerie things that transpired in my quest, you may call it coincidence. You may call it a figment of my imagination. But "if it's ME reading the signs"[23] as Jennifer Lawrence said emphatically in a recent movie, it's an instance of the a-causal and Jung's synchronicity. It is also, quite possibly, my beloved Grandpa Salvator's unspoken will to me, my cousins, and our children (Figure 29).

Notes

1. "Dumbo" was originally released in 1941. In the days before video tape, it was released once again to movie theaters in 1976.
2. Piaget (1964), p. 177.
3. The information that follows is part of the recorded video testimony from April 1987, filmed in Los Angeles at the Simon Wiesenthal Center. The recording is retained by my family and myself.
4. For further reading on Sephardic families and social conventions surrounding marriage in particular, in Salonica, one may refer to the research of Gila Hadar from The University of Haifa.
5. Although by 1943 there were already many transports of the Jewish population to Europe, the majority reaching Auschwitz, there is documentation of official orders throughout the month of March 1943 for transport of Jews to forced labor camps within mainland Greece. See Rivlin, p. 279.
6. In Ladino the word "Ija" means "child" (usually connoting "my child", female). In Spanish, the word is "hija" and is pronounced slightly differently. In Ladino, it sounds something like "Eeeezah" and is a term of endearment.
7. As expanded on by Hopcke in his fascinating chapter in his book of case studies from 1997. He devotes Chapter 2 to the explanation of Jung's concepts, this one in particular.

8 Forrer specifically states: "It took Jung 20 years to pluck up enough courage to make his thoughts on the matter public", (2015), p. 152.
9 Ibid, p. 152.
10 Ibid., p. 152.
11 "Cinema Paradiso" is a 1988 Italian film which recalls a Sicilian director's childhood and his close relationship with the projectionist from the movie theater in his home village. Ironically, the name of the main character is Salvatore.
12 The information regarding Benico Segura's work in advertising came at a later date, in 2021, while I was reading Rony Alfandary's work on Postmemory. It seems that his relative, Leon Cohen, was friends with Benico Segura and the two corresponded while Cohen was in France.
13 This information was obtained from a series of internet articles graciously provided by the Thessaloniki Cinema Museum in 2021.
14 The majority of these wonderful details were pieced together through interviews I conducted with Moshe's wife, Toni Hamburger Segura over the course of 2018–2019, until she passed away in 2020 at the age of 92. She was lovingly known as the "family encyclopedia", the holder of all the details and memories. Kelly Segura Barzilay also contributed countless gems of memories and details until her untimely death in the year 2021 as well. In an uncanny manner, Kelly passed away on 18/3/21, exactly three years to the reunion with Moshe Segura. Both Toni and Kelly are missed.
15 Alkazar is an Arabic word which was adopted into Spanish. It stems back to the Moors of Spain and means "palace" or "fortress".
16 The well-known line is from the 1939 film "The Wizard of Oz".
17 This pivotal line is from the 1994 movie "The Shawshank Redemption".
18 A plot changing line from the movie "Field of Dreams" (1989) wherein the main character, played by Kevin Costner, feels compelled to build a baseball field and summons his father's specter.
19 Much gratitude to my colleague and newfound friend, Anat Abraham of The Salti Institute, Bar-Ilan University where she serves as a research consultant and a doctoral candidate.
20 The touching but lesser-known film "Avalon" (1990) follows the interactions of a family, mainly the brothers and cousins of the Polish-Jewish Krichinsky line, who immigrated from the old country at the turn of the 20th century and ran a business together.
21 In their seminal work, from 1990 listed in the sources below, one may find theory and practice regarding this concept and many others.
22 Russel and Carey point out in their accessible and interesting article that the term was originally coined by Barbara Myerhoff (1982, 1986), who was an anthropologist who worked in a number of elderly Jewish communities in Southern California. She described the process as a "special type of recollection". Michael White popularized the term in 1997 when he introduced the term into Narrative Therapy. He and his colleague, David Epston, spoke about the "club of life" and the interchange between the witnesses who pick up on different aspects of the subjects' memories as well as the effect these "members" have on the quality and substance of those memories for the subject and the community alike.
23 Line from the popular 2012 movie "Silver Linings Playbook".

Bibliography

Alfandary, Rony, 2022. *Postmemory, Psychoanalysis and Holocaust Ghosts: The Salonican Cohen Family and Trauma Across Generations*. London and New York: Routledge/Taylor and Francis Group.

Forrer, Kurt, 2015. "Synchronicity: Did Jung Have It Right?", in *International Journal of Dream Research*, Vol. 8, No. 2, pp. 152–163.

Hadar, Gila, 2007. "Marriage as Survival Strategy among Sephardic Jews of Saloniki, 1900–1943: Continuity and Change", *in Mikan, Vol. 8/El Presente: Studies in Sephardic Culture*, Vol. 1, pp. 209–226.

Hopcke, Robert H., 1997. *There Are No Accidents: Synchronicity and the Stories of Our Lives*. New York: Riverhead Books.

Kornetis, Kostis, & Poulos, Panagotis C., 2021. "Moving Objects, Images, and Memories: Hamza Bey Mosque/Alcazar Cinema as an Affective Archive of Thessaloniki", *in Open Edition Journals,* Vol. 4. Accessed https://journals.openedition.org/bchmc/820

Piaget, Jean, 1964. "Cognitive Development in Children: Piaget, Development and Learning, Part I", in *Journal of Research in Science Teaching*, Vol. 2, pp. 176–186.

Rivlin, Bracha (Editor), 1998. *Pinkas HaKehillot: Encyclopaedia of Jewish Communities from their Foundation until after the Holocaust, Greece (Part 10)*. Jerusalem: Yad Vashem, The Holocaust Martyrs' and Heroes' Remembrance Authority. (Published in Hebrew).

Russell, Shona, & Carey, Maggie, 2002. "Re-membering: Responding to Commonly Asked Questions", in *The International Journal of Narrative Therapy and Community Work*, Vol. 3, pp. 23–31.

White, Michael, & Epston, David, 1990. *Narrative Means to Therapeutic Ends*. New York: W.W. Norton & Co.

Chapter 13

Writing the Erasure

Ilana Eilati Shalit

(In memory of my grandmother, Leah Greenstein 1903–1944, and in memory of many other grandmothers)

Terror

In this chapter, I discuss trauma and the possibility of its representation in art in general, and by writing a postmemory in particular. "Terror normally creates silence, but lengthy in-depth work may at times facilitate access to representation; then the capacity to say arises" (Yolanda Gampel, from "Those parents who live through me", 2005). I argue that in view of the danger of nullification and obliteration associated with experiences of the Holocaust, writing a postmemory is an attempt to perform a contrary (mental) act: an act of creating attendance and of continued development and growth. This act helps build a representation of the experience and engage in communication with respect to it.

I present an imaginary letter I wrote to my grandmother, whom I never met, and through it I discuss the psychological processes related to creating (concrete and symbolic) attendance in the events, creating an illusion of a responsive and beneficial internal presence, and through this, further processing the mirroring and containment processes cut short due to the Holocaust.[1] I claim that, in this way, writing a postmemory helps construct a representation of experiences related to the trauma and thus expands the possibility of communicating about them with one's surroundings.

Various theoreticians claim that the core of mental trauma is the experienced absence of a human empathic relationship. This experienced lack of an external empathic dyad[2] also leads to loss of contact with the inner other. Without such an inner other, no representation is possible.

The attempt to construct a representation of trauma involves a conflict, however, between the need to know the trauma and the need not to know it, between facing the memories and reluctance to do so. The conflict is intense and powerful, where time and again contrasting forces overcome one another.[3] In this conflict, the artwork has the capacity to create

DOI: 10.4324/9781003274650-15

the experience of an "other" who "holds", who provides a response to the absence of an internal object and to the abandoning of the listening and communication related to the traumatic experience, as well as to help with the conflict between the contrasting forces described. [4]

Shoshana Felman (1992) writes about this:

> it is only art that can henceforth be equal to its own historical impossibility ... [Art] alone can live up to the task of contemporary thinking and of meeting the incredible demands of suffering ... and yet escape the subtly omnipresent and the almost unavoidable cultural betrayal both of history and of the victims.
>
> (p. 34)

Writing specifically, as a type of art, involves coping with the issues described: the loss of the experienced internal object and the conflict between the need to know and the need to not know. When writing about trauma it is possible to create a private "memorial space" where one can explore and express a creative product and, in this way, give some form to the overwhelming chaotic experiences.

Moreover, in the writing process it is possible to build an illusion of a beneficial responsive presence, where the text itself can serve the writer as a therapeutic function: In the text it is possible to use free associations, using writing to create a mental movement between different needs and between contrasting situations: being and not being, silence and words, and so on. In addition, the text can be used to regulate painful feelings and to contain anxieties and impulses. In this way, the writer can observe the traumatic events from a safe distance, from different perspectives, and in a wider manner. [5]

Postmemory is described by Marian Hirsch as follows:

> I propose the term 'postmemory' with some hesitation, conscious that the prefix "post" could imply that we are beyond memory and therefore perhaps, ...purely in history. In my reading, postmemory is distinguished from memory by generational distance and from history by deep personal connection. Postmemory is a powerful and very particular form of memory precisely because its connection to its object or source is mediated not through recollection but through an imaginative investment and creation. This is not to say that memory itself is unmediated, but that it is more directly connected to the past. Postmemory characterized the experience of those who grow up dominated by narratives that preceded their birth, whose own belated stories are evacuated by the stories of the previous generation shaped by traumatic events that can be neither understood nor recreated. I have developed this notion in relation to children of Holocaust survivors, but I believe it

may usefully describe other second-generation memories of cultural or collective traumatic events and experiences.

(Hirch, 1999, p. 22)

Writing a postmemory is, in my perception, also capable of constituting a "memory space" for the next generations, in which various contrasting needs related to trauma and loss can be expressed, where the text might serve the reader to contain for insufferable feelings, while creating the illusion of a beneficial responsible presence. These elements can significantly facilitate mental coping with trauma, while transforming it into words.

In order to discuss this topic, I shall now present a postmemory text that I wrote, and then I shall discuss my understanding of the meanings of this writing for me. It is an "imaginary letter" that I wrote several years ago to my grandmother, whom I never met.

But first I shall describe the historical background essential for understanding the letter's context: At the beginning of World War II, my father was living with his family in Kovno, Lithuania. He was nine years old and he had a younger sister. His mother worked as a hospital nurse and was also a poet. His father was a teacher as well as a writer. When the war broke out, my father remained in the ghetto with his mother and sister, while his father was deported to a labor camp. Initially, there were 5000 children in the ghetto, but only 250 of them survived. My father's mother and sister did not survive. My father and my grandfather survived the war and later immigrated to Israel where they continued writing throughout their lives.

The Letter: A Gaze That Unravels Notes

Dear Grandmother, we don't know one another. That is, not in the usual sense of a grandmother and granddaughter who know each other. Because I am alive and I am here in the Land of Israel. And you are not and you are there, part of the "Land of the Slain". I think that only for children who grew up in Israel there is, in the imaginary atlas in their mind, another country among the countries of the world, the "Land of the Slain": a type of amorphous country that exists somewhere in the skies of Europe, whose gloomy Holocaust darkness overshadows all the continent's other countries. It does not have clear boundaries, but it is completely there. Perhaps similar to any loss, whose absent presence overshadows all other lands of existence.

So that is the kind of grandmother you are for me: "Grandmother from the Land of the Slain". And we don't know each other in the usual sense. I never sat on your lap; you did not stroke my hair. You didn't press your cheek against mine. I did not feel the touch of your fingers. I did not taste your steaming hot food. I did not sleep in your home. I did not share with you my day at pre-school and school. I did not have the chance to tell you when something was bothering me. You did not see me grow up and I, too, never met you. Neither in your essence nor in your transformation. I was not familiar with your posture, your bending, the emergence of wrinkles around your eyes, on your forehead, the white strands that appeared in your hair. I was never able to look at you, and you were prevented from looking at me. Perhaps the Land of the Slain should, in fact, be called the "Land of the prevented", where every person in the Land of the Slain, from whom so much was prevented, has an entire family in the Lands of existence.

Yet, we do know each other somewhat through my father, your son. Many things were certainly transmitted from you to him and from him to me, your granddaughter. So, in fact, we can also get to know each other through who I am. Because that is how it is with grandparents. One way or another, they leave their imprint upon their children and upon their children's children. Despite that which was prevented, that is the way of the world. In addition, you and we were lucky (if there is any point in talking about luck with regard to the Land of the Slain), for you wrote poetry, and some of your poems were published at the time in Lithuanian journals. Many years later in Israel, my grandfather and father found your poems and my father translated and published them, allowing your words to "make Aliyah" to Israel even after you were no longer alive. If not you, then at least your words. For apparently a Holocaust can be executed against people, but not against words. And through the words, you expressed yourself and conveyed to us too, your grandchildren, many years later, something of your thoughts, of your mind, of yourself.

The words reached us from Lithuania. There you lived with grandfather about 80 years ago. You were the young parents of two children. Grandfather was a Hebrew teacher and you worked as a nurse. And both of you wrote. You were occupied by your desire to express your creativity (believe it or not, your poems are now taught at universities). In 1936, when you were 33 years old, the Spanish Civil War broke out. Rumors of it must have reached you and you wrote. You wrote without knowing what was about to happen to you too.

"Blood in Spring"/Leah Greenstein

Blood in Spring
Blood in the sun...
A spray of blood
Splatters on the lily-white bud.
Blood?!
The tree shakes itself:
-Rain always falls upon me
But now – blood?
By what hand?
From which heart?
-The heart of murderers,

Writing the Erasure 179

The blood of children
Innocent, pure –
Rasps the bloody spray...
>(From: Leah Greenstein, "To Flicker". Carmel, 2010; originally translated from Yiddish into Hebrew by Shalom Eilati).

Or perhaps you did know? Could it be that even then, your "maternal instincts" already sensed what was about to rage into your world too in a matter of several years? Three years later, World War II broke out. Grandfather was exiled to a distant labor camp. Rumors spread like wildfire, and you remained alone with an eight-year-old son and a four-year-old daughter. You clung tightly to your work and to your varied contacts, and tried to maintain a family nest for your children. But the chariots of terror drew gradually nearer. People disappeared, and terrible stories reached your ears. You discerned the edges of events, yet tried to continue protecting your children and your home. But then, the ghetto closed in upon your home and your soul, and the worst of all happened: children were taken away. You understood that now you no longer had a choice, and that you must smuggle your children from within the ghetto to the other side, the side of life. Together with you it was not possible. So without you. You began to organize the escape. A parting of sorts, perhaps forever, in order to rescue them, perhaps forever. The "inconceivable" and the "unbearable" in one of their potential manifestations. At first, you smuggled out your daughter, and then your son as well. A while later, in a desperate attempt to escape from the ghetto, your efforts came to naught; you were caught and shot dead on the fence. As if frozen in the moment of your desperate effort to try and pass over to the side of life. You ultimately managed to save your son (my father), but not your daughter.

Later, your son was reunited with his father and they immigrated to the Land of Israel. Here he grew up, flourished, and started a family of his own, and alongside his work he began writing as well (your imprint, after all). Thus, 50 years later, through his talent and his words, he spun a painful and chilling description of your moment of parting. What is that moment like, the passage from the Land of the Slain to the Land of the Living? This is what he wrote:

>... In fact, I didn't really want to leave that morning. To emerge from the dim warmth of our only room, and my mother, to prepare to depart. But I had to.... Oars cut through the calm water, and I looked around me, wonderstruck. After years of the ghetto, suddenly a river, so much space, and me to sail upon it, like long ago at summer camp.
>
>As we neared the other bank, my mother quietly removed the two yellow patches, the threads of which she had previously cut and were now fastened only with a safety pin.
>
>Her instructions were clear: once we reached the other bank, I was to march without stopping through the Lithuanians standing there, cross the

road, and go up the path that led into the hills. All alone, I was to walk without raising suspicion and without looking back. Further up the path, a woman would meet me and tell me what to do.

...I proceeded according to my mother's instructions, going deeper into the hills, farther and farther from the riverbank and my Mother. Only then did a figure with a sealed face approach me, and as she passed me she whispered that I should continue slowly, she would soon return and join me... I am not sure even today that I have fully digested what happened to me that morning. But the next day I received the first letter from my mother, written on a rolled-up scrap of paper, to be read and then burned: "I watched you move away, my child", she wrote, "climbing all by yourself onto the bank of the river, walking past guards and people on your way to freedom. A day will come when a film will be made about your miraculous escape from the Ghetto.

(From "Crossing the River", Shalom Eilati,
University of Alabama Press, 2009)

I think to myself, what a courageous mother and what an impressive promise: "A day will come when a film will be made about your miraculous escape from the Ghetto". How were you able to send your son away at the moment of parting, which was surely torturous and accompanied by so much uncertainty, with a message of the wondrous future? How were you able to predict, as a mother, that not only would he survive, but it would become a remarkable story? It was as if you hid spiritual nutrition for him in his pockets that would accompany him along his journey into the unknown, saying: "My son, I must part from you now, but you are my hero. And now I am sending you over to the other side, the side of life. And you shall see, not only will you be saved, but you will have a magnificent future". It seems to me that my father's remarkable survival is connected to that note, to the message you gave him when you took leave of him, to your observation of him in those moments.

It seems to me that my father's knowledge of himself passed through your knowledge of him. And at the moment of parting, the very fact that he was able to see himself mirrored in your gaze as "getting through it safely", and even more so, getting through it "grandly, as a hero", and that one day it would become "a remarkable story", instilled in him the capacity to see and know himself as such and embedded within him inner resources that accompanied him on his continued journey towards life.

Thus, the note you wrote to him then in Lithuania – creased and shrunken, never to be read again and destined to be burned and nullified, endured, to be read 70 years later, transformed through the power of a gaze, at first hesitantly, but later expansively, opening a shaft to the world that had closed in on it and unrolling the form that had been enforced upon it, because every shrinkage is destined to expand!

This is an imaginary letter I wrote with regard to "unrolling the form that had been enforced" on the events. Writing a postmemory is for me an act that strives, through the writing process, against the dangers of nullification and eradication that are typical of the Holocaust. This is an attempt to perform acts of vitality: of creating attendance, development, and growth, which are the opposite of enforcing reduction and nullification, and which facilitate the processing of trauma, as I shall explain below.

Writing a postmemory involves an occupation with a concrete and symbolic process of attendance. In its concrete form, writing enables a process of concrete formation and attendance that contradict the forces of nullification and eradication that occurred during the Holocaust. Writing begins with a blank white page, and then, gradually, one word is written, followed by another. In this way, the page begins to fill up and the word that was written does not disappear, neither by gas nor by any other means of destruction. Even if the physical books are burnt, the meaning of the words is not eradicated, Thus, through words, it is possible to create an attendance that is not physically consumed.[6] The letter I wrote is now present, unshrinkable, unburnable, and unerasable.

Symbolically, the process of writing the postmemory expresses the need, through writing, to "fight back", even if in retrospect in the transitional space of the Holocaust.[7] This time we will use the "army of words", "tanks of imagery", "bullets of phrases".[8] In the letter I wrote, I symbolically gave my grandmother presence as an active, fighting, and persistent person who made every effort to fight the Nazis, even if unsuccessfully. For this purpose, I made use of family memories (stories about her), utilizing various images ("your imprint, after all"), and I explained that which had occurred through the "army of words".

Writing a postmemory makes it possible not only to give presence to memories and to symbolically fight in the transitional space of war through words, but also to form the illusion of a receptive, containing, mirroring, and holding mother figure, while creating an illusion of her endless presence.[9] Creating the illusion of this responsive and beneficial presence helps rehabilitate the representation of the internal "other", where as described, this representation had been weakened following the trauma.[10]

Writing a postmemory makes it possible to **imaginarily** continue the mental processes related to a connection with such a mother figure, severed due to the trauma of the Holocaust. I choose to relate to two processes that are most essential for healthy mental development, which exist between a mother and her infant and are revitalized in the writing process: mirroring processes and containment processes.[11]

With regard to the mirroring process, Winnicott described how the infant and the child see themselves when looking at their mother's face, as though she is a living mirror.[12] The infant sees the mother's face at an early stage of life, and through her gaze encounters himself. This act enhances in him the experience of being identified, of having his formation witnessed, of being comprehended, "thought", and thought about. In this way, not only is his self-existence created but, most importantly, it creates the knowledge that he is not being left alone with what he is and with what is forming within him, rather there is someone with him.[13]

It seems that through my imaginary observation of the figure of my grandmother who is no longer, I tried to observe her from up close. In this way, I tried to imagine how she would have observed me, what she would have seen in me, and through that what I would have seen in myself through my mirroring in her. Hence, the process of writing the postmemory is an attempt to observe the absent figure retrospectively and to imagine how we would be mirrored in them, an attempt that expresses the desire to mentally complete the "mirroring that never took place".

With regard to the process of containment, Bion described one of the mother's important functions in infancy as being a transforming container for her child.[14] The child projects at her the elements that assault his existence, and the mother, using her abilities, processes these experiences for him. These are experiences to which the child cannot give meaning on his own as they arouse in him chaotic and disassembling anxiety. When the mother is a significantly moderating and cleansing container, the infant will in time internalize her ability, and his mind will become capable of processing his experiences and of symbolization. In the mental process that accompanies writing the postmemory, an effort is made by using words to process and transform the experiences conveyed to the next generations after the Holocaust. In the letter to my grandmother, I also try to process various experiences related to the meaning of her absence following the Holocaust: the sadness, the shock, the pain, and the disaster, and alternately the resourcefulness, the courage, and the bravery.

In these manners, the letter becomes a type of holding container and framework, and in this way, it expands the possibility of observing the events in an integrative way that generates new meaning.

But this must be qualified by noting that writing in general and writing about trauma in particular, is based on the use of words, and words are limited in their ability to represent the entire experience. Hence, when using words to describe trauma, there will always remain a space – an area that cannot be mediated or transmitted through transformation.[15] A gap will forever remain between the written word and the experience, because at times, the word is not really capable of transporting us into the internal presence of things, but quite the opposite – it distracts in the presence of the void.[16]

In conclusion, I would like to refer to the letter I wrote as a message sent in a bottle.

"A poem, as a manifestation of language", writes Paul Celan, "and thus essentially dialogue, can be a message in a bottle, sent out in the – not always greatly hopeful – belief that somewhere and sometime it could wash up on land, on heartland perhaps. Poems in this sense too are under way: they are making toward something. To what? To something that stands open, available, maybe to a 'you' that can be spoken to, a reality that can be spoken about" (Paul Celan, in Felman & Laub, 1992, p. 126).

In this chapter, I am sending psychic materials packaged in the form of words, written by my family members and myself, in a bottle. I am sending them so that they will continue their transformation from the traumatic past of the Holocaust to potential others on the side of the living. This transformation will make it possible to construct for them representations about which it will subsequently be possible to speak to others.

Notes

1 Winnicott, 1971; Bion, 1962.
2 Laub & Podell, 1995; Caruth, 1990.
3 Caruth, 1995; Laub & Podell, 1995.
4 Laub & Podell, 1995; Rose, 1996.
5 Bion, 1962; Oppenheim, 2008; Richman, 2013.
6 Dreifuss-Kattan, 2016.
7 Winnicott, 1971.
8 Laub & Podell, 1995; Rose, 1995.
9 Dreifuss-Kattan, 2016; Freud, 1900; Turco, 2003a; Volkan, 1981.
10 Laub & Podell, 1995.
11 Bion, 1962; Oppenheim, 2008.
12 Winnicott, 1971.
13 Ofarim, 2013.
14 Bion, 1962.
15 Bromberg, 1998; Caruth, 1995; Grand, 2002; Langer, 1991; Laub & Auerhahn, 1987.
16 Bialik, 1915.

Bibliography

Bialik, C. N., 2000 [1915]. Revealment and concealment in language. In *Revealment and Concealment: 5 Essays*. Jerusalem: Ibis.

Bion, W. R., 1962. *Learning from Experience*. London: Karnac Books.

Bromberg, P. M., 1998. *Standing in the Spaces: Essays on Clinical Process, Trauma, and Dissociation*. Hillsdale, NJ: The Analytic Press.

Caruth, C., 1995. Introduction. In: C. Caruth (ed.), *Trauma: Explorations in memory* (pp. 3–13). Baltimore, MD: Johns Hopkins University Press.

Celan, P., 2001 [1958]. Speech on the occasion of receiving the literature prize of the free hanseatic city of Bremen. In J. Felstiner (trans.), *Poems and prose of Paul Celan*. New York: W.W. Norton.

Dreifuss-Kattan, E. D., 2016. *Art and Mourning: The Role of Creativity in Healing Trauma and Loss*. London and New York: Routledge.

Dudai, R., 2021. *Tongue of Fire: A Poetic Testimony to Holocaust Trauma*. Hebrew: Mofet Institute.

Eilati, S., 2009. *Crossing the River*. Tuscaloosa and Jerusalem: The University of Alabama Press, Yad Vashem.

Faimberg, H., 2005. Après-coup. *International Journal of Psycho-Analysis*, 86(1), 1–6.
Felman, S., 1992. Education and crisis, or the vicissitudes of teaching. In S. Felman and D. Laub (eds.), *Testimony: Crises of Witnessing in Literature, Psychoanalysis, and History* (pp. 1–56). New York and London: Routledge.
Felman, S., & Laub, D., 1992. *Testimony: Crises of Witnessing in Literature, Psychoanalysis, and History*. New York: Routledge.
Freud, S., 1896. Letter 52, 6 December 1896. In: Extracts from the Fliess papers. SE 1, p. 233.
Freud, S., 1900. The interpretation of dreams. In: J. Strachey (Ed. & Trans.), *The Standard Edition of the Complete Psychological Works of Sigmund Freud* (Vols. 4, 5). London: Hogarth Press.
Freud, S., 1917. *Mourning and Melancholia*. Standard Edition, 14: 243–258. London: Hogarth Press.
Gampel, Y., 2010. *Those Parents Who Live Through Me*. Keter Publication. (In Hebrew)
Grand, S., 2002. Between the reader and the read: Commentary on paper by Elizabeth F. Howell. *Psychoanalytic Dialogues*, 12(6), 959–970.
Greenstein, L., 2010. *To Flicker*. Editor: S. Eilati. Jerusalem: Carmel. (In Hebrew)
Hershberg, S. G., 2013. Coming out of hiding: How the analyst faces and transforms his or her story and its influence on clinical work: Commentary on papers by Clemens Loew and Sophia Richman. *Psychoanalytic Dialogues*, 23(3), 377–381.
Hirsch, M., 1999. Projected memory: Holocaust photographs in personal and public fantasy. In M. Bal, J. Crewe, & L. Spitzer (eds.), *Acts of Memory, Cultural Recall in the Present* (pp. 3–23). Lebanon, NH: University Press of New England.
Langer, L., 1991. *Holocaust Testimonies: The Ruins of Memory*. New Haven, CT: Yale University Press.
Laub, D., & Auerhahn, N. C., 1987. Play and playfulness in Holocaust survivors. *The Psychoanalytic Study of the Child*, 42, 45–58.
Laub, D., & Auerhahn, N. C., 1993. Knowing and not knowing: Forms of traumatic memory. *International Journal of Psycho-Analysis*, 74, 287–302.
Laub, D., & Podell, D., 1995. Art and trauma. *International Journal of Psycho-Analysis*, 76, 991–1005.
Mitrani, J. L., 2001. Taking the transference: Some technical implications in three papers by Bion. *International Journal of Psycho-Analysis*, 82, 1085–1184.
Ofarim, Y., 2013. Listening. In E. Perroni (ed.), *Play: Psychoanalytic Perspectives, Survival and Human Development*. Miskal-Yedioth Ahronoth Books and Chemed Books. (in Hebrew)
Oppenheim, L., 2008. Life as trauma, art as mastery: Samuel Beckett and the urgency of writing, *Contemporary Psychoanalysis*, 44(3), 419–442.
Ornstein, A., 2015. Memorial spaces: Further comments on mourning following multiple traumatic losses. In A. Tutter and L. Wurmser (eds.), *Grief and Its Transcendence: Memory, Identity, Creativity*. London: Routledge.
Richman, S., 2013. Out of darkness: Reverberations of trauma and its creative transformations. *Psychoanalytic Dialogues*, 23(3), 362–376.
Rose, G. J., 1996. *Necessary Illusion: Art as 'Witness'*. New York: International Universities Press.

Turco, R., 2003a. *Linking Objects.* Presentation to the American Academy of Psychoanalysis, May 2003. New Orleans, LA.

Turco, R., 2003b. *Psychoanalytic Aspects of Creativity.* Presentation to the American Academy of Psychoanalysis, May 11, 2003.

Volkan, V., 1981. *Linking Objects and Linking Phenomena—Complicated Mourning.* New York: International Universities Press.

Winnicott, D. W., 1971. *Playing and Reality.* London: Tavistock Publications.

Index

Note: *Italic* page numbers refer to figures and page numbers followed by "n" denote endnotes.

a-causal events 164–165, 172
active creators 83
Aeolia (Venezis) 53, 54
aesthetic distance 128, 129
affordances, to connective memory 92–93
Albert, Yael 114
Alfandary, Rony 1, 3, 29n10, 146, 173n12
Alkazar 167, 173n15
Alliance Israélite Universelle 16, 29n14, 29n15, 160
Amiliti/The Silent One (Trypani) 45
Amir, Dana 81, 82
Anatolia (Papadimitriou) 54
"Anatolian Catastrophe" (1922) 44, 52–55
Ancient Thebes 161, 167
And the Rat Laughed (Semel) 4, 124; emotional postmemory 127–128; impossibility of narrative memory of trauma 124–125; memory as an uncanny experience 127; relay race of remembrance 125–126; semiotic through poetic language 130–133; symbolic and semiotic realms 130; transition of emotional memory through art 128–129
animated documentary 146, 147, 149; functions of 153–154
animation and postmemory 150–151
Appelfeld, Aharon 134n18
Argaman, Iris: *Bear and Fred* 113, 115, 116
Argo (Theotokas) 53

art: representation in 175; transition of emotional memory through 128–129
Auschwitz Untold: in Colour 101
"Avalon" 171, 173n20

Balkin, Jack M. 56n12
Banville, John: *Birchwood* 51
Bar-Gil, Oshri 4
Baron Hirsch compound 161
Baumel-Schwartz, Judith Tydor 1, 3, 10; choices and understanding *goral* 41–42; dream that started it all off 35–36; giant leap forward 40–41; how i got there in first place 33–35; right person, right place, right time 38–39; timing is everything, 2g legacy 36–38; withdrawal to save professional life and personal sanity 39–40
Bear and Fred (Argaman) 113, 115, 116
belonging, concepts of 141–142
Ben-David, Anat 94
Bernhardt, Zvi 96
bibliotherapy process 82
big data, from digital memory to 99, 99–100
The Big House of Inver (Somerville and Ross) 51
Bion, W. R. 61, 182
Birchwood (Banville) 51
Boland, Eavan 47; "The Making of an Irish Goddess" 51
Bon Points 23, *24*
Borges, Jorge Luis 91
Bouletis, Tassos: *A Touch of Spice* 54
British empire 44–45

Index

Brooms Dancing in Winter (Leibovich) 113
Bukiet, Melvin Jules: *Nothing Makes You Free* 152–153
Bullough, Edward 128, 129

Canada 150, 151
Carey, Maggie 173n22
Celan, Paul 182
The Central Archives for the History of the Jewish People in Jerusalem (CAHJP) 29n17
Certeau, Michel de 91, 95
Chakrabarty, Dipesh 51
Chika the Dog in the Ghetto (Dagan) 114, 115
Children of the Holocaust (Epstein) 37
Chinweizu 45
Chirac, Jacques 15
choices 32–33
Chomsky, Martin 42n10
Cieślak, Aleksandra 121n12
"Cinema Paradiso" 167, 173n11
cloud affordances, for memory 93–94
cloud-based digital memory 92
The Cohen Family: Benjamin's secrets 17, *18–27,* 20, 23, 25, 27–28; collection 10–12; Ines Cohen Matarasso 16; Isaac Cohen 15; Leon Cohen 14–15; Rita Cohen Parenti 16–17; story of 12–14
collective memory 90–91, 101
collective social memory 90
concentration camps 15–17, 148, 152, 159
connective memory 91; affordances to 92–93; from digitally mediated memories to 94; from digital memory to *99,* 99–100; human role in 94–95; materially mediated memory to 96; places and events list 106–107
"consensual self-validation" 95
Constantinople 52–53
container-contained model 61
containment 5, 175, 181, 182
contemporary Israeli children's picture books 113; as collective postmemory representations 111–112; re-taking picture of war and paradox tuning postmemory 116–119; visualizing history, portraying postmemory 113–116
controversial issue 111

creating attendance 5, 175, 181
"Creating memory" program 3–4, 75; connecting through gazes 80; disconnection 78–79; entanglement 77–78; images and metaphors in texts 81–83; purpose of study 75–76; research method 76

Dagan, Batsheva 119, 121n12; *Chika the Dog in the Ghetto* 114, 115
databases, emergence of 87
David (Holocaust survivor case study) 61–63, 68–70; post-traumatic memories, restricting family from processing postmemory 63–65; therapy partly unraveling mother's postmemory 65–67
Deane, Seamus 48
Death of a Naturalist (Heaney) 51
Degel Sion 29n17
Derrida, Jacques 11
digitally mediated memories 94
digital memory: to big data and connective memory *99,* 99–100; materially mediated memory to 96; from material to 96, *97–98;* proliferation of 92
digitization, of memory 93
disconnection, "Creating memory" program 78–79
discrimination, lifelong struggle against 142–143
Doukas, Stratis: *A Prisoner of War's Story* 53
dreams, representation of 149–153
Druya memorial book 100
Dudai, Rina 134n7, 134n18
"Dumbo" 157, 172n1
Durrell, Lawrence 54

Eichmann, Adolf 155n11
Eichmann trial (1961) 152
Eisenstein, Bernice 5, 146, 148–154
ELAS (Greek partisan organization) 162
Elytis, Odysseas 49
emotional memory 4, 127–128, 133; transition through art 128–129
emotional postmemory 127–128
England 44–45
English language 10, 141
English-language Jewish Studies survey course 38

entanglement, "Creating memory" program 77–78
epigenetic memory 57n52
epiphylogenesis 92
epistemophilia 152
Epstein, Helen: *Children of the Holocaust* 37
Epston, David 172, 173n22
Europe, Jewish communities in 149
Evans, E. Estyn 50
evocation 147, 149–150; animation and postmemory 150–151; effects of secondary trauma 152–153; visualizing Holocaust obsession 151–152; wishful postmemory 151
externalization, of memory 93

factual-realistic dimension 129
family, concepts of 141–142
Famine (Murphy) 51, 52
Famine (O'Flaherty) 51–52
"Famine echoes" project 50
Farewell Anatolia (Sotiriou) 53
fate 31, 33
Felman, Shoshana 75, 176
Figley, Charles 147
Finkler Institute of Holocaust Research 38, 42
Fleming, Ann Marie 146, 150; *I was a Child of Holocaust Survivors* 146–153
Fools of Fortune (Trevor) 51
Forrer, Kurt 164
France 15, 27
Francesco Tirelli's Ice Cream Shop (Meir) 114–115
Frankel, Alona 119; *Why Joshua's Name Is Joshua* 117–118
French Commission for the Compensation of Victims of Spoliation Resulting from the Anti-Semitic Legislation in Force during the Occupation 15
French *Labortorie Bouty* 20, *22*
French language 11
Freud, S. 61, 72, 74, 80, 127
Frosh, Stephen 44, 61

Gampel, Yolanda 60, 134n5, 134n7
genocide 50
German Jewish refugee 140, 141
Gershon, Karen 4, 137; concepts of home, family, and belonging 141–142; language and creative expression 140–141; lifelong struggle against prejudice and discrimination 142–143; postmemory 138–139; transmission and translation of memories 140; "We Came as Children" 138; writing and therapy 139–140
Gibbons, Luke 46
Gibson, James 92
Gilder, Kineret 115, 116, 118
Gioconda (Kokántzis) 29n16
Givner, Maria 118
goral 3, 31, 33, 36–40; making choices and understanding 41–42
"Great Famine" (1845–1852) 44, 46–47, 49–52
The Great Hunger (Kavanagh) 51, 56n27
Greece 45; "Anatolian Catastrophe" (1922) 44, 52–55
Green, Gerald 42n10
"grey zone" concept 73
Grossman, David 73, 74, 79. *See under: Love* 74, 79

Halbwachs, Maurice 90
hallucinations, representation of 149–153
Hand, Derek 51
Heaney, Seamus 56n27; *Death of a Naturalist* 51
Hebrew alphabet 28n2
Hebrew books: characteristic of 114; *see also* contemporary Israeli children's picture books
Hebrew Shoah books 112
Heller, Erga 4
Hirsch, Marianne 32, 44, 60, 61, 151, 176
historical narratives 112
Hitler 33, 34
Hoffman, Eva 60
Holocaust 2, 3; and the "Anatolian Catastrophe" 51; contemporary visual representations of 111; graphic interpretation 111; transitional space of 181; visual documentation and memory of 117; visual knowledge of 111; writing for children about 113
Holocaust children's literature *see* contemporary Israeli children's picture books
Holocaust education: importance in Israel 120n7; Israeli education system toward 119

Holocaust literature: literary criticism of 73; representing trauma in 111; for young readers in Israel 118–119
Holocaust memory 4, 80, 87, 93
Holocaust Museum in Washington 90
Holocaust obsession 151–152
Holocaust-related family history 3
Holocaust survivor 2, 3; case study (*see* David (Holocaust survivor case study)); Savta Hannah (*see* Savta Hannah (Holocaust survivor)); and testimonies 72
home, concepts of 141–142
Honess Roe, Annabelle 147, 149, 153
Hopcke, Robert H. 173n7
Hoskins, Andrew 91, 94, 95
A Hug of Love (Mazliah-Liberman) 113, 116

identification 41, 69, 73, 76, 77; projective 68; traumatic 61; visual 115
illustration 115, 117; in Hebrew children's books 114; Holocaust 114; in Israeli picture books 4; visual 111; in *Why Joshua* 118
immersion 87, 102
impression memory 91
intergenerational transference 60, 69, 73, 80, 81
internalize 68, 182
Ireland 44–45; "Great Famine" (1845–1852) 44, 46–47, 49–52
"Irish Famine in Literature" (Kelleher) 51
Irish Folklore Commission 49, 52
Irishness 50–51
Israeli culture, narrative of Holocaust 111
Israeli education system 119
Israeli Independence Proclamation Scroll 112
I was a Child of Holocaust Survivors (Fleming) 146; animation and postmemory 150–151; effects of secondary trauma 152–153; production of 147; representing thoughts, dreams, and hallucinations 149–153; subjective memories of un-filmed events 147–148; visualizing Holocaust obsession 151–152; wishful postmemory 151
Izmir (Smyrna), Turkey 53, 167

Jewish communities, in Europe 149
Judaism 33
Jung, Carl 164–165

Kaleidoscope (Nissimov) 115
Kalvaria Friedman, Ariela: *There was a Castle* 118
Karnezis, Panos: *The Maze* 53
Katz, Avi 114–116, 118, 121n12
Kavanagh, Patrick: *The Great Hunger* 51, 56n27
Kelleher, Margaret: "Irish Famine in Literature" 51
Kellermann, N. P. F. 57n52
Kindertransport 137, 138, 141
Klarsfeld, Beate 11, 15
Klarsfeld, Serge 11, 15
knowledge, development and gathering of 158
Kokántzis, Níkos: *Gioconda* 29n16
Kotsias, Tilemachos 46, 53
Kristeva, Julia 130, 134n20

La Capra, Dominic 151
Ladino language 10, 11, 170, 172n6
La Grande Marque Française 20, 22
Landsberg, Alison 90, 91, 94, 95, 102n5
language 10–11; and creative expression 140–141; encounter between trauma and 76; materialistic and formative aspects 132
The Last Conquest of Ireland (Perhaps) (Mitchel) 50
Latour, Bruno 94
Laub, Dori 134n6
Lawrence, Jennifer 172
Leibovich, Hadas 119; *Brooms Dancing in Winter* 113
letters 175–183
Levi, Primo 73
Librairie Hachette 20, 21
Lisses-Topaz, Michelle 5
literature, orature to 46–48
Lloyd, David 50
Loewenthal, Kaethe 4
Lyotard, Jean-François: "The Postmodern Condition" 134n21

Machon 37–41
Macken, Walter: *The Silent People* 51
"The Making of an Irish Goddess" (Boland) 51

materially mediated memory, to digital and connective memory 96
material objects: of memory 91; use of 91
The Maze (Karnezis) 53
Mazliah-Liberman, Gila: *A Hug of Love* 113, 116
McBride, Ian 49
McHugh, Roger 49
McLean, Stuart 50, 51, 57n32
mediated memory 90
Megáli Idéa 52–54
Meir, Tamar 119; *Francesco Tirelli's Ice Cream Shop* 114–115
melancholia 72, 74, 80
"memorial candle" 37, 73, 80
memory 5, 32–33; as an uncanny experience 127; cloud affordances for 93–94; externalization and digitization of 93; of Famine 50; intermixing of 78; material objects of 91; as means to power and control 95–96; personal story of 96; poetic solution to coping with 83; of Savta Hanna *88, 88–89, 89*; social construction of 90; transmission and translation of 140
memory media 90
memory obsession 152
memory space 177
Memory Studies Association conference 102n5
mental experience 139
metamorphosis 47
metaphorical witnessing mode 81–82
metaphors 47; image of memory as 54; for Sabbath and Jewish holidays 114; in texts 81–83
Milner, Iris 151
Miłosz, Czesław 45–46, 51; two Europes 48
mimetic substitution 147, 150, 154
mirroring 5, 31, 62, 69, 175, 181, 182
Mitchel, John: *The Last Conquest of Ireland (Perhaps)* 50
momentary peeking 80
mourning 72, 74, 75
Moustafades 162
Murphy, Tom: *Famine* 51, 52
Myerhoff, Barbara 173n22

narrative 12; biographical 112; communal 47; literary 49; personal 72, 74, 119, 120; public and private 48; repetitive 62, 64, 65; textual 44; verbal 113, 115; visual 111, 113, 115, 117
narrative memory 4, 74, 127; of trauma 124–125
Ngũgĩ wa Thiong 45
Night (Wiesel) 152
Nissimov, Chava 119; *Kaleidoscope* 115
non-mimetic substitution 147, 150, 154
Nothing Makes You Free (Bukiet) 152–153

Ó Ciosáin, Niall 56n31
O'Connor, Sinéad 50
Ofer, Avi 116, 118
O'Flaherty, Liam 47; *Famine* 51–52
ontological absence 151
oral culture, transmission of 49
"Organization of Children of Holocaust Survivors in Israel" 37
Orlev, Uri 112–113, 115, 119
Orwell, George 95
"The Other Mind of Europe" (Sherard) 48

Palestine 9, 11–13, 15, 16, 115, 160
Papadiamandis, Alexandros 50
Papadimitriou, Elie: *Anatolia* 54
Paran, Noa 113
Parc Zoologique de Paris 20, *21*
the Parenti family 9, 13, 16–17, 28
Paris 11, 12, 14–16, 20, 25, 27, 28, 160
Passover Seder 159, 165
personal memory 101
personal narrative 72, 74, 119, 120
the "Phoney War" 27
Piaget, Jean 158
picture book *see* contemporary Israeli children's picture books
Pine, Richard 3
poetic language 79, 129, 130, 133; semiotic through 130–133
Poland 1, 34, 87, 118, 163
Portéir, Cathal 49
"post-imperial guilt" 45
postmemorial activity 2, 5
postmemorial work 3, 10, 42, 146; as form of working through 61
postmemory 2, 5, 10, 32–33, 60, 176–177; animation and 150–151; defined as 55n1; dimension of 9; as form of traumatic identification 61; Karen

Gershon 138–139; of Platform Age 88; processing of 69; theory of 44
postmemory representations 111–112
"The Postmodern Condition" (Lyotard) 134n21
post trauma 61, 63, 64, 68, 75
post-trauma symptoms 75
predestination 32–33
pre-Holocaust 3
prejudice, lifelong struggle against 142–143
pre-verbal semiotic communication 130
A Prisoner of War's Story (Doukas) 53
Program for Basic Jewish Studies 38, 39
projective identification 68
prosthesis 92
prosthetic memory 90, 91, 94
psychic deadness 64
psychoanalysis 2, 72
psychological scars 78
psychotic transference 69

radioactive fallout 60
reconstruction 62–65, 68, 139
Refael, Shmuel 32
repetition compulsion 3
repetitive narrative 62, 64, 65
representation: cultural 73; Holocaust 74, 111; of inner world 154; legitimacy and limits of 74; metonymical 78; of personal trauma 5; of Shoah's postmemory 4, 111; of subjective memory 148; of trauma 175
Reshef, Naama 4
Ross, Martin: *The Big House of Inver* 51
Russell, Shona 173n22

Sagi, Bella 3–4
Salonica (Greece) 16, 159; Jewish community of 29n12; Nazi invasion of 160
Santner, Eric 72
Sanyal, Debarati 73
Savta Hannah (Holocaust survivor) 101–102; affordances to connective memory 92–93; cloud affordances for memory 93–94; collective memory 90–91; from digitally mediated memories to connective memory 94; from digital memory to big data and connective memory 99, 99–100; materially mediated to digital and connective memory 96; from material to digital memory 96, 97–98; memory of 88, 88–89, 89
search engines, emergence of 87
secondary trauma 149, 151–153
secondary traumatic stress disorder 147
second generation (2g) 60, 61; of Holocaust descendants 119; Holocaust representation by 74; timing is everything 36–38; in United States 36
second-generation Holocaust survivors 5, 146
second-generation postmemory 5
second-generation survivors 73, 74, 77, 151
Second World War 111, 113, 177
See under: Love (Grossman) 74, 79
Semel, Nava 134n4, 134n7; The Parents Who Live Through Me 134n5; *And the Rat Laughed* 4, 124–134
"semiotic chora" 134n20
semiotic language 130–133
semiotic realms 130
"The Sensorimotor Period" 158
separation 3, 33, 41, 61, 64, 66, 68, 141
Sephardic Jews 162, 170
Sephardi script 28n2
shadows 10, 28, 60–70, 146, 147, 149
Shakine, Esther 120n7
Shalit, Ilana Eilati 5
shared memory 92
Sherard, Philip: "The Other Mind of Europe" 48
Shloshim 149
Shmuel, Naomi 4
Shoah: collective visual memory of 120; Hebrew picture book about 114; postmemory of 117; shift of contemporary Israeli picture books 112–113
Shoham, Maia Jessica 3
Shulman, David 101
The Silent People (Macken) 51
silent witnesses 83
Skoller, Jeffrey 154
Smith, Cecil Woodham: *The Great Hunger* 56n31
Solitreo 10, 28n2
Somerville, Edith: *The Big House of Inver* 51
Sotiriou, Dido: *Farewell Anatolia* 53

Index

Steir-Livny, Liat 5
Stiegler, Bernard 92, 95
storytelling 47
subjective memories, of un-filmed events 147–148
Sullivan, Harry Stack 95, 100
symbolic language 130–133, 134n21
symbolic realms 130
synchronicity 164; sparks desire to discover 165, *166*, 167–171, *169, 170*

Tal-Kopelman, Judy 119
technologically-mediated memory 91
terror 175–177
testimonies 72, 73
textual narrative 44
Theodore Herzl Association 16, 29n17
Theotokas, George: *Argo* 53
the "Phoney War" 27
There was a Castle (Kalvaria Friedman) 118
The Thing in the Dark 113
third-generation survivors 77, 79
thoughts, represention of 149–153
A Touch of Spice (Bouletis) 54
Tower of Babel 11
transference 68, 69; intergenerational 60, 69, 73, 80, 81
transformation 2, 61, 182, 183
transgenerational postmemory 2
translation, of memory 140
transmission, of memory 140
transmitted emotional memory 128
transposition 47
trauma 2; encounter between language and 76; Greek collective memory 45–46; impossibility of narrative memory of 124–125; obliterating force of 72; pain of 72; pathological-psychological ordeal of 129; powerful transfer of 68; representation in art 175
trauma materials 60, 61
trauma-related language, modes of 81–82

traumatic capsule 68, 69
traumatic experience 60, 64, 69
traumatic identification 61
traumatic impressions 62, 68
traumatic lacuna 82
traumatic memories 60, 63, 68
Trevor, William: *Fools of Fortune* 51
Trypani, Dimitra: *Amiliti/The Silent One* 45
Tustin, Francis 68
two Europes 48
Tziovas, Dimitris 53

uncanny 1, 3, 11, 113, 127, 139
UNRRA (United Nations Relief and Rehabilitation Administration) 163

Van Dijck, Jose 90
Venezis, Ilias: *Aeolia* 53, 54
verbal narrative 113, 115
virtual memories 102n5
visual identification 115
visual narrative 111, 113, 115, 117

Wardi, Charlotte 73
Waters, John 48, 50
"We Came as Children" (Gershon) 138
White, Michael 172, 173n22
Why Joshua's Name Is Joshua (Frankel) 117–118
Wiesel, Elie: *Night* 152
Wikipedia 100
Wilde, William 50
Winnicott, D. W. 82, 181
wishful postmemory 151, 154
working through 61
writing 2; for children about Holocaust 113; letters 175–183; postmemory 181, 182; and therapy 139–140

Yadin, Orly 147
Yad Vashem 17, 96, 99
Yad Vashem archive *98,* 99
Yom Kippur 163
Yom Kippur War 33

Printed in the United States
by Baker & Taylor Publisher Services